New Policies for Mandatory Defined Contribution Pensions

New Policies for Mandatory Defined Contribution Pensions

INDUSTRIAL ORGANIZATION MODELS AND INVESTMENT PRODUCTS

Gregorio Impavido,
Esperanza Lasagabaster, and
Manuel García-Huitrón

THE WORLD BANK
Washington, D.C.

ISBN-13: 978-0-8213-8276-9
eISBN: 978-0-8213-8317-9
DOI: 110.1596/978-0-8213-8276-9

Library of Congress Cataloging-in-Publication Data
Impavido, Gregorio.

New policies for mandatory defined contribution pensions : industrial organization models and investment products / Gregorio Impavido, Esperanza Lasagabaster, Manuel García-Huitrón.

p. cm.—(Latin American development forum series)
Includes bibliographical references and index.
ISBN 978-0-8213-8276-9—ISBN 978-0-8213-8317-9 (electronic)

1. Defined contribution pension plans. 2. Pensions. 3. Industrial organization. I. Lasagabaster, Esperanza. II. García-Huitrón, Manuel. III. Title.

HD7105.4.I47 2011
331.25'2—dc22

2010013119

Cover design by ULTRAdesigns

Latin American Development Forum Series

This series was created in 2003 to promote debate, disseminate information and analysis, and convey the excitement and complexity of the most topical issues in economic and social development in Latin America and the Caribbean. It is sponsored by the Inter-American Development Bank, the United Nations Economic Commission for Latin America and the Caribbean, and the World Bank. The manuscripts chosen for publication represent the highest quality in each institution's research and activity output and have been selected for their relevance to the academic community, policy makers, researchers, and interested readers.

Advisory Committee Members

Alicia Bárcena Ibarra, Executive Secretary, Economic Commission for Latin America and the Caribbean, United Nations

Inés Bustillo, Director, Washington Office, Economic Commission for Latin America and the Caribbean, United Nations

José Luis Guasch, Senior Adviser, Latin America and the Caribbean Region, World Bank; and Professor of Economics, University of California, San Diego

Santiago Levy, Vice President for Sectors and Knowledge, Inter-American Development Bank

Eduardo Lora, Chief Economist (a.i.) and General Manager, Research Department, Inter-American Development Bank

Luis Servén, Research Manager, Development Economics Vice Presidency, World Bank

Augusto de la Torre, Chief Economist, Latin America and the Caribbean Region, World Bank

Titles in the Latin American Development Forum Series

New Policies for Mandatory Defined Contribution Pensions: Industrial Organization Models and Investment Products (2010) by Gregorio Impavido, Esperanza Lasagabaster, and Manuel García-Huitrón

The Quality of Life in Latin American Cities: Markets and Perception (2010) by Eduardo Lora, Andrew Powell, Bernard M. S. van Praag, and Pablo Sanguinetti, editors

Discrimination in Latin America: An Economic Perspective (2010) by Hugo Ñopo, Alberto Chong, and Andrea Moro, editors

The Promise of Early Childhood Development in Latin America and the Caribbean (2010) by Emiliana Vegas and Lucrecia Santibáñez

Job Creation in Latin America and the Caribbean: Trends and Policy Challenges (2009) by Carmen Pagés, Gaëlle Pierre, and Stefano Scarpetta

China's and India's Challenge to Latin America: Opportunity or Threat? (2009) by Daniel Lederman, Marcelo Olarreaga, and Guillermo E. Perry, editors

Does the Investment Climate Matter? Microeconomic Foundations of Growth in Latin America (2009) by Pablo Fajnzylber, José Luis Guasch, and J. Humberto López, editors

Measuring Inequality of Opportunities in Latin America and the Caribbean (2009) by Ricardo de Paes Barros, Francisco H. G. Ferreira, José R. Molinas Vega, and Jaime Saavedra Chanduvi

The Impact of Private Sector Participation in Infrastructure: Lights, Shadows, and the Road Ahead (2008) by Luis Andres, José Luis Guasch, Thomas Haven, and Vivien Foster

About the Contributors

Gregorio Impavido is a Senior Financial Sector Expert at the International Monetary Fund, which he joined in 2007 after nine years at the World Bank. In his work, he delivers policy advice on financial stability, regulation, and supervision of private pensions and insurance markets. He has written on these topics for the several multilaterals and published in refereed journals and books. He earned a PhD and a MSc in economics from Warwick University and a BSc in economics from Bocconi University. A partial list of his publications is available at http://ssrn.com/author=429651.

Esperanza Lasagabaster is a Senior Financial Economist at the Latin American and Caribbean Region of the World Bank and formerly worked as an economist in other regional departments of the World Bank, Inter-American Development Bank, and the Institute of International Finance. She has researched and advised on pension policy to governments in Eastern Europe and Central Asia, Latin America, and South Asia. She earned a PhD in economics from Cornell University.

Manuel García-Huitrón is a Manager of Strategic Planning of Afore XXI, a Mexican pension fund administrator. He has worked in different capacities for the World Bank, the International Finance Corporation, the Yale School of Management, and the Ministry of Finance of the Federal District in México. He was adjunct professor of microeconomics at Pontificia Universidad Católica and Adolfo Ibañez Business School, both in Chile. He has received several awards for his research and consulting on social security and pension systems. Manuel earned a BA in economics from Instituto Tecnólogico Autómo de México and a Masters in international and development economics from Yale University.

Contents

TABLES

Foreword

The recent financial crisis is challenging the reform approach to mandated pension schemes that has emerged over recent decades across the world. This reform approach is characterized by a move toward multipillar pension systems and includes the creation or extension of a mandatory funded pillar with defined contribution design. The rationale and viability of such a pillar is contingent on an enabling environment and the delivery of high risk-adjusted net rates of return that beat the natural benchmark, which is the internal rate of return that an unfunded mandated scheme is able to achieve. The (mostly temporary) decline in asset prices of mandated funded pillars, which have been introduced in more than 30 countries, has caused the mind to refocus and ask for innovative policies that are better able to shield individuals from the vagaries of financial markets while providing the expected retirement income.

Two key aspects of mandated and funded defined contribution schemes have been under discussion and investigation since dedicated pension funds were created: (a) the high fees levied by privately organized pension funds and the consequence for the net rate of return and (b) the investment products of these funds and their capability to address the investment risks and to deliver the expected retirement income in a life-cycle context. To this end, country policies have experimented with a variety of approaches to improve outcomes with some important leads but overall modest results.

This book proposes to take a fresh and highly innovative look at both policy issues. It suggests stepping back and looking at the underlying causes of the issues at stake instead of merely trying to address their symptoms. In addressing the high fees of pension funds, it focuses on the less-than-ideal conditions—inert consumers facing firms with market powers—and proposes to apply solutions derived from industrial organization models and pricing methods that better reflect the cost structure of the supply of pension services. In addressing the investment risks, it asks how to improve fund managers' risk-adjusted investment performance when participants are inert. The book proposes moving beyond the current default options and suggests a rule-based or risk-based framework, depending on the enabling framework and the level of financial market development.

The proposed new policies are very timely and highly encourage enrichment of the pension design and reform discourse. They are based on sound economic thinking and empirical evidence, and they reflect the deep experience of the authors in pension design and implementation issues. Yet the presentation is fully accessible to a broader audience interested in pension reform.

Robert Holzmann
Research Director and Senior Adviser
World Bank
March 2010

Acknowledgments

This book is the result of a policy research project designed and coordinated by Gregorio Impavido and finalized with Esperanza Lasagabaster and Manuel García-Huitrón. The book is part of the regional studies series sponsored by the Chief Economist' Office of the Latin American Vice Presidency of the World Bank.

Among other sources, the book draws on four background papers that were commissioned specifically for it: (a) Blake, Cairns, and Dowd (2008) review the literature on strategic asset allocation and develop a proposal for linking the accumulation and payout phases through the use of target annuitization funds; (b) Dayoub and Lasagabaster (2008) survey trends in competition policy and investment regulation in Latin American countries; (c) Raddatz and Schmukler (2008) analyze the asset allocation patterns and investment strategies of Chilean pension fund managers; and (d) Valdés-Prieto (2007) discusses policy trade-offs in the use of ad hoc regulations and alternative industrial organization structures. The authors are grateful to the authors of these papers; their analysis provided valuable inputs to this book.

The authors wish to thank the Chief Economist' Office of the Latin American and Carribean Region of the World Bank—especially Tito Cordella, Augusto de la Torre, and Alan Ize—for helpful inputs during all the phases of the project. Thanks are also due to Gustavo Demarco, Alejandro Reveiz, and Heinz Rudolph (of the World Bank) and Carlos Herrera (of BBVA), for their role as internal reviewers, and to two external anonymous reviewers. Finally, the authors wish to express their gratitude to Richard Hinz, Eduardo Levi-Yeyati, Rafael Rofman, and Dimitri Vittas (of the World Bank); Moisés Schwartz and Roberto Calderón (of the Comisión Nacional del Sistema de Ahorro para el Retiro of Mexico); Lorena Masías and Elio Sanchez (of the Superintendencia de Banca, Seguros y AFP of Peru); Alain Jousten (of the Institute for the Study of Labor); and Marcos Souto (of the International Monetary Fund) for their comments and advice. Finally, the authors wish to acknowledge the support received by the International Monetary Fund.

The usual caveat applies: all remaining errors are the authors' only.

References

Blake, David, Andrew J. G. Cairns, and Kevin Dowd. 2008. "Turning Pension Plans into Pension Planes: What Investment Strategy Designers of Defined Contribution Pension Plans Can Learn from Commercial Aircraft Designers." Discussion Paper PI-0806, Pensions Institute, Cass Business School, City University, London. http://www.pensions-institute.org/workingpapers/wp0806.pdf.

Dayoub, Mariam, and Esperanza Lasagabaster. 2008. "General Trends in Competition Policy and Investment Regulation in Mandatory Defined Contribution Markets in Latin America." Policy Research Working Paper 4720, World Bank, Washington, DC.

Raddatz, Claudio, and Sergio Schmukler. 2008. "Pension Funds and Capital Market Development: How Much Bang for the Buck?" Policy Research Working Paper 4787, World Bank, Washington, DC.

Valdés-Prieto, Salvador. 2007. "State-Supported Defined Contribution Pensions: Quasi-Markets or Procurement?" Pontificia Universidad Católica de Chile, Santiago.

Abbreviations

AFORE	*administradora de fondos para el retiro*, or pension fund administrator
AFP	*administradora de fondos de pensiones*, or pension fund administrator
CONSAR	Comisión Nacional del Sistema de Ahorro para el Retiro, or National Commission for the Pension System (Mexico)
CPPI	constant proportion portfolio insurance
DB	defined benefit
DC	defined contribution
GDP	gross domestic product
OECD	Organisation for Economic Co-operation and Development
PAYG	pay-as-you-go (scheme)
PPM	Premiepensionsmyndigheten, or Premium Pension System (Sweden)
TIAA-CREF	Teachers Insurance and Annuity Association–College Retirement Equities Fund
VaR	value-at-risk (limit)

1

Introduction

Recent Developments

The pension reforms of the past few decades had almost inevitably three key objectives:[1]

- To improve the actuarial features of the pension system in a way that would also increase its intergenerational fairness[2]
- To reduce the defined benefit (DB) and increase the defined contribution (DC) component in financing retirement income with the objectives (among others) of (a) diversifying the financing mechanisms for pensions, (b) strengthening the consumption-smoothing component of the system, and (c) increasing the risk-adjusted return on pension contributions
- To increase the level of funding in the system as a means of increasing the value of the collateral behind the pension promise and of promoting national savings[3]

In many countries, these objectives were achieved through the introduction of second pillars. *Second pillars* are occupational or personal, fully funded plans targeting formal sector workers, with mandatory participation and with financial assets as the funding or collateral of the pension promise (Holzmann et al. 2005).

Currently, mandatory DC pension second pillars are present in a large number of economies, with coverage easily exceeding 100 million participants.[4] In Latin America, economies include, but are not limited to, Chile, Colombia, Mexico, and Peru.[5] In Europe, economies include Bulgaria, Denmark, Hungary, Poland, Sweden, Switzerland, and the United Kingdom.[6] In Asia and Oceania, economies include Australia; Hong Kong, China; and New Zealand.

Many of these countries used the Chilean reform of 1981 as a model. This reform was influential in achieving a radical paradigm shift in the way pension income is considered best financed. The new paradigm is based on a larger role for markets and on individual savings complementing intergenerational risk sharing. In addition, reducing the fiscal pressure created by generous mandatory DB plans is considered essential. Finally, the new paradigm is believed to be more resilient to demographic shocks, although this resilience, in reality, can be achieved only by policies aimed at increasing labor productivity and future per capita gross domestic product.

The Objective of This Book

This book has three main objectives: (a) to discuss the main implications that consumers' inability to make rational choices can have on the functioning of second pillars, (b) to describe how jurisdictions have tried to address these problems through ad hoc policy interventions, and (c) to propose new policy directions that potentially could address these concerns more effectively.

The common thread throughout the book is the limited capacity of individuals to choose what is best for them. This problem stems from a combination of lack of financial education, bounded rationality, and use of simplistic "rules of thumb" in the decision-making process.

This limited capacity of individuals to make rational choices has two main implications for the functioning of second pillars: (a) pension firms enjoy disproportionate market power that translates into administrative fees that exceed average costs and socially undesirable high levels of marketing expenditures, and (b) consumers—especially those close to retirement—can be exposed to excessive investment risk.

These two policy concerns increase the costs of financial intermediation for contributors as measured by lower risk-adjusted expected net rates of return. Disappointing ex post risk-adjusted net rates of return imply disappointing ex post replacement rates (that is, the value of pensions relative to salaries). The latter, in turn, may imply higher than expected levels of poverty among elderly individuals and raise concerns about the advantages of an individual account pension system. Hence, policies aimed at either lowering fees or increasing risk-adjusted expected returns will strengthen the rationale for introducing mandatory DC pensions as a key element of a pension system.

The rest of this section summarizes (a) the nature of these two policy concerns, (b) the policy interventions typically adopted in many jurisdictions to address those concerns, and (c) new policy directions for exploiting individuals' inertia and the biases in their decision-making process to help improve the performance of second pillars.

The Concern about Firms' Market Power

Pension markets are characterized by high barriers to entry, and consumers do not typically react to price signals such as administrative fees and risk-adjusted rates of return because of their lack of financial education or simple lack of interest.[7] When they do react, they tend to follow rules of thumb that are not rational according to the standard economic theory. These factors, jointly with a production function for pension services that is characterized by important economies of scale, create market power, which, in turn, leads pension firms to treat their clients as captive and to choose prices well above average production costs. High prices finance excessive marketing activity, thereby further increasing barriers to entry, or they translate into supernormal profits for pension firms.

Administrative fees are clearly not without limits. For instance, one upper limit is determined by the desire to minimize entry, which can be costly for incumbents because of the ensuing marketing wars. An alternative upper limit is determined by fears of government intervention stemming from the public reaction to welfare losses for participants. However, these limits are not related to cost structures, and equilibrium prices are significantly above average production costs.

The divergence between prices and average production costs is socially undesirable because it redistributes rents from consumers to pension firms. Such redistribution potentially reduces the value of pensions relative to preretirement earnings (expected replacement rates) and undermines the policy objectives that had justified introducing second pillars in the first place.

The Concern about Investment Risk

The recent financial crisis has reignited the debate on whether pension participants bear excessive investment risk. The debate is particularly relevant within the component of mandatory DC pensions, where participants fully bear such risk, especially in the case of cohorts who are close to retirement and would not have sufficient time to recuperate from adverse market shocks.

What is important for the objective of this book is whether risk-adjusted rates of returns are low ex post because individuals expose themselves to excessive investment risk by being unable to choose the right investment strategy or fund over their life cycle. Ample evidence indicates that even in normal times individuals generally lack the necessary skills to monitor portfolio management; therefore, they tend to make an uneducated selection of portfolios during their life cycle. In addition, the lack of a long-term target for pension fund managers appears to leave too many degrees of freedom to asset managers in implementing the strategic asset allocation. This problem is compounded by the lack of a connection between the accumulation phase and the retirement phase, which exposes individuals to annuitization risk. In other words, the institutional mechanism to force asset managers to invest consistently with participants' long-term preferences is weak.

Policy Responses to These Two Key Concerns

Jurisdictions seeking to protect individuals against pension firms' market power have introduced measures aimed at reducing administrative fees and redistributing rents in favor of consumers. The policy menu has generally included (a) soft interventions such as prohibiting firms from charging different individuals different prices for the same services, reducing the number of fees that can be charged, and bundling pension services; (b) more draconian interventions such as imposing price controls, imposing restrictions or bans on switches, and informally accepting market agreements aimed at avoiding marketing wars; and (c) specific institutional arrangements such as using centralized agencies or auction mechanisms for certain pension services and using automatic assignation rules for undecided consumers.

The key problem with these measures is that they have been often ad hoc in the sense that they have tried to achieve simultaneously conflicting objectives. In other words, while addressing one problem, they have often created other problems.

Jurisdictions seeking to protect individuals from their ability to expose themselves to excessive investment risk have adopted some form of life-cycle funds as default investment choices for undecided individuals. Jurisdictions that have introduced these investment products appear to have managed to shield individuals close to retirement from the high market volatility of the last two years, relative to jurisdictions that have not yet introduced these investment products.

Nonetheless, several issues arise with these default investment choices. First and foremost, very few jurisdictions have introduced these measures. Second, the way in which undecided individuals are assigned to investment funds by default could be further improved to promote better intertemporal risk diversification. Finally, such measures leave individuals exposed to annuitization risk when they need to convert cash balances in annuities at retirement.

New Policy Directions

The book acknowledges the usefulness of financial education programs as a means of improving individuals' rationality. However, it contends that rationality is in the end bounded and that individuals' decision-making process will inevitably be dominated by the use of rules of thumb. These heuristic solutions are not rational according to traditional economic theory but are broadly predictable; therefore, they display systematic biases. These biases can be exploited (rather than corrected) by policy makers to design interventions that are more effective at protecting individuals from themselves than are the ad hoc policy interventions that are currently used.

The book provides clear recommendations on new policy directions for exploiting individuals' inertia and the biases in their decision-making process in order to promote a reduction in administrative fees and an increase in risk-adjusted expected returns over the life cycle. In addition, it provides a clear distinction between policies that can be safely adopted by the majority of jurisdictions and other policies that, while promising, require further research or present more marked trade-offs.

The new policy menu recommended in the book, to be used selectively by different jurisdictions, includes (a) more use of flat fees to increase pricing efficiency and reduce incentives for marketing and cream skimming; (b) introduction of transparent flat subsidies from the budget to pursue equity policy objectives; (c) more use of hybrid industrial organization models, together with unbundling of pension services, to address the problem of participants' inertia; (d) use of cost-based tariffs where price controls cannot be avoided; (e) generalized adoption of life-cycle funds default investment options to improve intertemporal risk diversification and to protect inert individuals who are near retirement from market risk; (f) identification and adoption of long-term investment targets to benchmark asset managers' performance; and (g) introduction of life-cycle-based investment products that mitigate annuitization risk by reconnecting the accumulation phase with the retirement phase without reintroducing liabilities for pension asset managers.

The Structure of This Book

The rest of this book has the following structure. Chapter 2 begins with an analysis of the key characteristics of the demand and supply of mandatory DC pensions. It provides factual and empirical evidence on the outcome of the interaction between a demand for pension services that is highly inelastic to prices and a supply that is characterized by important fixed costs and economies of scale. The key characteristics are market concentration, market power, low volume of transfers across pension firms, high administrative fees, high levels of marketing expenditure, and supernormal profits. It also provides a simple theoretical framework to explain the interaction among market power, concentration, and elasticity in a Cournot oligopoly setup. Finally, it provides an in-depth discussion of the literature on switching costs to justify the inertia of individuals and explain why pension firms have incentives to invest excessively in marketing.

Chapter 3 discusses the trade-offs that policy makers face in introducing ad hoc policies and regulations aimed at offsetting the price distortions created by market power. These policies include various experiments with narrowly focused regulations aimed at increasing demand elasticity, redistributing rents in favor of consumers with low income or net worth, exploiting economies of scale in select pension services, lowering barriers to entry, rendering markets more contestable, reducing the incentives to spend on marketing, and capping prices charged by pension firms.

Two key messages stem from the analysis conducted in chapter 3. First, the policy interventions aimed at reducing administrative fees have been narrowly devised; hence, while they may partially address a problem, they often create new challenges. This problem arises because they typically attempt to address the consequences rather than the causes of price distortions. Second, more fundamental and market-based policies should be pursued. In general, specific policies with negligible trade-offs that could be pursued include (a) flat fees, (b) flat subsidies, (c) unbundling of pension services, and (d) hybrid industrial organization models that combine public procurement techniques for inert participants and choice for participants with a higher elasticity of demand. Thus far, only a few countries have started experimenting with such policies.

Chapter 4 discusses investment choice in mandatory DC plans, describes in detail the design characteristics of life-cycle default funds adopted in selected Latin American countries, and analyzes the strengths and weaknesses of those funds. It then considers the impact of the subprime financial crisis that started in 2007 on DC pension markets and makes a preliminary evaluation of how life-cycle funds have fared under the crisis. It finally discusses policies aimed at increasing risk-adjusted expected returns. Thus, the chapter supports the progressive liberalization of the regulatory framework for investments and the adoption of life-cycle funds. Such an approach has been observed in Latin American and Eastern European countries in recent years to promote financial innovation and offset participants' inertia.

The analysis conducted in chapter 4 conveys two key messages. First, the chapter suggests that, even within a rule-based framework, welfare gains can be achieved by (a) reviewing investment rules spanning the universe of investment products, (b) mandating the use of deferred annuities and long-term duration bonds toward retirement as a way to better hedge annuitization risk, and (c) increasing the number of default investment options. Second, additional welfare gains for participants can be achieved only within a risk-based framework by reconnecting the accumulation phase with the retirement phase through the use of target retirement date annuitization funds without introducing liabilities for private providers.

Chapter 5 concludes by summarizing the lessons that can be drawn from the discussion of the previous chapters and by indicating important areas for future research.

The Audience of This Book

This book is relevant to a wide audience, which includes the following:

- *Policy makers in countries with an important or rapidly growing DC component.* Policy makers in countries with a high or rapidly growing value of assets under management will find the book particularly useful. Information on some of these countries is given in figures 1.1 and 1.2.

Figure 1.1 Assets in DB and DC Private Plans, Various Years

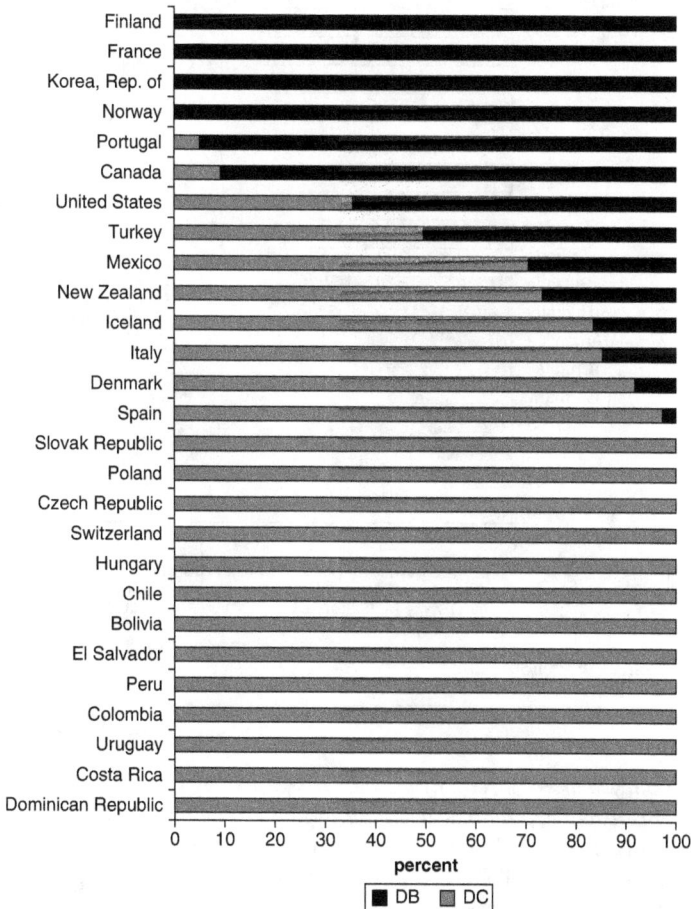

Source: Organisation for Economic Co-operation and Development and International Organization of Latin American Pension Supervisors.

Figure 1.2 Role of Financial Assets in Overall Income
Retirement Financing

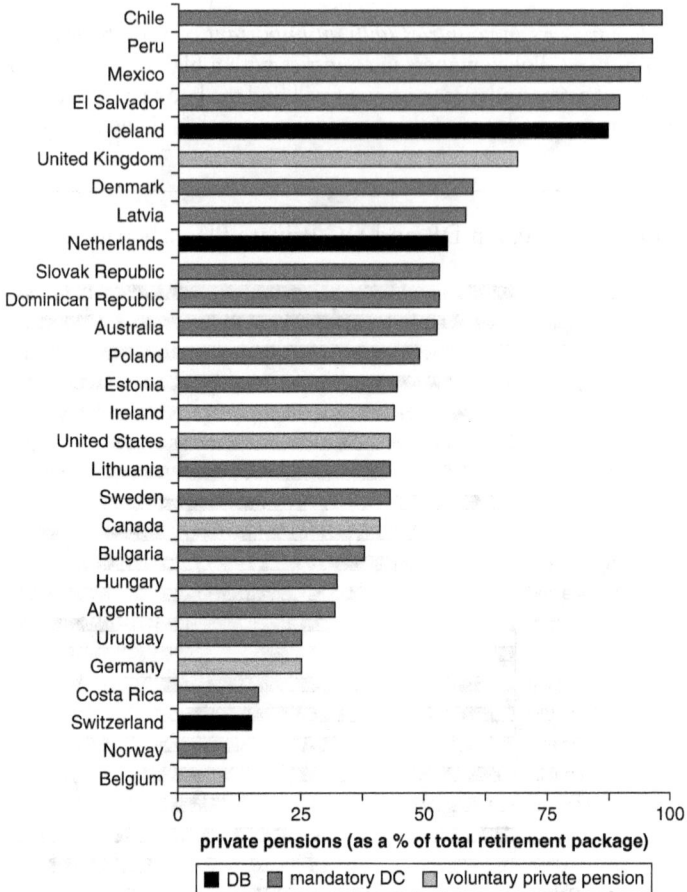

Source: Whitehouse 2007.

- *Policy makers in countries with a smaller DC component or unso-phisticated capital markets.* Size should not be interpreted in absolute terms. Thus, the book is also relevant to countries where pension systems have a small DC component and a limited amount of assets under management but the industrial organization of local financial services or the lack of sophistication of local capital markets makes competition policy issues and long-term asset allocation and investment risk management issues important for reasons of financial stability. Information on some of these countries is given in figures 1.1 and 1.2.

- *Policy advisers working in the areas of pension regulation and supervision, competition policy for financial services, capital market development, and financial stability.* The book is relevant to policy advisers who want to develop a detailed understanding of the strengths and limitations of the policies adopted by many jurisdictions to lower administrative fees and to improve expected long-term performance in mandatory DC pensions.

- *Academics who are interested in identifying underresearched pension policy issues.* The book is relevant to academics because it identifies numerous policy issues that so far have not received adequate theoretical or empirical attention and that represent promising areas of future research. In addition, although essential policy material is provided in the main text of the book, more academically inclined readers will find relevant supporting technical discussions in the annexes that accompany each chapter.

Notes

1. For a review of country-specific reforms and general trends, see Feldstein and Siebert (2002); Fultz (2003); Holzmann, Orenstein, and Rutkowski (2003); Holzmann and Palmer (2006); Lindbeck and Persson (2003); and OECD (2000).

2. The literature here distinguishes between *actuarial balance* and *actuarial fairness.* The former feature, more macroeconomic, relates to the long-run financial stability (viability) of the pension systems (Diamond 2002). The latter feature, more microeconomic, relates to the link between benefits and contributions (Fenge 1995; Kotlikoff 1996, 1998).

3. Many countries with very mature systems (Italy, Latvia, Poland, and Sweden) have improved actuarial fairness and balance by introducing notional defined contribution systems that combine partial funding with individual accounts.

4. The International Organization of Latin American Pension Supervisors (Asociación Internacional de Organismos de Supervisión de Fondos de Pensiones) reports around 73 million participants for Latin America only. There are also around 40 million participants from Australia; Bulgaria; Denmark; Hong Kong, China; Hungary; the Netherlands; New Zealand; the Slovak Republic; Sweden; and Switzerland.

5. The effective years of implementation of initial reform in Latin America are Chile (1981), Peru (1993), Argentina and Colombia (1994), Uruguay (1996), Bolivia and Mexico (1997), El Salvador (1998), Costa Rica (2001), Nicaragua (2002), and the Dominican Republic (2003). Two more countries have passed a reform but either have not yet implemented it or are in the early stages of implementation: Ecuador (2001) and Panama (1999 and 2006). Finally, in late 2008, the Argentine parliament enacted a law nationalizing the second pillar and reverting to the system in place before the 1994 reform.

6. The effective years of implementation of the initial reforms in Eastern Europe are Hungary and Poland (1998); Latvia (2001); Bulgaria, Croatia, Estonia, Kosovo, and the Slovak Republic (2005); and the former Yugoslav Republic of Macedonia

(2006–07). In addition, Lithuania implemented a reform in 2002 that is voluntary for new entrants.

7. In reference to this concept, this book often mentions that the demand for pension services is highly inelastic to prices.

References

Diamond, Peter A. 2002. *Social Security Reform.* London: Oxford University Press.

Feldstein, Martin, and Horst Siebert, eds. 2002. *Social Security Pension Reform in Europe.* Chicago: University of Chicago Press.

Fenge, Robert. 1995. "Pareto Efficiency of the Pay-as-You Go Pension System with Intergenerational Fairness." *FinanzArchiv* 52 (3): 357–63.

Fultz, Elaine. 2003. "Recent Trends in Pension Reform and Implementation in the EU Accession Countries." Paper presented at the Informal Meeting of Ministers at the International Labour Organization's International Labour Conference, Geneva, June 10.

Holzmann, Robert, Richard Hinz, Hermann von Gersdoff, Indermit Gill, Gregorio Impavido, Albert R. Musalem, Robert Palacios, David Robalino, Michal Rutkowski, Anita Schwarz, Yvonne Sin, and Kalanidhi Subbarao. 2005. *Old-Age Income Support in the 21st Century: An International Perspective on Pension Systems and Reform.* Washington, DC: World Bank.

Holzmann, Robert, Mitchell Orenstein, and Michal Rutkowski. 2003. *Pension Reform in Europe: Process and Progress.* Washington, DC: World Bank.

Holzmann, Robert, and Edward Palmer, eds. 2006. *Pension Reform: Issues and Prospects for Non-financial Defined Contribution (NDC) Schemes.* Washington, DC: World Bank.

Kotlikoff, Laurence J. 1996. "Privatizing Social Security: How It Works and Why It Matters." In *Tax Policy and the Economy*, vol. 10, ed. James Poterba, 1–32. Cambridge, MA: MIT Press.

———. 1998. "Simulating the Privatization of Social Security in General Equilibrium." In *Privatizing Social Security*, ed. Martin Feldstein, 265–306. Chicago: University of Chicago Press.

Lindbeck, Assar, and Mats Persson. 2003. "The Gains from Pension Reform." *Journal of Economic Literature* 41 (1): 74–112.

OECD (Organisation for Economic Co-operation and Development). 2000. *Reforms for an Ageing Society.* Paris: OECD.

Whitehouse, Edward. 2007. *Pensions panorama: Retirement Income Systems In 53 Countries.* Washington DC: World Bank.

2

Industrial Organization Issues and Their Consequences

This chapter analyzes the nature of the markets for mandatory defined contribution (DC) pensions, the characteristics of the supply of and demand for pension services, and their consequences for consumers.

The supply and demand for pension services have very specific characteristics that make mandatory DC pension markets unlike any other market. On the supply side, the provision of important pension services is characterized by large fixed costs and economies of scale.[1] On the demand side, consumers' participation is mandatory and is characterized by inertia.

On the one hand, economies of scale create barriers to entry and promote concentration. On the other hand, inertia limits the extent to which consumers can impose market discipline by switching across pension firms.[2] A key consequence is that pension firms in mandatory DC markets enjoy a considerable amount of market power. Facing a pool of captive consumers, providers are encouraged to charge fees substantially above what would be observed in competitive markets.[3]

In addition, pension firms engage in strategic behavior aimed at preserving market share and power. For instance, providers invest excessively in marketing to attract and retain consumers. In addition, they use loyalty bonuses or discounts to lock in consumers. These forms of expenditure are essentially fixed costs[4] that increase barriers to entry and, therefore, market power.

This chapter is organized as follows. The next section defines the quasi-market nature of mandatory DC pensions. The two sections that then follow discuss the characteristics of the demand and supply. The penultimate section considers the outcomes that result from the interplay of the supply and demand for pension services. Conclusions follow in the final section.

This chapter also lays the foundation for the rest of the book by presenting empirical evidence and many technical concepts that are repeatedly referred to and used in chapters 3 and 4.

The Nature of Mandatory DC Pension Markets

Systemic pension reforms have introduced mandatory second pillars in many Latin American and Eastern European countries in the past three decades. These reforms have all shared the following characteristic: individual workers are still required to participate, but the state has essentially reduced its role as both the funding agent and the provider of pension services. In second pillars, participants are required to purchase services from a variety of private or public sector providers, all operating in competition with one another. In other words, the reforms have created a quasi-market for pension services.[5]

A pension quasi-market is a "market" because competitive, independent, and often specialized entities provide some or all services. It is "quasi" because it differs from a conventional market on both the demand and the supply side. On the demand side, consumption is mandatory,[6] and purchasing power is expressed by vouchers, which are often subsidized by an earmarked state budget.[7] On the supply side, providers do not necessarily maximize profits, and their governance structure includes both private and public sector firms, as well as for-profit and mutual associations.[8] These special demand and supply characteristics of quasi-markets create inherent inefficiencies, as explained in box 2.1.

The Demand for Pension Services

The demand for pension services is characterized by inertia on the part of individuals. A well-functioning market for mandatory DC pensions requires consumers to react to relevant price parameters, such as administrative fees and gross rates of return. However, ample evidence indicates that they do not do so. In Argentina, for example, about 80 percent of new members were assigned to pension firms by the pension supervisory agency in 2006. In Mexico, 74 percent of new members in 2006 were automatically assigned to a pension fund administrator (*administradora de fondos para el retiro*, or AFORE) by the supervisor.[9] Similarly, in Chile, the regulator had automatically assigned about 70 percent of the 8.63 million registered individuals by April 2007. Despite ample evidence of inertia, table 2.1 shows a trend of increasing consumer activism when switches are measured as a share of active contributors. This trend is often explained (as in the case of Peru after 2004) by the relaxation of existing switching rules combined with the offset of consumer inertia by efforts of the marketing and sales forces.

Box 2.1 Are Quasi-Markets Efficient?

Because of the different nature of demand and supply, the welfare analysis for consumers participating in quasi-markets is far from obvious. The classic concerns relate to the ability of quasi-markets to produce X-efficiencies and improve allocation efficiency. With X-efficiencies, the indeterminacy of firms' objectives (profits, market share, participants' welfare, and so forth) creates ex ante uncertainty about how firms will react to market incentives. For instance, because of the inertia of participants, providers engage in excessive marketing and are encouraged to create switching costs for participants to defend their investments, with an ambiguous effect on overall costs. With allocation efficiency, quasi-markets are expected to increase consumer choice and improve the quality of service with respect to monopolistic state providers. Although it is a priori unclear why, more choice of financial services clearly is not necessarily Pareto improving.[a] Indeed, consumers of financial services are not always rational and are often disinterested. Even when rational, they frequently lack the financial education to process the relevant information and lack the willpower to implement their decisions consistently. In the specific case of pension services, one may question whether individual consumers are best equipped to solve the relevant intertemporal strategic asset allocation problem to maximize their expected replacement rates. Maybe the solution to this problem is best left to professionals, as suggested in chapter 4.

a. Given a set of alternative allocations of, say, goods, income, or—in this case— choice for a set of individuals, a change from one allocation to another that can make at least one individual better off without making any other individual worse off is called a *Pareto improvement*.

Consumers are inert in two important dimensions: (a) consumers should switch to firms with a more favorable combination of fees and returns, but they tend not to react to these price signals,[10] and (b) once consumers choose a firm (if a choice is made), they tend to ignore portfolio choice, when available. In other words, the decision patterns of consumers have systematic biases.[11] The subsections that follow summarize the underlying reasons for the inertia phenomenon in pension markets and present evidence from a variety of studies of the low magnitude of demand elasticity.

Underlying Causes of Inertia in Pension Markets

Recent developments in economic theory explain inertia as a consequence of the following key causes: (a) irrational consumer behavior, (b) high switching costs, and (c) information problems. These causes are not necessarily mutually exclusive and are clearly interrelated.

Table 2.1 Number of Transfers across Pension Firms, 2000–07

Country	Transfers (thousand)							
	2000	2001	2002	2003	2004	2005	2006	2007[a]
Argentina	401	413	331	364	711	243	432	460
Bolivia	n.a.	n.a.	n.a.	3	3	4	4	4
Chile	256	235	229	275	212	235	235	270
Colombia	—	—	170	123	80	73	67	64
Costa Rica	n.a.	6	n.a.	75	74	97	99	140
Dominican Republic[b]	n.a.	n.a.	n.a.	n.a.	1	1	1	1
El Salvador	135	78	41	53	37	68	10	5
Mexico	99	117	133	431	1,205	2,438	3,849	3,869
Peru	7	5	9	9	10	129	643	640
Uruguay	—	0	1	1	0	1	1	1
Total transfers	898	854	914	1,334	2,334	3,289	5,341	5,454
Total contributors[c]	18,618	20,075	24,070	25,719	26,885	28,724	30,490	31,996
Turnover[d]	4.82	4.25	3.79	5.18	8.67	11.45	17.51	17.04

Source: Author calculations based on data from the Asociación Internacional de Organismos de Supervisión de Fondos de Pensiones.

Note: — not available; n.a. = not applicable.

a. June 2006 to June 2007.

b. Switches were allowed starting only in 2004.

c. Country-specific definition for the month preceding the reference month, with the exception of Mexico, where the data refer to the two months preceding the reference month.

d. Number of switches measured as a percentage of contributors.

Standard economic theories on lifetime savings assume that individuals follow a pattern of rational behavior. They assume the following: (a) savers accumulate and spend assets to maximize some form of utility function over their lifetime that may include bequests or inheritance, (b) savers have the necessary financial education to optimize their investment and savings strategies, and (c) savers have sufficient willpower to implement the optimal investment and savings strategy consistently over their lifetime. However, the literature on behavioral economics and financial education suggests that these assumptions are highly suspect (see box 2.2). Even if consumers do act, they often act on wrong information, perhaps because they are not adequately informed about their pension system, or they fail to act in a consistent fashion.[12]

In addition, switching costs are an important cause of individuals' inertia. *Switching costs* are the real or perceived costs that consumers incur when changing supplier but that are not incurred when remaining with the current supplier. These costs render consumers captive ("locked in") to the pension firms, which can then price services above production costs. As a result, price competition is rare or nonexistent. See box 2.3 and annex 2D for a more detailed treatment of the issue of switching costs.

Inertia is often compounded by regulations restricting, banning, or increasing the cost of switches across pension firms. Policy makers in Latin America, for example, have used these regulations as a tool (a) to control what is perceived as excessive switching caused by marketing wars between pension firms (Chile in various episodes) or (b) to prevent such marketing wars (Mexico from 1997 to 2003).

Although newer versions of these regulations recognize that a complete ban on switches is detrimental to consumers, so is unfettered switching in response to the incentives that pension firms have to invest in salespeople to increase their market share.[13] Indeed, although salespeople can play a role as providers of financial education, especially in contexts where participant choice is required (Papke 2004), the use of high-pressure sales tactics and even fraud has often been problematic.

Finally, information problems are pervasive in mandatory DC markets. Either consumers are misinformed about the pension products they are forced to consume, or products are too complex to understand and monitor in a systematic way.[14] Twenty-eight years after the reform, consumers in Chile remain uninformed of critical factors in the system. The 2004 Social Protection Survey indicated that only 50 percent of respondents claimed to know their pension account balances and less than 2 percent knew about their fund's fixed or variable fees (Arenas de Mesa et al. 2008). Surveys of members of U.S. corporate pension plans show low financial literacy too (Gustman and Steinmeier 2001a). Such comprehensive surveys are not yet available throughout Latin America, but one can presume that other countries in the region and other emerging markets face similar challenges.

Box 2.2 Behavioral Economics Lessons for Mandatory DC Pensions

The literature on behavioral economics identifies several key patterns (or anomalies) of investment retirement behavior (Barberis and Thaler 2003). For instance, when presented with a choice of investment strategies, pension plan members appear to have relatively weak preferences for the asset portfolio they choose (Benartzi and Thaler 2002); that is, individuals lack firm preferences. In addition, investment decisions are affected by framing effects; hence, the response of individuals changes depending on how the same information is presented to them (Benartzi and Thaler 1999, 2001, 2002). Alternatively, investment decision making is affected by anchoring effects; that is, the initial conditions used to justify a decision remain important over time even when the decision is irrational (Mitchell and Utkus 2004). Anchoring is also consistent with the significant inertia and procrastination in investment decision making by pension plan members, as documented by Choi et al. (2002) and Madrian and Shea (2001). Another anomaly is that asset allocations in DC pension plans tend to be driven by past performance rather than by expected future returns and risks (Benartzi 2001).

Additionally, there is some reason to suspect that individuals do not maximize expected utility in practice. According to prospect theory developed by Kahneman and Tversky (1979), individuals maximize some form of nonlinear value function that differs from expected utility maximization in two key ways: (a) individuals judge how their decisions affect incremental gains and losses to their wealth, rather than how they affect their total wealth as required by standard utility theory, and (b) individuals treat gains and losses asymmetrically. Individuals tend to be overconfident about the future and to make excessively optimistic forecasts (Barber and Odean 2001; De Bondt 1998; Goetzmann and Kumar 2008). Investors are reluctant to cut their losses, and they keep loss-making positions in the hope that they will recover their original investment, as reported by Benartzi and Thaler (1995), Gneezy and Potters (1997), Odean (1998), and Rabin and Thaler (2001).

Finally, overconfidence and loss aversion are exacerbated by narrow framing effects, also known as *mental accounting*, that individuals seem to use to keep track of financial transactions and evaluate them (Barberis and Huang 2001; Barberis, Huang, and Thaler 2006; Kahneman and Tversky 1984, 2000; Thaler 1985, 1999).

Information problems provide a rationale for policy interventions in the design and delivery of tailored financial education programs to consumers of mandatory DC plans. Indeed, a general consensus exists that important benefits can be derived from financial education programs when they are well tailored and carefully delivered (Martin 2007).[15]

Box 2.3 What Are the Effects of Switching Costs in Pension Markets?

The presence of switching costs has implications for the dynamics of mandatory pension markets and can explain many commonly observed business practices in pension markets. For instance, switching costs can explain why pension firms focus their business strategies on building and maintaining their market share, because the presence of switching costs discourages switching and thus can mean the existence of a pool of captive consumers. Switching costs allow pension firms to price above cost to consumers who are already clients and are locked in because they would incur a cost if they changed to a different pension firm. As a result, price competition is rare or nonexistent, whereas competition for the market is pervasive, particularly when a sales force and other marketing tools are used.

Given that pension firms are usually constrained to charge a single price to all customers, when setting prices they have to balance the incentive to price high to extract the rewards from their customer base against the incentive to price low to attract new customers who will be valuable in the future. Consequently, a firm's price depends on its market share and on the stage of growth of a market. A firm with a high market share is more likely to find that the incentive to harvest the rewards from its current customer base outweighs the incentive to invest by pricing low to obtain new customers.

The existence of switching costs also helps explain some usual patterns in pension market history. When a mandatory DC pension market is created, usually pension firms compete intensively for clients. In the presence of switching costs, this dynamic diminishes competition later on when the market matures (that is, when most customers are already locked in). This view fits the experience of the Chilean pension market, for example.[a] According to Reyes and Castro (2008), three phases can be identified since the start-up of the Chilean market in 1981. The initial phase (1981–90) was characterized by high fees and costs for pension firms, very little churning of firms, and rapidly rising profit levels toward the end of the phase. The intermediate competitive phase (1991–97) was characterized by the entry of new companies, a consolidation of the industry through mergers and acquisitions, greater concentration, a decreasing level of profits, and rising commissions in real terms. The third phase (from 1998 to the present) is characterized by a steady state and higher market concentration and market power levels. It also fits the history of the Mexican pension market, as discussed by García-Huitrón and Rodríguez (2002) and Meléndez (2004).

Annex 2D offers a more technical analysis of what is known about switching costs, and the regulatory challenges that switching costs impose are covered in chapter 3.

a. The match is not perfect because of regulatory changes along the way, but it is a good approximation. It is also a neat approximation of the Mexican pension market start-up.

This book recognizes the importance of financial literacy. It acknowledges that both the content and the form of delivery of information are critical, but contends that financial literacy is a complex policy issue that merits separate research.[16] Indeed, financial education cannot by itself fully compensate for the limited capacity of individuals to process information, let alone offset behavioral biases and switching costs. Hence, policies aimed at addressing consumers' inertia need to focus on (a) institutional industrial organization models and (b) investment solutions that exploit the aforementioned behavioral biases (rather than try to correct them) to improve consumers' welfare.[17]

Empirical Evidence of Low Responsiveness to Changes in Prices

Several studies on the responsiveness of consumers to changes in prices have been conducted for selected countries, using a variety of methodologies. Results are mixed. They generally point to low demand elasticity with respect to prices, but elasticity increases with investment by firms in marketing and with the level of consumers' income.

For Chile, a series of papers investigated the effects of regulations that limited the role of sales agents. Berstein and Micco (2002) estimated demand elasticity for the periods covering 1995–97 and 1998–2002, before and after a regulatory reform. In the first period, which was characterized by aggressive competitive strategies through sales agents, net transfers were found to be positively correlated with differentials in rates of return and negatively correlated with differentials in fees. The number of sales agents increased the elasticity of demand to rates of return and decreased the elasticity of demand to fees. In the second period, after new regulations came into effect reducing both the number of salespersons and transfers across funds, parameters related to fees were not found to be significantly related to the elasticity of demand. These findings suggest that net switches among pension funds are mainly determined by the number of sales agents and that the presence of sales agents increases the elasticity of demand with respect to fees and returns. Berstein and Ruiz (2005) confirm that the large number of salespersons during 1995–97 helped increase elasticity with respect to price variables—in particular rates of return. They also confirm widespread misinformation about the market for mandatory DC pensions. Misinformation is more acute among women, young individuals, and individuals with low income or education. Cerda (2006) shows that the rate of churning of contributors is positively correlated with the market share of the pension fund and its ranking in terms of asset management performance. Finally, Berstein and Cabrita (2007) reconfirm, using individual data, that despite relatively low demand elasticity with respect to prices (fees and returns), elasticity increases considerably when associated with sales agent involvement.[18]

In Mexico, consumers seem to be particularly sensitive to the marketing strategies of pension funds. García-Huitrón and Rodríguez (2002) estimate the demand elasticity function for Mexico and find that the only significant parameters are those related to marketing, especially the number of sales agents, whereas parameters related to fees and rates of return are neither significant nor significantly different from zero. Meléndez (2004) estimates AFORE demand functions and finds that neither fees nor returns explain affiliation. In addition, members' decisions to transfer their accounts across Mexican pension firms are highly associated with the sales efforts of the pension firm and less associated with fees and rates of return. However, the importance of these last two factors has significantly increased over time. Armenta (2007) analyzes the determinants of switches from one AFORE to another and finds that the number of switches is statistically correlated with the changes in the fees charged on contributions but less affected by the fees charged on the asset base.

In Peru, Masías and Sánchez (2006) find positive and significant correlations between transfers to a pension fund administrator and the number of sales agents. However, they also find that transfers are positively and negatively correlated to real rates of return and commissions, respectively, which would suggest a positive demand elasticity to relevant price variables.[19]

Chisari et al. (1998) find similar results for Argentina. As in the previous cases, they find a positive and statistically significant correlation between the activity of sales agents and the probability of switching to another firm. They also find that high-income consumers are more responsive to fees and returns than are low-income consumers, presumably because high-income consumers are also better equipped to make financial decisions.

In sum, this section shows that consumers in mandatory DC markets do not behave according to the rationality paradigm typically assumed in the economic literature. In fact, they are typically very insensitive to differences in prices among pension firms. However, their price elasticity is positively correlated with the number of salespeople, marketing expenditures, and disposable income. Finally, policy makers have often restricted switching as a means of preventing marketing wars and excessive marketing expenditures, which are deemed socially undesirable. However, as discussed in the next chapter, these interventions have tried to address only the symptoms, rather than the causes, of these problems.

The Supply of Pension Services

High barriers to entry (box 2.4) characterize the supply of pension services in mandatory DC systems, because (a) most jurisdictions allow only specialized entities to provide pension services in a heavily regulated

---

Box 2.4 Barriers to Entry in Pension Markets

Barriers to entry are factors that prevent or deter the entry of new firms
into an industry even when incumbent firms are earning excess profits.
Bolivia, where only two firms are allowed to participate in the market, provides an example of a regulatory barrier. Nonregulatory barriers
encompass a broad class, including structural and strategic barriers.
Structural barriers to entry arise from basic industry characteristics
such as technology (like economies of scale), costs (like sunk costs), and
demand (like product differentiation). For the pension markets, economies of scale and sunk costs are of particular relevance. Strategic barriers
to entry arise from the behavior of incumbents. In particular, incumbents
may act to strengthen structural barriers or may threaten to retaliate
against entrants if they do enter. Such threats must be credible, however,
in the sense that incumbents must have an incentive to carry them out if
entry does occur.

---

environment and (b) the typical pension services provided in mandatory
DC markets are characterized by large fixed costs and important economies of scale. Indeed, the empirical literature finds unambiguous evidence
of economies of scale in the supply of pension services.

Structure and Governance of Pension Firms

The structure of firms offering mandatory DC plans varies across countries, but most emerging markets allow only specialized, sole-purpose
pension firms whose own assets are legally separated from the assets under
management.[20] The widespread use of sole-purpose providers among
emerging markets has its origins in the 1981 introduction of mandatory
privately managed individual accounts in Chile. A specialized pension fund
manager (pension firm) was considered easier to supervise, and potential
conflicts of interest and risks could be more adequately controlled, resulting in enhanced consumer protection.[21]

Other countries in Latin America and Eastern Europe have adopted
similar models requiring specialized pension firms, although the specific
governance structure differs across countries (box 2.5). However, jurisdictions with more mature financial markets, such as Australia, Sweden,
and the United Kingdom, have permitted a wider range of financial
institutions to manage mandatory DC plans (Bateman 2000; Palmer 2004,
2006). In Australia, for example, financial service providers granted a
superannuation trustee license by the Australian Prudential Regulation
Authority can offer mandatory DC plans. Employers can also sponsor

Box 2.5 Governance Structure of Pension Firms in Selected Emerging Markets

Governance structure varies among countries, including private providers often sponsored by large financial holding companies (in Latin America) or insurance companies (Poland), public providers, and open mutual associations. Argentina, Costa Rica, Mexico, and Uruguay have also allowed the operation of public pension firms.[a] In Hungary, although the governance structure is designed to grant decision-making powers to fund members, this outcome does not materialize in many plans. The nature of open mutual associations and the absence of capital requirements imply that in most cases local mandatory pension funds need a sponsor to meet start-up costs. As a result, the Hungarian mandatory DC pension industry is divided into three groups of pension fund managers: (a) those sponsored by financial institutions, (b) those sponsored by large employers, and (c) independent plans (that is, without a sponsor) (Impavido and Rocha 2006). In Poland, the pension fund industry has ownership links with the insurance sector and is largely operated by foreign companies. For example, insurance companies control the seven largest managers, and banks control three managers. Two other managers, whose controlling companies are not linked to active financial sector holding groups, also exist.

a. In particular, the Mexican government has had a stake in a pension firm (Afore XXI) targeted at private sector workers since the start of the system in 1997. With the federal civil servants' pension reform of 2007, another government-owned pension firm was created (PensionISSSTE). For an initial period of three years, PensionISSSTE is allowed to provide services exclusively to federal civil servants and other public sector employees who may choose the DC system over the traditional defined benefit system for public servants. After this transition period, PensionISSSTE will operate like any other pension firm; that is, private sector workers may choose PensionISSSTE, and public sector workers will be allowed to change to a different pension firm.

plans for their employees. Industry-specific funds and self-managed funds (funds with fewer than five members, where each member is also a trustee of the fund) are also allowed. As a result, Australia had about 575 pension firms (superannuation entities) at the end of 2007 (see chapter 4 for more details).

In addition to the sole-purpose requirement, the typical regulatory environment imposes strong licensing criteria. Typically, it requires a minimum amount of capital, a fit-and-proper test, and a business plan. The minimum capital usually ranges from about US$150,000 to US$1 million, although the European Union has set the minimum capital requirement as high as €2.5 million. The minimum capital often increases with membership. In the case of Chile, for example, the minimum capital required for a license is close to US$150,000, and the minimum increases with the number of members but does not exceed US$500,000.

Finally, some jurisdictions require a minimum level of reserves to support a guarantee on the rate of return. Argentina (until 2008), Bulgaria, Chile, Colombia, the Dominican Republic, El Salvador, Hungary, Lithuania, Peru, Poland, the Slovak Republic, and Uruguay are examples of countries where guarantees on the rate of return exist. In most cases, the guarantee is defined as an industry's *relative rate of return guarantee*.[22,23] Any pension firm with a rate of return below a band around the industry's average rate of return has the obligation to meet the shortfall with its own compulsory reserves. In Chile, for example, compulsory reserves are equivalent to 1 percent of assets under management, so the whole industry holds reserves amounting to 0.75 percent of gross domestic product (GDP). These compulsory reserves are meant to cover any difference between realized returns and a benchmark defined in relation to a band around the average rate of return of all pension funds over a rolling 36-month period.[24] If the rate of return is lower than the lower band, the asset manager needs to make up for the difference from its own minimum reserves.[25]

Historically, the sole-purpose provider requirement and licensing criteria have not constituted major entry barriers for reputable pension fund administrators in Latin America and Eastern Europe. Reserve requirements appear to constitute more burdensome entry barriers than do minimum capital requirements. However, market concentration is also high in jurisdictions without minimum reserve requirements to support guarantees. This finding suggests that nonregulatory barriers to entry are far more important in explaining market concentration and market power.

Types of Services Provided by Pension Firms

The typical services provided by pension firms in mandatory DC pension markets are summarized in the following list. Most of these services are characterized by high economies of scale.

- *Collection of contributions.* This function covers the physical collection of contributions and the reconciliation of total collections with amounts collected for each participant. Therefore, it is closely related to record keeping. Many countries, such as Argentina, Bulgaria, Colombia, Mexico, Poland, Sweden, and—more recently—Hungary, have centralized this service either through the tax administration authority or the social security institutions.
- *Record keeping.* This service includes maintaining the registry of flows into (mainly contributions) and out of each individual account,[26]

determining the end-of-period value of the account, and managing the transfer of accounts from one pension fund to another.

- *Asset management.* This function is often conducted in house but can usually be subcontracted.
- *Benefit payment.* This function includes the determination of benefits and their payments. Often, it also covers the provision of advisory services on retirement options to participants. These tasks are frequently shared with other institutions within the financial group.
- *Insurance.* In many jurisdictions, pension firms are also involved in the provision of disability and survivorship insurance benefits. Sometimes, pension firms simply negotiate contracts with insurance companies on behalf of consumers. More often, they act as insurers and buy reinsurance from insurance companies. In a few jurisdictions, such as Mexico, separate entities manage disability insurance.
- *Treasury operations.* The provision of all of these services requires the support of treasury functions.
- *Provision of information.* Most jurisdictions establish minimum information requirements in relation to each participant's account, such as sending annual statements with details of the flows in and out of the account, fees, and rates of return.[27] The rate of return is often benchmarked against the industry's performance.
- *Marketing.* Marketing is part of the strategic behavior of pension firms to preserve or increase market power and is regulated by pension supervisors. Box 2.6 explains why marketing expenditures increase economies of scale and the market power of pension firms. Marketing typically includes the maintenance of a sales force and the design and launching of public information campaigns through mass media or by subcontracting of these services to specialized agencies. Most mandatory pension systems restrict the cross-sale of services (that is, the sale of pension services along with other financial services or vice versa), although it is often permitted for voluntary plans.

Empirical Evidence of Economies of Scale

The empirical literature finds unambiguous evidence of economies of scale, especially in functions such as collection of contributions, record keeping, and marketing. Economies of scale promote concentration, thereby reducing the scope for entry to the market and giving incumbents greater market power, as further discussed in the next section.

A summary of the literature on the cost functions of pension funds in Latin America follows. The general trends are consistent with international empirical evidence for members of the Organisation for Economic Co-operation and Development or middle- to high-income countries.[28]

Box 2.6 Marketing as a Means of Preserving and Increasing Market Power

Pension firms typically engage in marketing as part of their strategic behavior to preserve and increase market power. Other tools typically used by pension firms to preserve market power include discounts on fees for length of membership, which discourage participants from switching to other funds. Marketing expenditure, which is a key component of average fixed costs, increases barriers to entry, reduces contestability of the market, and gives incumbents additional market power.

The rationale for why marketing expenditure increases market power is simple and is better understood by noting the following:

- *Marketing expenditures are fixed costs.* Marketing outlays are determined by comparing the marginal benefit and the marginal cost of additional marketing efforts—in the form of either more messages or a larger sales force (Rasmussen 1952). Thus, such outlays are typically proportional to the volume of transfers of individuals across pension firms for a given market size and *not* to the level of production or clients. For this reason, marketing expenditures are regarded as fixed costs.
- *Marketing expenditures create endogenous economies of scale.* When the effectiveness of marketing efforts is proportional to the volume of transfers and not to the level of clients, marketing becomes endogenous in the sense that it is part of the firm's internal strategy to maximize profits. The part of economies of scale explained by endogenous fixed costs is known as *endogenous economies of scale* (Sutton 1991). By contrast, some fixed costs are exogenous in the sense that they have to be incurred and are outside the control of the firm. For instance, some fixed costs related to the establishment of a pension firm.
- *Marketing expenditures increase market power.* A major policy implication of the two previous points is that economies of scale intensify when marketing expenditure rises (Comanor and Wilson 1967). Increased economies of scale imply that any potential competitor would need to achieve a larger market share to make its entry profitable. Threats of triggering a marketing war on entry are a further deterrent. The key consequence is the increased market power of incumbents. Market power is discussed later in this chapter.

Apella and Maceira (2006), Chisari et al. (1998), and Ferro (2003) for Argentina; Barrientos and Boussofiane (2001) and Marinovic and Valdés-Prieto (2004) for Chile; and Meléndez (2004) for Mexico find that there are significant economies of scale in the mandatory DC pension industry and that marketing expenditures contribute to raising economies of scale.

Marinovic and Valdés-Prieto (2004) show that without marketing costs the minimal efficiency scale in the Chilean pension industry declines substantially from about 1 million contributors (or 2 million registered individuals) to about 150,000 contributors (or 300,000 registered individuals).[29] Similarly, Apella and Maceira (2006) found that economies of scale in the Argentine pension industry declined after 1997 in response to a regulatory change that restricted the transfers of members across administrators and resulted in a decline in the sales force. Despite the decline in economies of scale after 1997, they remained significant. Apella and Maceira (2006) reconfirmed the existence of economies of scale in the Argentine pension industry and found that the minimum efficiency scale was reached at 1 million affiliates. Without marketing costs, the minimal efficiency scale declined to approximately 800,000 affiliates. These results are consistent with previous estimates in Chisari et al. (1998) and Ferro (2003).

Although unambiguous evidence indicates the presence of economies of scale, their exact magnitude is subject to debate. For Mexico, Meléndez (2004) found that the minimum efficiency scale is close to 1.15 million members for pension fund managers who belong to a financial conglomerate and 1.05 million members for managers who do not belong to a financial conglomerate. Nevertheless, Aguilera and Velázquez (2008) suggest that previous studies used wrongly specified cost curves. By using a semiparametric cost function, they found that economies of scale are lower in Mexico (about 800,000 members or 2 percent of the market share) and that the industry has dramatically reduced its costs since 2002, when the authorities started introducing regulatory changes aimed at promoting competition in fees.

The differences in the results of studies in the economies of scale stem from three main weaknesses: (a) lack of reliable data to analyze cost determinants, in particular disaggregated accounting cost data and inconsistencies in cost allocations across countries; (b) methodological difficulties inherent in the definition of outputs produced by a pension firm; and (c) possible misspecification in some studies (namely, omitted variables) attributable to data inconsistencies across countries.

The decrease in average administrative costs of pension funds over time in Latin American countries also suggests the presence of economies of scale (table 2.2). Expenditures were particularly high in the early years of the reform because of both small asset and member bases but have experienced a dramatic decline over the years; high setup costs also help explain this trend.[30] A similar trend is found in other emerging markets that established mandatory DC pillars in the 1990s or early 2000s.

Despite the observed economies of scale, many jurisdictions require that mandatory pension services be bundled as a package. Hence they forgo opportunities for increasing efficiency and promoting further declines in

Table 2.2 Operational Expenses in Latin America, 2000 and 2007

	Per member (US$)		Over assets (%)	
Country	2000	2007	2000	2007
Argentina	75.80	35.37	3.12	1.27
Bolivia	18.16	5.42	1.37	0.20
Chile	34.52	42.12	0.60	0.31
Colombia	—	44.28	—	1.40
Costa Rica	n.a.	17.73	n.a.	2.09
Dominican Republic	n.a.	7.35	n.a.	1.27
El Salvador	76.43	16.06	13.44	0.64
Mexico	42.22	25.60	4.34	1.30
Peru	31.32	43.21	2.60	0.89
Uruguay	53.14	24.58	3.79	0.56
Mean	47.37	23.85	4.18	1.15
Standard deviation	22.32	12.46	4.29	0.73

Source: Data from Asociación Internacional de Organismos de Supervisión de Fondos de Pensiones.

Note: — not available; n.a. = not applicable.

administrative fees. However, others have unbundled services with high fixed costs (such as contribution collection and disability insurance) from services with lower economies of scale (such as asset management). For example, the mandatory DC pillar in the Swedish model separates asset management, which is subject to low entry barriers and high competition, from collection and record-keeping functions, which are centralized. This model has allowed pension fund managers to operate with modest fees. Other countries in Latin America and Eastern Europe (for example, Hungary and Poland) have centralized the collection of contributions, which has allowed pension firms to operate more efficiently in providing other pension services (see chapter 3).

Consequences of Inertia and Barriers to Entry

The interplay of demand and supply with such special characteristics as described in the previous sections has led to concentrated pension markets and a situation in which pension firms enjoy considerable market power; consequently, they tend to charge fees above average costs. This section explores those outcomes.

Concentration

The market for mandatory DC pension funds in emerging markets, which allow only specialized pension firms, is typically fairly concentrated (table 2.3) in comparison with countries with more mature financial markets such as Australia, Sweden, and the United Kingdom, which allow a wider set of providers. Industry concentration is also related to market size. Concentration is particularly high in emerging markets with a small membership, such as Bolivia and El Salvador, where two managers cover the entire market.[31]

For the most part, concentration has increased through mergers and acquisitions in emerging markets as the mandatory pension system has matured (table 2.3). In 2007, for example, Chile had six pension firms, with the two largest managing about 55 percent of assets or about 40 percent of GDP. This high concentration followed an intensive industry consolidation in the late 1990s, characterized by the exit or acquisition of a large number of small and mostly inefficient operators.[32] Argentina and Mexico, with a larger market, show greater diversification. Concentration in Argentina declined during the mid-2000s because of regulatory changes that facilitated the entry of newcomers, but it started to increase following the regulatory amendments that came into effect in March 2008.[33] Regulations appear to have influenced concentration levels.

High concentration is also the general pattern in emerging countries outside Latin America. In Hungary, the number of local mandatory provident funds declined from 38 in 1998, the year after the pension reform, to 18 in 2004, while assets under management in the 6 largest funds averaged 83 percent over the same period (Impavido and Rocha 2006). In Poland, the three largest pension firms accounted for about 64 percent of the assets under management in the system in 2005; this share was about 76 percent for the Slovak Republic in 2006 (Rudolph and Rocha 2007). In contrast to emerging markets that have focused on specialized pension firms, high-middle-income countries such as Australia, Sweden, and the United Kingdom have a more diversified industry.[34]

The only jurisdiction in table 2.3 that shows both an increasing number of pension firms and a decreasing asset concentration ratio over time is Mexico, especially between 2003 and 2006. This trend was the result of a series of reforms that began in 2002, which led to a much more contestable market.[35] However, in the view of some observers (Valdés-Prieto 2007), this result came at the cost of introducing distortionary subsidies in favor of funds with potentially low-quality asset management without sufficient incentives to improve asset management quality. By 2009, most reforms were reversed.[36]

Table 2.3 Concentration Indicators in Selected Emerging Markets, Selected Years

Country	Number of pension firms					C2 (%)[a]				
	2002	2003	2005	2006	2007	2002	2003	2005	2006	2007
Latin America										
Argentina	12	12	11	11	11	53	42	39	38	37
Bolivia	2	2	2	2	2	100	100	100	100	100
Chile	7	6	6	6	6	62	56	55	55	55
Colombia	8	6	6	6	6	77	51	51	52	52
Costa Rica	9	8	8	8	8	55	66	61	59	57
Dominican Republic	n.a.	8	7	7	5	n.a.	60	61	60	61
El Salvador	5	2	2	2	2	79	100	100	100	100
Mexico	11	13	16	21	21	45	44	39	36	35.5
Peru	4	4	5	5	4	59	59	57	61	61
Uruguay	6	4	4	4	4	77	75	74	74	74
Eastern Europe										
Bulgaria	n.a.	8	8	9	9	n.a.	61	56	53	53
Hungary	18	18	18	19	19	43	44	44	44	44

Sources: Data from Asociación Internacional de Organismos de Supervisión de Fondos de Pensiones; Dayoub and Lasagabaster 2008; Impavido and Rocha 2006; Rudolph and Rocha 2007.

Note: n.a. = not applicable. All data are from December of the year indicated.

a. C2 refers to the share of assets managed by the two largest administrators.

Market Power

A highly concentrated market can lead to excessive market power, which produces important distortions on both the demand and the supply side. Market power implies (a) price distortions,[37] (b) losses in social welfare,[38] and (c) rent redistribution from consumers to firms.[39]

A strong correlation seems to exist between market concentration and market power in mandatory DC pension systems in Latin America, at least in countries for which data are available (table 2.4).[40] Concentration is measured in terms of assets under management by the Herfindahl-Hirschman index.[41] Market power is measured by the Lerner index,[42] here approximated by the average administrative income fee (net of disability insurance premiums where needed) and average administrative expenses.[43]

As noted earlier, concentration is correlated to market size and is also affected by regulatory changes that facilitate the entry of new firms or encourage mergers and acquisitions as well as the exit of firms. Although market power tends to be more volatile than market concentration, table 2.4 suggests significant correlations between the two indexes. Correlations tend to be lower at points when a firm entry or exit occurs (or the threat of entry because of a regulatory change) but tend to resume thereafter. The correlation between concentration and market power is not as strong in the case of Argentina because of the severe crisis of the early 2000s and its negative impact on the performance of pension funds and the profits of pension firms for several years thereafter.

- *Mexico*. In Mexico, two distinct periods can be identified: (a) a period of increasing concentration and average market power until 2003 and (b) a period of decreasing concentration and market power afterward, caused by a series of policy reforms aimed at easing entry for potential competitors and increasing competition in the market.[44,45] At the peak of market concentration in 2003, firms were on average charging a relative markup of about 50 percent of fee income, as indicated by the Lerner index.
- *Argentina*. Argentina showed increasing levels of concentration through the period 1998–2006, and concentration was significantly higher than in Mexico, especially toward the end of the sample. Yet average relative markups were much lower[46] than in Mexico, especially during the period 2002–05, when the economic crisis severely hit the profitability of pension firms (Rofman 2007).
- *Chile*. Chile's market also shows a correlation between market concentration and market power, with the relative markup rising to more than 30 percent during the period 2000–07, following a sharp reduction in the number of firms and an increase in the market concentration ratio.[47]

Table 2.4 Concentration and Market Power in Latin America, 1998–2007

	1998	1999	2000	2001	2002	2003	2004	2005	2006	2007
Mexico										
Firms[a]	14	13	13	13	11	12	13	16	21	21
HHI[b]	1,318	1,257	1,232	1,170	1,424	1,410	1,336	1,209	1,110	1,093
LI[c]	–7	26	30	37	47	49	39	25	10	16
Argentina										
Firms[a]	17	15	13	13	12	12	12	12	11	11
HHI[b]	1,282	1,313	1,298	1,542	1,581	1,550	1,490	1,432	1,526	1,509
LI[c]	12	27	28	17	–1	0	–17	–15	9	8
Chile										
Firms[a]	14	16	8	7	7	7	6	6	6	6
HHI[b]	1,578	1,306	2,066	2,089	2,091	2,136	2,140	2,144	2,147	2,162
LI[c]	15	22	32	37	39	30	34	31	35	39
Peru										
Firms[a]	5	5	4	4	4	4	4	5	5	4
HHI[b]	2,293	2,310	2,661	2,653	2,647	2,639	2,629	2,500	2,667	2,718
LI[c]	9	21	45	52	53	52	55	25	9	12

Source: Author calculations based on data from the respective supervisory authorities.
Note: HHI = Herfindahl-Hirschman index; LI = Lerner index.
a. Number of pension firms.
b. The Herfindahl-Hirschman index is calculated on the basis of assets and scaled by 10,000.
c. The Lerner index is weighted by assets.

- *Peru.* Although Peru has significantly fewer firms than Argentina and Mexico, a similar pattern of increasing market power can be observed. Again, pension firms charged on average a 50 percent relative markup until 2004 and, on average, charged more than in Argentina. However, a sudden drop in profit margins took place after 2005 when Prima AFP entered the market as the direct competitor of Profuturo AFP and AFP Unión Vida. This competition sparked a marketing war in which the incumbents had to defend their market shares. The drop in relative markups in 2006 could be explained by the huge loss of Prima AFP, which had already reached 27 percent of the market in 2006, and at the same time by the fact that marketing expenditure had doubled in the same year, greatly reducing profit margins for all firms. The marketing war seems to have stopped in 2007 following the merger of AFP Unión Vida and Prima AFP during the second half of 2006.

Poor Price Performance

Very few studies have attempted to compare price performance across countries in a systematic manner because cross-country comparisons are hampered by several factors. Ideally, fees should be compared in relation to the cost structure of pension firms, which is likely to differ across and within countries because of the heterogeneous industrial organization of pension services. Unfortunately, a systematic cross-country analysis of cost structures has not been conducted, because of the unavailability of accounting data disaggregated by cost functions. In addition, differences in key parameters, such as retirement age, density of contributions, contribution rates, salary bases, and assets under management, further render international comparisons problematic.

Despite those caveats, several key policy issues emerge from cross-country comparisons: (a) fee structures are heterogeneous across countries; (b) comparable measures of fees are highly variable both within and across countries; and (c) fees charged by pension firms do not always compare positively with fees charged for similar services in nonmandatory markets, resulting in excessive returns on equities.

Countries that charge uniform fee rates mostly on earnings. Most countries require pension firms to charge fees in the form of uniform rates applied to different bases, such as earnings, contributions, or assets.[48] Because these fee bases vary across individuals, this pricing scheme redistributes from high- to low-base participants, which relieves the latter from the burden of paying fees.[49]

As of early 2006, all pension firms in Latin American countries charged fees as a percentage of the locally relevant earnings base (on flows), and in some countries, other types of fees were also charged. These charges are reported in table 2.5, which compares average first-floor fees[50] charged by pension firms in Latin America.

In Chile, firms could charge first-floor fees only on flows, but de facto they also charged second-floor fees on assets under management (on the stock). Indeed, participants' accounts were credited only the net rate of return from the management of foreign assets.[51] In addition, pension firms in Chile and Uruguay charged flat fees on every flow, irrespective of its size. Pension firms in Bolivia and Mexico charged additional fees on assets under management, and those in Costa Rica included additional charges on nominal returns. The Dominican Republic is the only country where pension firms had additional charges on excess benchmark returns. Finally, discounts were offered in a number of jurisdictions according to the number of years a consumer either participated in the system or was the client of a pension fund.

Table 2.5 Average First-Floor Fees in Latin American Countries, 2006

Country	Proportional charge on flows (% of salary)[a]	Fixed charge on flows (US$)	Charge on assets under management (%)	Charge on nominal returns (%)	Charge on excess returns (%)
Argentina	1.27	n.a.	n.a.	n.a.	n.a.
Bolivia	0.50	n.a.	0.2285[b]	n.a.	n.a.
Chile	1.60	0.90	n.a.	n.a.	n.a.
Colombia	1.57	n.a.	n.a.	n.a.	n.a.
Costa Rica	0.14	n.a.	n.a.	7.50	n.a.
Dominican Republic	0.50	n.a.	n.a.	n.a.	28.57
El Salvador	1.40	n.a.	n.a.	n.a.	n.a.
Mexico[c]	1.20	n.a.	0.34[d]	n.a.	n.a.
Peru	1.81	n.a.	n.a.	n.a.	n.a.
Uruguay	2.07	0.26	n.a.	n.a.	n.a.

Source: Corvera, Lartigue, and Madero 2006.
Note: n.a. = not applicable.
   a. Where the rate is applied to contributions, it has been converted as a rate applied to earnings.
   b. Different charges apply depending on the fund size.
   c. In 2007, Mexico banned fees proportional to flows.
   d. The fee applies to the excess return paid over the interest rate of commercial banking cash deposits.

Fee structures that are very heterogeneous. The other characteristic of prices in mandatory DC pensions is that they tend to be highly heterogeneous across and within countries. Corvera, Lartigue, and Madero (2006) develop a methodology to facilitate the comparison of different fee structures across countries by estimating "equivalent fees" on assets or on the flows.[52] They calculate the equivalent asset-based fee for 67 pension managers in Latin America and find that dispersion for pension management fees is large, both across and within countries. Cross-country dispersion in fees can be partially explained by differences in the services that pension managers are forced to provide as well as by the degree to which pension system architecture in each country takes advantage of economies of scale. However, Corvera, Lartigue, and Madero (2006) find that intracountry fee dispersion seems to be related to inadequate competition and the presence of state-owned managers, which tend to charge lower fees.

The fees of the most expensive firms are about two to three times higher than the least expensive one. Corvera, Lartigue, and Madero (2006) find that Argentina, Mexico, and Peru have the most expensive firms, calculated with a 25-year horizon (table 2.6 and figure 2.1).[53] Argentina, Costa Rica, and Mexico have the most expensive firms, calculated with a 40-year horizon (table 2.7 and figure 2.2). Bolivia, Colombia, and El Salvador have

Table 2.6 Latin America: 25-Year Assets under Management, Equivalent Fees

Country	Minimum (%)	Maximum (%)	Weighted average (%)	Standard deviation (%)	Coefficient of variation (%)
Argentina	1.20	1.45	1.35	0.09	6.89
Bolivia	0.53	0.53	0.53	0.00	0.20
Chile	0.98	1.21	1.07	0.08	7.31
Colombia	0.81	1.01	0.92	0.08	8.44
Costa Rica	0.75	1.10	1.02	0.16	15.26
Dominican Republic	0.81	1.01	1.01	0.09	8.95
El Salvador	0.86	0.86	0.86	0.00	0.00
Mexico	0.67	1.51	0.89	0.20	22.48
Peru	0.94	1.22	1.10	0.13	11.64
Uruguay	0.74	1.14	0.90	0.19	20.93

Source: Based on Corvera, Lartigue, and Madero 2006, with updated data as of June 2007.

Figure 2.1 Latin America: 25-Year Assets under Management, Equivalent Fees (Dispersion)

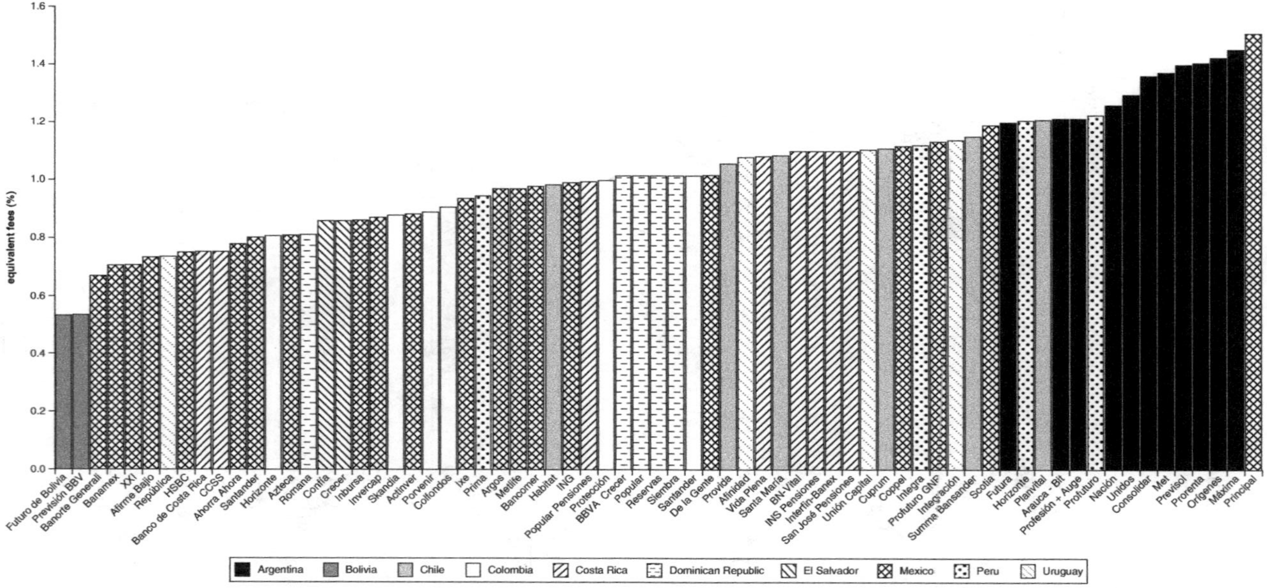

Source: Based on Corvera, Lartigue, and Madero 2006, with updated data as of June 2007.

Table 2.7 Latin America: 40-Year Assets under Management, Equivalent Fees

Country	Minimum (%)	Maximum (%)	Weighted average (%)	Standard deviation (%)	Coefficient of variation (%)
Argentina	0.69	0.83	0.77	0.05	6.87
Bolivia	0.39	0.39	0.39	0.00	0.27
Chile	0.56	0.69	0.61	0.04	7.29
Colombia	0.46	0.58	0.53	0.04	8.42
Costa Rica	0.69	0.98	0.92	0.13	14.01
Dominican Republic	0.64	0.84	0.84	0.09	10.80
El Salvador	0.49	0.49	0.49	0.00	0.00
Mexico	0.46	0.88	0.62	0.12	18.96
Peru	0.54	0.70	0.63	0.07	11.62
Uruguay	0.42	0.65	0.51	0.11	20.89

Source: Based on Corvera, Lartigue, and Madero 2006, with updated data as of June 2007.

the least expensive plans and present low price dispersion across firms.[54] Corvera, Lartigue, and Madero (2006) also find that fees have largely stagnated over the years and are unlikely to decline in the medium term because of insufficient competition, especially in Bolivia and El Salvador, which have a duopoly market structure.

Some mandatory pension plans in Eastern Europe with similar structures to the ones in Latin America also display high fees. The methodology developed by Corvera, Lartigue, and Madero (2006) was also applied to countries such as Hungary, Poland, and the Slovak Republic.[55] For Hungary, where the calculations have been applied to the system before Hungary introduced caps on fees in 2007, the 25- and 40-year assets management equivalent fees are much higher than for other countries in Eastern Europe and Latin America. Equivalent fees for Poland show a decline to 40 and 24 basis points by 2030 and 2045, respectively, and are similar to the least-cost Latin American firms operating in Bolivia. Equivalent fees for the Slovak Republic are comparable to the ones obtained for Latin American countries (table 2.8 and figures 2.3 and 2.4).

Finally, the charges applied by pension firms in both Latin America and Eastern Europe do not positively compare to the 50 and 100 basis points that large U.S. occupational funds and mutual funds charge, respectively, or to the Swedish mandatory DC plan.[56] For instance, the average fee for

Figure 2.2 Latin America: 40-Year Assets under Management, Equivalent Fees (Dispersion)

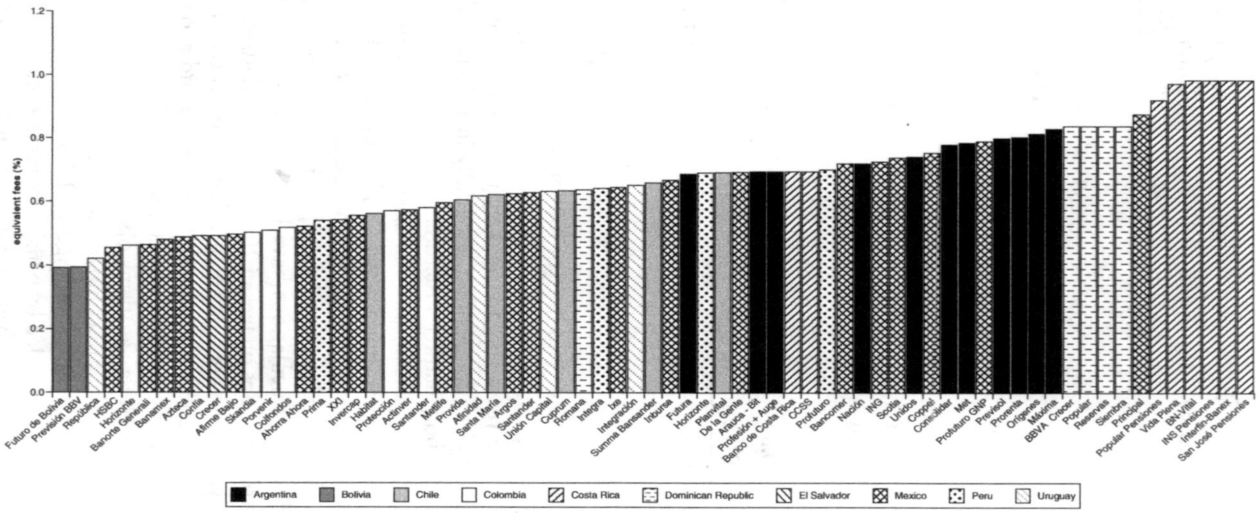

Source: Based on Corvera, Lartigue, and Madero 2006, with updated data as of June 2007.

Table 2.8 Eastern Europe: 25- and 40-Year Assets under Management, Equivalent Fees

Country	Minimum (%)	Maximum (%)	Weighted average (%)	Standard deviation (%)	Coefficient of variation (%)
25-year equivalent fee					
Hungary	0.39	1.44	1.15	0.34	29.56
Poland	0.39	0.41	0.40	0.01	2.51
Slovak Republic[a]	0.90	1.00	0.95	0.04	4.21
40-year equivalent fee					
Hungary	0.24	1.29	1.00	0.34	34.02
Poland	0.23	0.26	0.24	0.01	4.17
Slovak Republic[a]	0.85	0.96	0.91	0.05	5.49

Source: Author calculations based on Corvera, Lartigue, and Madero 2006.
a. Unweighted.

stock funds, bond funds, and money market funds in the United States (more relevant comparators given the portfolio structure of pension firms) are about 30 to 70 basis points (table 2.9).[57] The Swedish mandatory DC plan, in operation since 2000, charges fees close to 77 basis points, and the authorities expect those fees to decline to less than 30 basis points by 2025 (Rudolph and Rocha 2007).

Pension firms that enjoy exceptional profits. Because of the previously mentioned price distortions, pension firms in many Latin American countries have registered exceptionally high rates of return on equity. In Chile, for example, operating costs fell significantly after 1997 because of reduced expenditures on marketing services. However, the corresponding decrease in fees was substantially smaller, leading to a remarkable increase in firms' returns on equity, which reached 51 percent in 2000. Returns started to fall thereafter, partly to absorb an increase in insurance premiums. In El Salvador, a small country with a duopoly market, the returns on equity in 2005 were as high as 39 percent. By contrast, returns on equity have decreased in Mexico since 2002, when competition started to rise because of regulations that facilitated the entry of low-cost operators and switches across pension firms. Similarly, the returns on equity have been declining in Peru since 2004, mostly because of regulatory changes and the entry of new operators (figure 2.5).

Figure 2.3 Eastern Europe: 25-Year Assets under Management, Equivalent Fees (Dispersion)

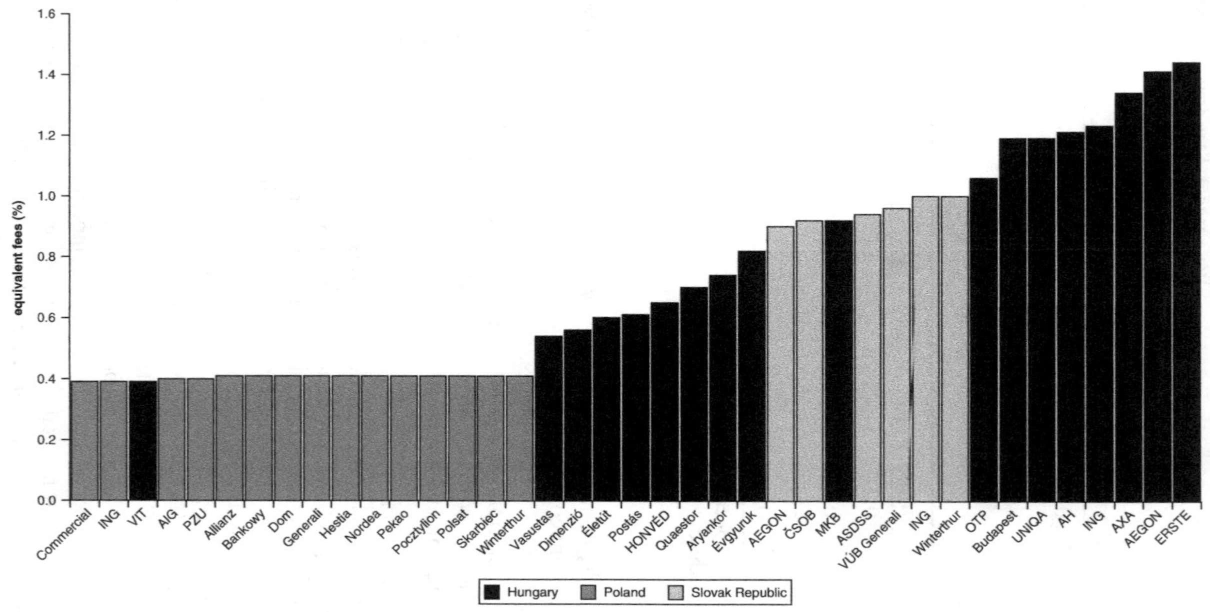

Hungary   Poland   Slovak Republic

Source: Corvera, Lartigue, and Madero 2006.

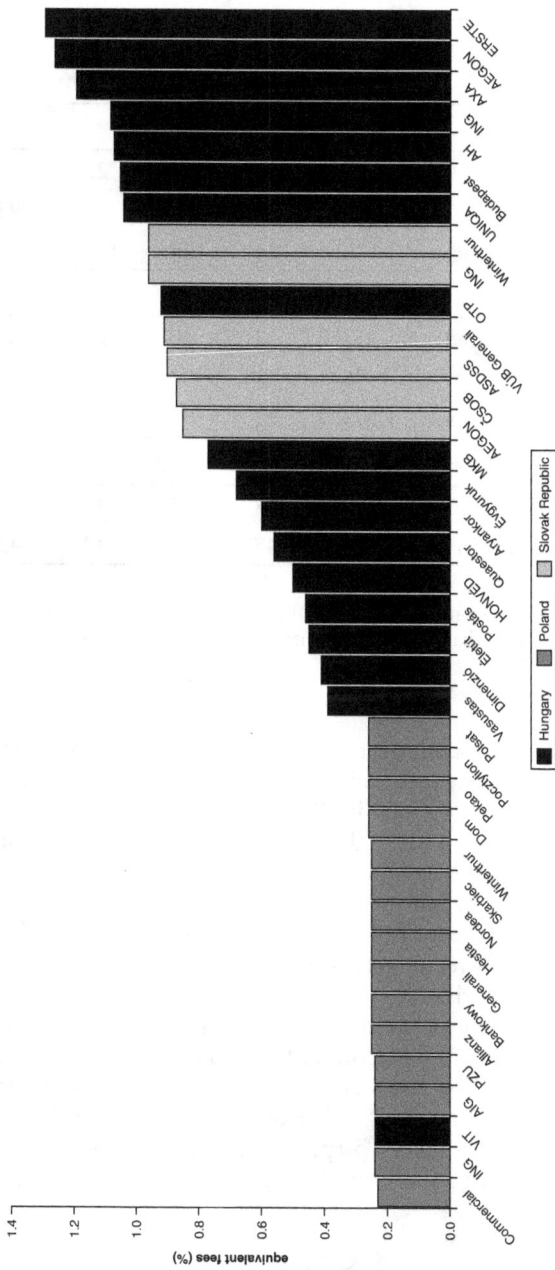

Figure 2.4 Eastern Europe: 40-Year Assets under Management, Equivalent Fees (Dispersion)

Source: Corvera, Lartigue, and Madero 2006.

Table 2.9 Mutual Fund Fees and Expenses in the United States, 2000–05

	Basis points					
Fees and expenses	*2000*	*2001*	*2002*	*2003*	*2004*	*2005*
Stock funds						
Load fees (annualized)	30	25	24	23	22	22
Expense ratio	98	99	100	99	95	91
Total fees and expenses	128	124	124	122	117	113
Bond funds						
Load fees (annualized)	27	22	20	20	20	20
Expense ratio	76	74	73	74	72	70
Total fees and expenses	103	97	93	94	92	90
Money market funds						
Expense ratio	49	47	45	43	42	41
Total fees and expenses	49	47	45	43	42	41

Source: ICI 2006.
Note: Fees are measured as asset weighted averages. The expense ratio is the amount of expenses that a fund charges its shareholders every year.

In Eastern Europe, pension firms were able to recover their start-up costs within a few years and have generated high returns on equity in recent years. For example, in 2004, the returns of Hungarian pension firms were about 16 percent. In Poland, they were 22 percent in 2004 and 24 percent in 2005 (Rudolph and Rocha 2007). More interesting, average returns on equity of pension firms in Latin America have been higher than average returns on equity of banks (except for Mexico), which are subject to stricter capital requirements, manage a more complex business, and bear much higher risks (figure 2.6).

An alternative measure of profitability is given by returns on assets. However, this measure is more difficult to calculate because net returns should be divided by assets at replacement costs which, in turn, require special data adjustments.[58] Using this methodology, Valdés-Prieto and Marinovic (2005) estimate a 50 percent annual return on assets for Chilean pension firms during the 1999–2003 period.

Conclusions

Mandatory DC pension markets can be characterized as quasi-markets, differing from standard markets in important ways. On the demand side,

Figure 2.5 Returns on Equity of Pension Firms in Select Latin American Countries, 1995–2005

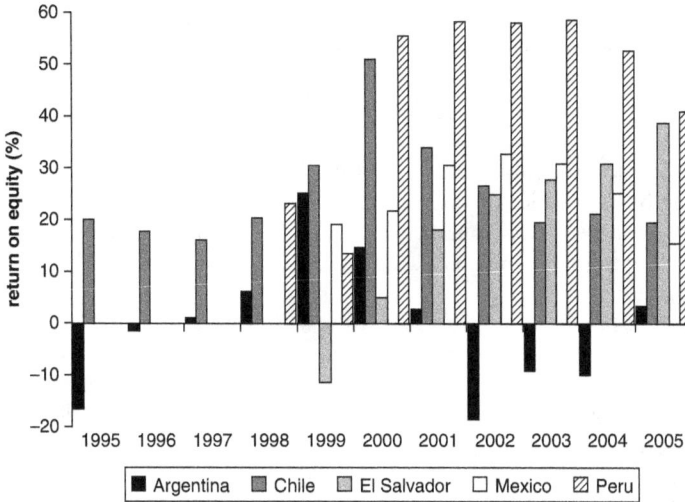

Source: Data from Asociación Internacional de Organismos de Supervisión de Fondos de Pensiones.

Figure 2.6 Returns on Equity of Pension Firms and Banks, 2005

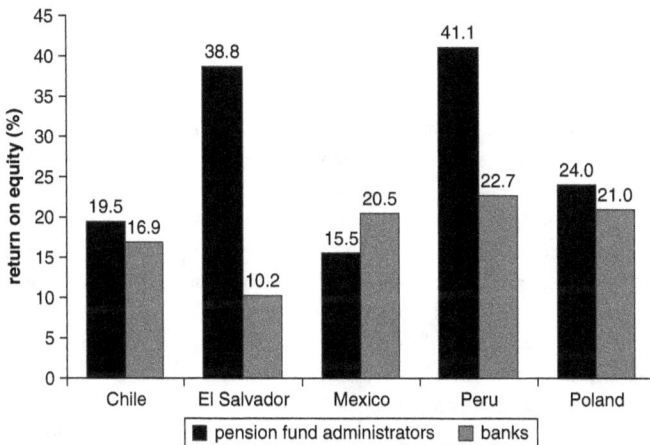

Sources: Data from Asociación Internacional de Organismos de Supervisión de Fondos de Pensiones; BankScope; Fitch Ratings.

consumption is mandatory, and purchasing power is expressed by vouchers, which are often subsidized by earmarked state budgets. On the supply side, providers do not necessarily maximize profits, and their governance structure includes both private and public sector firms, as well as for-profit and mutual associations. In addition, both the demand and the supply of pension services have specific characteristics.

On the demand side, consumers are typically very insensitive to changes in prices because of misinformation or difficulty in processing complex financial decisions. In other words, the demand for pension services is highly inelastic to prices. In addition, individuals choose on the basis of rules of thumb, thus introducing systematic biases into their investment decisions. In other words, consumers do not behave according to the rationality paradigm typically assumed in the economic literature.

On the supply side, specialized firms with strong licensing criteria typically provide pension services. In addition, certain pension functions, such as collection of contributions and record keeping, are characterized by important fixed costs and economies of scale. In addition, most countries require firms to bundle pension services into a single package. Hence, important barriers to entry characterize the market. Finally, pension firms engage in strategic behavior to preserve market share, such as investing in marketing to further increase barriers to entry.

Because of the interplay of these demand and supply characteristics, mandatory DC pension quasi-markets are not contestable; in fact, they are concentrated, and concentration has increased over time through mergers. Pension firms enjoy considerable market power, which is evidenced by firms charging prices well above average costs and by prices that are generally highly variable both within and across countries. In other words, pension firms extract substantial rents from their oligopoly position at the expense of consumer welfare.

This situation provides a strong rationale for policy intervention to help consumers recapture such rents in at least three areas: (a) financial literacy of consumers, (b) overall industrial organization of pension services, and (c) design of investment options to which inert individuals are assigned by default.

This book endorses the broad consensus on the value of financial literacy, and it acknowledges the importance of identifying the most relevant content and delivery mechanisms to influence behavior. Although these topics merit further research, this book does not examine them. Instead, it focuses on industrial organization models and default investment options that exploit the systematic biases of the decision-making process of individuals to promote permanent changes in behavior that can result in improved expected replacement rates. Chapters 3 and 4, respectively, address these themes in more detail.

Annex 2A: Know Your Plan and the Role of Financial Education

To arrive at optimal saving decisions, workers rely on accurate knowledge regarding their likely retirement benefits and consumption needs (Skog 2006). However, the lack of key financial information can cause individuals to prepare inadequately for retirement (Lusardi and Mitchell 2006). Little is known about individuals' reasons for acquiring financial knowledge. Older people may know more simply because they are closer to retirement, healthier people may know more because they expect to live longer in retirement, and wealthier or more educated individuals may know more than do the poor or less educated because they will need to rely more on their pensions in retirement.

Studies in the United States show that financial misinformation or lack of information is the norm (Gustman and Steinmeier 2001a). However, men tend to know more about their retirement benefits than do women; the older, wealthier, or healthier the individual, the more financially literate he or she is (Chan and Stevens 2004; Gustman and Steinmeier 2001b; Mitchell 1988). Individuals who are the most likely to rely on social security are the least informed, whereas those who are most likely to rely on their pensions are the best informed (Luchak and Gunderson 2000). Studies of members of the Organisation for Economic Co-operation and Development generally find that financial understanding is correlated with education and income levels. In Australia, the lowest levels of financial literacy are associated with low levels of education (10 years or fewer), unemployment or low-skilled work, low incomes, low levels of savings, being single, and being at either end of the age profile (18- to 24-year-olds and those age 70 or older). In the United Kingdom, individuals in the lower social grades and the lowest income band, as well as people ages 18 to 24, are likely to be the least receptive consumers. By contrast, individuals in the higher social grades, those with a higher income, young couples, and older respondents with no family are more likely to be sophisticated financial consumers, knowing how to get the information they need and understanding the advice they receive. In the Republic of Korea, scores broken down by demographic characteristics indicated that students from families with less educated parents or students who have low professional expectations score the lowest (OECD 2005).

Relatively few analysts have examined the question of pension knowledge outside the United States. Arenas de Mesa et al. (2008) used Chilean data from the Social Protection Survey of 2004 to examine trends of financial literacy variables across social groups, showing that 25 years after the reform, consumers in Chile remain unapprised of critical factors in the system. The 2004 Social Protection Survey indicated that only 50 percent of respondents claimed to know their pension account balances and less than 2 percent knew about their fund's fixed and variable fees. In addition,

Skog (2006) shows that the older, healthier, more educated, married male workers know more about the system. Union members, those with higher incomes, and employees of larger companies are also more financially informed. Finally, he finds that knowledge varies by subject area; accordingly, it is important to ascertain what literacy shortfalls must be targeted before determining what education efforts might be useful. Individuals become more pension literate as that knowledge becomes more useful.

A general consensus exists that some benefits can be derived from financial education if education programs are carefully tailored and delivered; however, some authors question whether financial education improves the rationality of investment decision making. For instance, Caskey (2006) argues that personal financial management education cannot be considered an effective mechanism for helping lower-income households accumulate financial assets or improve their credit histories. Also, Bell and Lerman (2005) argue that the success of financial education programs may be due to simple self-selection. By contrast, Hilgert, Hogarth, and Beverly (2003) present suggestive evidence on the value of financial literacy by demonstrating that individuals with greater measured levels of financial knowledge are more likely to behave in ways consistent with recommended financial behavior. Moreover, Bernheim, Garrett, and Maki (2001) find that households exposed to financial literacy education in the United States increased asset accumulation, and Bernheim and Garret (2003) find that employer-provided financial education stimulates savings. Finally, in his review of the literature, Martin (2007) makes the following conclusions: (a) although some households make mistakes with personal finance decisions, mistakes are more common for low-income and less educated households; (b) a connection exists between knowledge and behavior, with increases in knowledge positively affecting personal finance behavior (that is, the causality runs from knowledge to behavior); (c) because low-income and less educated households tend to make more mistakes, they also benefit the most from financial education; (d) other groups that appear to benefit disproportionately include minorities, single parents, and women; (e) the benefits of financial education appear to span a number of areas, including retirement planning, savings, homeownership, and credit use; (f) financial education programs are most effective when they are tailored to the needs of the recipient and include face-to-face time, either with a counselor or in a classroom setting; (g) financial education programs that cover specific topics and teach skills are better than those covering more general subjects; and (h) the outcomes of financial education efforts are often described as "better" for households, though increased financial knowledge may also result in seemingly worse outcomes, such as the increased use of mortgage default in certain circumstances.

As far as delivery is concerned, salespeople can play a role as providers of financial education, especially in contexts where participant choice is required (Papke 2004). However, the use of high-pressure sales tactics and even fraud have often been problematic. This factor provides a rationale for policy interventions in the design and delivery of tailored financial education to consumers of mandatory DC plans.

Annex 2B: Evidence of Behavior Based on Rules of Thumb

As discussed earlier, from 2003 to 2007, pension firms in Mexico saw a decline in market power and high turnover of contributors in comparison with other countries in Latin America. These trends were largely the result of regulatory reforms issued around 2002 and 2003 that facilitated switches among pension funds, automatically allocated undecided individuals to the funds with the lowest equivalent fees, and abolished time restrictions for switches when such switches occurred from higher- to lower-fee funds. These reforms lowered barriers to entry by securing a pool of accounts for low-fee pension firms and increased the productivity of sales forces by facilitating switching by individuals from one fund to another, which led to higher demand elasticity.[59]

The increased number of transfers in the system, however, does not imply higher expected net rates of return until retirement, because individuals consistently make mistakes when choosing their pension funds. The standard economic theories of lifetime saving are based on several implicit rationality assumptions: (a) savers accumulate and spend assets to maximize some form of life-cycle utility function, which may include bequests; (b) savers have the financial education to solve the necessary optimization problem; and (c) savers have sufficient willpower to implement the strategy that stems from the solution to the intertemporal optimization problem. However, all these assumptions are highly suspect.

Not only do individuals act in an irrational way and make mistakes, but they also do so in a very inconsistent and unpredictable way. Individuals tend, in practice, to adopt simple rules of thumb to solve optimization problems and subsequently implement their choices, leading to systematic biases.

The experience of Mexico exemplifies the behavior based on contributors' rules of thumb in choosing their pension firms, and it highlights the critical role played by information and the way it is provided. Calderón-Colín, Domínguez, and Schwartz (2008) analyze the choice of pension fund providers by Mexican contributors and the role played by the sales force of each fund in this selection process. Like many other studies, this paper finds that the number of sales agents hired by the receiving pension fund manager affects the number of switches. In addition, it notices a high increase in switches among pension firms between 2003 and 2006, coupled with a substantial increase in marketing expenditures, especially after 2003.[60] Finally, nearly 40 percent of switches were made to pension funds with lower historical returns and higher fees (see figure 2B.1).

Figure 2B.1 Consumer Confusion in the AFORE Market

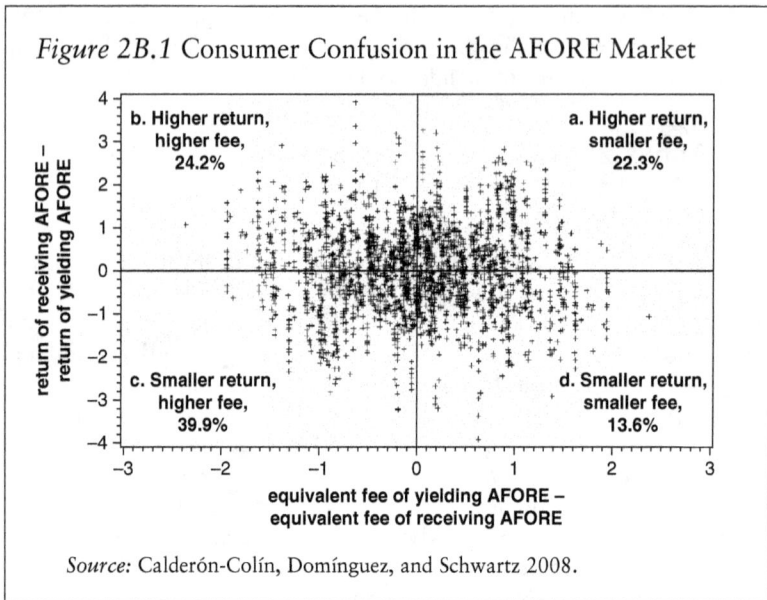

Source: Calderón-Colín, Domínguez, and Schwartz 2008.

The Mexican authorities were naturally concerned about the expo-
nential trend in turnover, the parallel increase in marketing expenditure
that did not directly benefit consumers, and the surprisingly high number
of switches toward firms with lower net rates of return. As a result, the
Mexican authorities decided in 2007 to curtail (albeit not to halt) switches
to essentially once a year and to base the automatic assignment rule on net
rate of returns. However, whether the Mexican policy response (adopted
for similar reasons in other countries) is optimal remains unclear. Historical returns are not representative of future returns, which suggests that the
alleged wrong choice today may turn out to be the right choice tomorrow.
Notwithstanding this concern, retirement investment behavior is characterized by all the aforementioned anomalies, suggesting that consumers
had likely made mistakes.

Behavior based on the rules of thumb of individuals points to a strong
rationale for policy intervention in the design of pension plan options.
Consumer behavior can be altered by merely changing the options available, especially the default option, and the way pension services are
organized. For instance, in the United States, employers' decisions on
automatic enrollment, automatic saving, and default investment funds of
401(k) plans have been critical in shaping retirement savings. Thaler and
Sunstein (2003) argue that the solution to modify permanently consumer
behavior is a strategy of paternalistic libertarianism, in which individuals

can have some choice, but the choices are predetermined by a paternalistic plan designer.

Annex 2C: Market Power, Demand Elasticity, and Welfare

This technical annex aims to develop the relationship between the concentration and market power indexes used in the chapter, as well as their relationship with demand elasticity and welfare.

Market Power and Demand Elasticity

The inverse relationship between market power, measured by the Lerner index, and the elasticity of demand is easily shown in the case of a profit-maximizing Cournot oligopoly of n different firms producing a single homogeneous good. Let $p(Q)$ be the inverse demand function with $Q = \sum_i^n q_i$ being the total output produced by the n firms. Let $C_i(q_i)$ be the supply function of the ith firm—that is, the cost (different for each firm) incurred by ith firm to produce q_i units of the good. Assume that both the demand and the supply functions are differentiable with $p' < 0$ and $C_i' > 0$. Firm i maximizes its profits by taking the quantities produced by the other firms as given. Therefore, the problem for the ith firm implies choosing the quantity q_i^c such that

$$\max_{q_i} \Pi_i(Q) = [p(Q)_{q_i} - C_i(q_i)]$$

This quantity is found by solving the system of reaction functions $q_i^R(Q_{-i}) = q_i$ jointly with the other $n - 1$ firms. This yields the Nash equilibrium $q_i^R(Q_{-i}^c) = q_i^c \ \forall i = 1, \dots, n$ sold at the equilibrium price $p^c = p(Q^c)$.

Notice in particular that the Lerner index for firm i is derived directly from the first-order condition $\dfrac{\partial p}{\partial q_i} q_i + p - \dfrac{\partial C_i}{\partial q_i} = 0$. In other words,

$$LI_i = \frac{p - C_i'}{p} = -\frac{p_i' q_i}{p} = \frac{1}{\varepsilon_i}$$

where the left-hand side of the last equation is the relative markup, also known as the Lerner index, charged by firm i, and ε_i is the elasticity of the residual demand faced by firm i.

In equilibrium, the market power of firm i is inversely proportional to the elasticity of its residual demand. For given q_i^c, firm i will have a low market power if its residual demand is very elastic. It will have a high market power if its residual demand is very inelastic.

Concentration and Market Power

The Herfindahl-Hirschman index is defined as the sum of the market shares squared:

$$HHI = \sum_{i=1}^{n} (s_i)^2$$

where simply $s_i = q_i / Q$ is the market share of the ith firm.

The previous section showed that in the case of the profit-maximizing Cournot oligopoly of n different firms producing a single homogeneous good, the Lerner index for firm i can be expressed as the inverse of the price elasticity of its residual demand. One can further manipulate this finding to express the firm's Lerner index as the inverse of the elasticity of the market demand weighted by the firm's market share:

$$LI_i = \frac{1}{\varepsilon_i} = \frac{p' q_i}{p} \frac{Q}{Q} = \frac{s_i}{\varepsilon_Q}$$

where ε_Q is the elasticity of the market demand.

The *market Lerner index* is defined as the average of the firm Lerner indexes weighted by their market shares:

$$LI = \sum_{i=1}^{n} s_i LI_i = \sum_{i=1}^{n} \frac{s_i^2}{\varepsilon_Q} = \frac{HHI}{\varepsilon_Q}$$

which gives the relationship between market concentration and market power.

Market power is directly related to market concentration, and the strength of this relationship is inversely proportional to the demand elasticity. If market demand is very elastic, changes in concentration will not have very large effects on pricing and, hence, market power. If demand is very inelastic, changes in concentration can have large effects on pricing and, therefore, produce important distortions on both the demand and the supply side, as mentioned in the text.

Market Power and Social Welfare

A social welfare loss arises when the combined surplus of producers and consumers decreases—in other words, when the surplus of the consumer decreases by more than the increase in the surplus of the producer. The social welfare loss is also a function of the demand elasticity, but contrary to the case of price distortions, the welfare loss is not necessarily monotonically decreasing with it; this will depend on the interaction between demand and supply. Finally, in the case of mandatory DC pensions, concerns arise about the distribution of rents. With a highly inelastic demand, price changes do not affect quantities consumed very much but elicit large monetary transfers from consumers to firms. This outcome is not particularly desirable for either policy makers, who mandate consumption, or for pension providers, because rent redistributions that are deemed socially unacceptable elicit strong political responses, which can easily jeopardize profit margins.

Market power can also have perverse effects on the supply side. These more subtle distortions take the following forms: (a) X-inefficiencies (Leibenstein 1966) and (b) rent-seeking behavior. In general, unless shareholders can perfectly monitor the activities of the firm's employees (executives and workers) and credibly threaten to sanction deviations, firms are likely to engage in X-inefficiencies. The corporate governance literature (Becht, Bolton, and Röell 2003) indicates that a whole series of mechanisms (including a board of directors, compensation packages, and—more generally—yardstick competition[61]) can be useful in mitigating the problem of separation between ownership and control. However, most of these mechanisms are not available for pension funds. In addition, market power and concentration reduce the scope and effectiveness of yardstick competition in ensuring alignment of incentives between owners and managers. In other words, market power makes it easier for the manager to slack and increase production costs. These extra costs would add to the welfare loss that arises in the presence of price distortions.

The other supply distortions relate to rent-seeking behavior. Firms in a noncompetitive market will incur strategic and administrative expenses to increase and maintain their market power. Research and development, lobbying, patent fees, legal fees for defense against charges of antitrust violations, and marketing expenditures that raise barriers to entry by increasing endogenous switching costs[62] are all examples of such expenses. For instance, marketing expenses (salespeople, agency networks, and advertising) create market power by intensifying economies of scale (Comanor and Wilson 1967), and these expenses have been particularly high in mandatory DC pensions. However, whether they amount to socially wasteful spending depends on the circumstances. In the case of financial services, sales agents typically play both a positive and a negative role. On the one hand, they help consumers make educated choices in the purchase of financial services. On the other hand, they can create noise and engage in persuasion and high-pressure sales tactics, not necessarily for the benefit of consumers. Whether rents are socially wasted to produce noise or used to educate consumers is a matter for further empirical estimation.

Annex 2D: Markets with Switching Costs

The presence of switching costs can explain many commonly observed business practices, such as why businesses appear so concerned with their market share and why firms give generous introductory offers to new customers.[63] Switching costs also affect the structure of prices. Policy makers should be concerned with switching costs for three reasons: switching costs can (a) affect the mechanics of competition, (b) raise the average price level, and (c) distort the pricing structure.[64]

Switching costs are defined as the real or perceived costs that are incurred when changing supplier but not incurred when remaining with the current supplier. Thus, a customer who has previously bought a product from one firm may incur extra costs in purchasing an otherwise identical product from a new firm, even if that product is sold at the same unit price. The existence of such costs leads to economies of scale in repeated purchasing (Farrell and Klemperer 2006).

The literature identifies a series of switching costs that includes transaction costs, compatibility costs, learning costs, contractual switching costs, uncertainty costs, and psychological costs. Some of these appear to be more relevant to the pension fund industry:

- *Transaction costs.* For some products, transaction costs apply when changing suppliers that are not incurred when staying with the existing supplier. For example, changing pension funds can involve significant costs in terms of time and direct financial costs.
- *Contractual switching costs.* Because switching costs can increase a firm's market power, firms can sometimes artificially create switching costs to discourage customers from changing supplier. These switching costs include frequent flyer programs, loyalty cards, loyalty discounts, joining fees for gyms, and exit fees in mutual funds or pension funds. These switching costs are also known as *endogenous switching costs* because firms create them to differentiate their products.
- *Uncertainty costs.* If the product is an experience good (that is, a good for which its quality or suitability for the consumer can be known only after consumption), consumers may be reluctant to switch to untested brands because they are uncertain whether the product will suit them. Typically, changing a pension fund involves changing the asset manager for one's individual accounts. Doing so can create uncertainty costs, in addition to the fact that future rates of return can be predicted only with a margin of error.

Firms and Individual Behavior in the Presence of Switching Costs

Klemperer (1995) contains the basic reference model in the literature to describe firm and individual behavior in the presence of switching costs. With switching costs, firms face two types of consumers: old types, who face switching costs, and new types (new entrants), who do not face switching costs. The model assumes firms cannot price discriminate among customers, which is a good assumption for the pension fund industry.

In a one-period setup, pension funds typically attract new customers by "compensating" them for the transaction costs through gifts of various sorts. If switching costs are sufficiently high, each firm acts as a monopolist to its customer base and needs to compensate them for not switching. In Klemperer (1995), such compensation would involve each firm giving up more profit on its own customer base than it would gain by stealing its rivals' customers. Hence, no switching takes place in equilibrium.[65] In a two-period setup, firms have an incentive to "harvest" their customer base.[66] Farrell and Shapiro (1988) find that, in the second period, firms with higher market shares price higher than rivals with low market shares. They do so because the more locked-in customers a firm has, the more it benefits by increasing prices to reap the rewards from these customers, rather than reducing prices to compete for uncommitted customers.[67,68]

Extensions to the Basic Switching-Costs Model

Introducing new entrants. The existence of new customers creates a trade-off for the firms in the market (Klemperer 1995). In the second period, either firms can set a high price to exploit their locked-in existing customers (*harvesting*), or firms can set a low price to attract new customers (*investing*). The direction of this trade-off critically depends on a firm's market share. For a firm with a large market share, the profits gained by charging a high price to its locked-in customers are likely to be sufficiently higher than the gains made by setting a low price to attract new customers. However, firms with fewer existing customers are likely to price more aggressively. As a result, firms with higher market shares tend to charge higher prices than do firms with lower market shares.

Switching costs and prices. Assuming that firms cannot price discriminate between locked-in and uncommitted customers, in a market where both types of consumer coexist, prices could, in principle, be either higher or lower than in an otherwise identical market in the absence of switching costs. On the one hand, the existence of a locked-in customer base that firms could exploit induces firms to charge higher prices. On the other hand, firms may have an incentive to price low to build a customer base and thus ensure their profitability in the future. It is difficult, a priori, to determine which of the two effects will prevail in equilibrium. However, one would expect the level of prices to be higher when switching costs are present for at least three reasons: (a) discounting,[69] (b) aggressiveness of competitors,[70] and (c) elasticity of demand.[71]

Switching costs and market shares. Perhaps contrary to conventional wisdom, the presence of switching costs need not lead to stable market shares (Beggs and Klemperer 1992; Klemperer 1987a, 1987c). Market shares exhibit certain inertia because consumers are reluctant to switch suppliers. However, the literature consistently finds that the firms with larger customer bases price much higher than do their smaller counterparts. Consequently, the smaller firms succeed in attracting the business of consumers with low or no switching costs. Smaller firms see their shares grow as a result, whereas large firms see their shares eroding over time. Leadership is therefore only temporary. In a multiperiod market with switching costs, both prices and market shares tend to fluctuate over time. Stability is the exception rather than the norm.

Introducing search costs. Search costs arise when a customer has to invest effort in finding a new supplier. Although search costs can be considered a form of transaction switching cost, they differ from switching costs in that switching costs arise only after one has purchased a product from a supplier (that is, switching costs make previously homogenous products differentiated), whereas search costs arise even before one has purchased from a supplier. Some types of switching costs exist even if all products and suppliers are identical and known to the buyer; however, search costs can exist even when products, suppliers, or both are differentiated and the buyer has imperfect information about which one is a better or worse alternative. Search costs can also arise with homogenous products when effort has to be invested in finding the best price. Moreover, though switching costs are paid only if a customer actually switches, search costs are incurred whether or not a customer finally decides to remain with the current supplier. Search costs and switching costs often arise together.[72]

Market contestability. As Farrell and Klemperer (2006) note, perhaps the most significant effect of switching costs is on entry. Although at first sight lock-in costs would appear to deter entry—and they indeed do so in many cases—switching costs can be conducive to entry in some cases. Whether they do so depends on (a) the size of switching costs,[73] (b) the scale of entry,[74] (c) the market dynamics,[75] and (d) the existence of economies of scale.[76] The interaction of economies of scale and switching or search costs in the pension fund industry has strong implications for the competitive behavior of firms.

Product differentiation. In addition to affecting pricing behavior, the presence of switching costs can have implications on which products a firm chooses to produce. Economic theory finds that product differentiation tends to reduce price competition as firms compete on aspects other than price. In the presence of switching costs, however, product differentiation can actually *increase* price competition if consumers value variety. With identical products, a customer has no reason to pay the switching cost, but with differentiated products, the desire for product variety gives the customer a reason for paying it. If a customer is already purchasing from more than one firm, he or she may become relatively more sensitive to price competition. Consequently, product differentiation can increase price competition in markets with switching costs, and firms may choose to compete head to head rather than to differentiate their products. Finally, the literature also finds that firms can face incentives to create switching costs to increase oligopoly power (see, for example, Farrell and Klemperer 2006; Klemperer 1995). These incentives are likely to be greater in markets with homogenous products, given that product differentiation mitigates some of the lock-in effects of the switching cost. These artificial switching costs are likely to be particularly harmful to overall economic welfare, because they usually lead to higher prices and firms waste productive resources when creating them.

Notes

1. Economies of scale exist when per unit average costs decrease with the increase in the magnitude of the output being produced by a firm. The level of production at which the average costs are at a minimum is called the *minimum efficient scale*.

2. Switches are probably the most important way in which the market disciplines pension firms: when consumers are dissatisfied with the performance or the quality of services, they can switch to another pension firm. To exert such discipline, consumers need to be well informed and to make rational decisions on the basis of such information. In short, the demand for pension services needs to be highly responsive to prices.

3. The text refers to this situation as *price distortion*.

4. As discussed later in this book, the literature defines these expenditures as *endogenous fixed costs* to differentiate them from the *exogenous fixed costs* that characterize the supply of services.

5. The term *quasi-market* was introduced and used by Glennerster (1991), Le Grand (1991), Le Grand and Bartlett (1993) to describe and assess the welfare effects of the education reforms of the Margaret Thatcher government in the United Kingdom. Indeed, the idea was actually put into practice well before the Thatcher government by the replacement of concessionary fares with transport vouchers almost two decades earlier, and it can be traced back to the education vouchers originally proposed by Milton Friedman.

6. A quasi-market may also emerge in the absence of formal compulsion if incentives for participation lead to the creation of a de facto captive clientele. These incentives can be financial (as in the case of tax deductions, subsidies, and exemptions) or nonfinancial (as in the case of mandatory participation cum opt-out clauses, stigma, or addiction).

7. In the case of mandatory DC pensions, the voucher is financed by mandatory contributions from the beneficiary and is often subsidized by an earmarked state budget or a combination that includes a subsidy and exemptions from labor tax.

8. For simplicity of exposition in what follows, this chapter uses the terms *market* and *quasi-market* interchangeably when referring to mandatory DC pensions, unless otherwise noted.

9. According to the National Commission for the Pension System, the total number of workers in the system increased by 2.1 million in 2006, 1.6 million of whom were assigned by the supervisor.

10. Economists label consumers' responsiveness to price signals as *price elasticity*. Hence, the terms *inertia* and *low elasticity* are used interchangeably in this book. Chapter 3 is fully dedicated to policies aimed at exploiting the causes of low price elasticity to protect consumers from their inability to choose.

11. Chapter 4 is fully dedicated to policies aimed at exploiting these systematic biases in investment decisions to protect consumers from their inability to choose the right investment strategy.

12. The literature refers to this as "irrational" or "heuristic" behavior. For a survey of examples of inconsistent behavior of individuals in relation to retirement savings, see Benartzi and Thaler (2007). See also box 2.2 and annex 2B.

13. For instance, Mexico introduced a rule in 2008 whereby a switch to an AFORE that offers a higher net rate of return is allowed at any time; otherwise, the consumer can move to a different AFORE only after 12 months.

14. See Barr and Diamond (2008) for a detailed treatment.

15. See annex 2A for more details about this and other studies.

16. To advance this agenda, the World Bank has initiated a program that seeks to develop standard methodologies for the assessment of financial literacy and skills; formulate guidelines for the design, delivery, and evaluation of financial literacy improvement programs; pilot these programs in several emerging markets; and disseminate the results. The program started in January 2009 and will run through December 2012. Parts of the program will be conducted in conjunction with the Organisation for Economic Co-operation and Development.

17. These topics are the focus of chapters 3 and 4, respectively.

18. See annex 2A for more on the role of sales agents and the importance of information.

19. The study covers the period January 1998 through January 2001.

20. The legal separation of pension firms and pension funds in mandatory DC markets aims to reduce potential conflicts of interest, to ensure the security of the operation of the system, and to better control the investment of pension funds.

21. At the time of the reform, experience with pension fund management was limited, which raised strong concerns about principal-agent problems in the pension industry, and a high premium was given to ease of supervision. Therefore, the Chilean pension law (Decree No. 3,500/1980) specified the creation of new financial entities with the exclusive purpose of managing pension funds (pension plan administrators or pension firms). Certain types of institutions, in particular banks, were prohibited from participating directly in the ownership of pension firms.

22. Switzerland is an exception because an absolute rate of return guarantee is applied. Pension firms must meet a minimum nominal investment return of 2.75 percent. Absolute return guarantees are more common in voluntary DC pensions, as in Belgium and Germany. Absolute return guarantees eliminate any possibility of bad investment returns translating into lower benefits for plan participants. In addition, such guarantees force pension funds to invest in a cautious manner to avoid having to cover any return shortfall with additional contributions from employers (or employees). The main drawback is that setting a suitable return guarantee is very complex. For a detailed analysis, see Antolin et al. (2009).

23. In Hungary, the benchmark is not defined around an industry's average return or an absolute return, but around a rate of return target that is determined primarily by a basket of long-term government securities. If the rate of return exceeds the upper band, the excess would need to be placed in the liquidity reserve. If the rate of return is lower than the lower band, it should be increased to the minimum with transfers from the liquidity reserve. The liquidity reserve cannot be larger than 4 percent of total assets. Therefore, the rate of return guarantee in Hungary seems to be an internal smoothing device, designed to avoid extreme fluctuations relative to the benchmark.

24. Specifically, each pension firm must guarantee that the average real rate of return in the past 36 months is not lower than the lesser of (a) the average real return of each fund minus 2 percentage points for funds C, D, and E and 4 percentage points for funds A and B or (b) 50 percent of the average real return of all the funds.

25. If the return is higher than the upper band, the difference is placed in a profitability reserve in the pension fund, called the *reserve for fluctuations on returns*. According to article 193, paragraph 7, of Chile's Social Insurance Code, if the rate of return achieved by a universal or a professional pension fund exceeds by more than 40 percent the average rate of return achieved for the respective type of pension fund or exceeds the average by 3 percentage points (whichever of the two figures is greater), the resources resulting from a return above this percentage must be set aside for a reserve by the respective fund.

26. Voluntary pension programs often allow early withdrawals for personal loans.

27. In some jurisdictions, information is provided more than once a year. For instance, in Mexico, AFOREs are obliged to provide information three times a year, and in Chile, pension fund managers (*administradoras de fondos de pensiones*, or AFPs) are required to do so on a quarterly basis.

28. For instance, Tapia and Yermo (2008) compare administrative fees across countries in Central and Eastern Europe, Latin America, Australia, and Sweden and make the link with economies of scale. Impavido and Rocha (2006) present evidence of rapidly decreasing fees as a percentage of asset management in Hungary, indicating the presence of important fixed costs and, therefore, economies of scale. Dobrogonov and Murthi (2005) report evidence of economies of scale for Croatia, Hungary, Kazakhstan, and Poland.

29. *Contributors* are individuals who are registered and have paid into the fund at least once in the preceding 12 months; *registered individuals* have paid at least one contribution. They might be unemployed or not pay their contributions, but they are below retirement age.

30. International comparison of operational expenses as a share of assets or per member should not be directly interpreted as a measure of relative efficiency because the ratios are highly influenced by coverage and asset volume. Also, costs in mature systems should not be compared with costs in younger systems because of start-up costs.

31. In Bolivia, the government initially granted operating licenses to two pension firms with an exclusivity period of five years through an international bidding process. In El Salvador, five pension fund managers were initially set up in 1998. Two years later, three managers merged, and the license of a fourth manager was revoked for operating without sufficient capital.

32. In the early 1990s, a large number of small and mostly inefficient operators entered the market, which unleashed an aggressive competition war and resulted in higher costs and inefficiencies. At the peak in 1995, there were as many as 21 operators. The lack of viability of the small operators and changes in regulations led to a wave of mergers and acquisitions and, as of July 2007, six managers were operating in Chile.

33. Concentration in Mexico declined from 2003 through 2007. Recent regulatory changes in 2009 may reverse this trend.

34. In general, trends toward higher concentration are typical of the asset management industry. For instance, industry concentration, measured by the assets under management of the world's largest 500 fund managers, has grown in recent years, and the share of the largest 20 of these fund managers increased from 29 percent in 1996 to 36 percent in 2004 (IFSL 2006).

35. Reforms were then partially reversed in 2008. See note 44 for more information.

36. Chapter 3 analyzes extensively the effect of regulations aimed at promoting competition.

37. Price distortions arise when a relative markup is imposed and therefore consumption takes place at a higher price relative to the competitive equilibrium. The magnitude of price distortions can be measured by the Lerner index, and such magnitude is monotonically decreasing with the elasticity of demand to prices, as explained in annex 2C.

38. A social welfare loss arises when the combined surplus of producers and consumers decreases—in other words, when the surplus of the consumer decreases by more than the increase in the surplus of the producer. The social welfare loss is also a function of the demand elasticity, but contrary to the case of price distortions, the welfare loss is not necessarily monotonically decreasing with it; this result will depend on the interaction between demand and supply.

39. The concern about the distribution of rents arises in the case of mandatory DC pensions because, with a highly inelastic demand, price changes do not affect quantities consumed very much but elicit large monetary transfers from consumers to firms. This outcome is not particularly desirable for either policy makers, who mandate consumption, or pension providers, because rent redistributions that are deemed socially unacceptable elicit strong political responses, which can easily jeopardize profit margins.

40. In fact, market concentration and market power differ only by a factor inversely proportional to the price elasticity of demand, as shown in annex 2C.

41. The *Herfindahl-Hirschman index* is a measure of concentration computed as the sum of the squares of the relative size of all firms in the industry. See annex 2C for a more detailed explanation.

42. The magnitude of price distortions is measured traditionally by subtracting a firm's marginal cost from its price and then dividing the result by the firm's price. This measure of market power is known as the *Lerner index*. See annex 2C for a detailed explanation.

43. The approximation underestimates market power in the presence of economies of scale (decreasing marginal costs).

44. The Mexican supervisory authority, the National Commission for the Pension System (Comisión Nacional del Sistema de Ahorro para el Retiro, or CONSAR), introduced a series of reforms starting in 2002 and 2003 aimed at facilitating switches to low-cost funds. These reforms included the following: (a) eliminating the requirement for the ceding fund to intervene in transfers, (b) reducing the transfer period from three months to 13 days, (c) simplifying the documentation requirements for transfers, (d) centralizing the transfer validation in a single agency (Procesar), (e) allowing individuals to initiate transfers over the Internet, (f) improving the quality of information disclosure at the level of individual consumers and on the Web site of CONSAR, (g) automatically assigning undecided individuals to low-fee funds, and (h) eliminating the time restriction on switches from higher-fee to lower-fee funds. During the second half of 2007, an amendment to the Mexican pension law changed the rule for assigning unallocated affiliates from the lowest fee to the highest net rate of return. The new measures came into effect in March 2008. CONSAR created the Index of Net Rate of Return (Indice de Rendimiento Neto) to facilitate the comparison of pension firms for the switching and assigning decisions. In 2009, CONSAR again tightened switching requirements between AFOREs.

45. Prior to 1999, the correlation between market power and concentration was low or negative because of the high expenditures incurred by pension firms in the early years of operation of the system.

46. The Lerner index was calculated here by subtracting from both income fee and total costs the premium for disability and survivorship insurance. The

presence of the public pension fund operation in Argentina may have explained why the markups in Argentina were generally lower than in Mexico even though concentration tended to be higher.

47. In Chile, three phases can be identified. See box 2.3.

48. Similar to a tax base, a *fee base* is the monetary base on which the fee is levied. Standard fee bases are earnings contributions, assets, or excess returns on reference indexes (performance fees). In pension jargon, fees levied on earnings or contributions are usually called *flow fees* because the base is a flow into the individual account. Fees levied on assets accumulated in the individual account are usually called *stock fees*.

49. Rate uniformity regulation requires each pension firm to apply a single commission schedule to all its customers, with the aim of creating an implicit redistributive scheme in which high-base participants pay more than low-base participants.

50. *First-floor fees* include all fees charged by pension firms to participants for services provided directly by them. *Second-floor fees* include fees charged by service providers to pension firms, which, in turn, pass them on to participants.

51. Following the 2008 reform, Chilean pension firms can charge fees only on asset management.

52. The equivalent asset fee is calculated as the annualized charge over assets that would have generated the same final asset accumulation as the actual combination of charges on the flows, assets, and returns applied to the individual retirement account of a representative consumer during a given period of time (say, 25 and 40 years, as reported in tables 2.6 to 2.8 and figures 2.1 to 2.4). To make the calculations as comparable as possible across countries, Corvera, Lartigue, and Madero (2006) must assume the same accumulation periods, rates of return, and contribution density, but allow for country-specific average wages and contribution rates. The uniform assumptions provide a reasonable trade-off between comparability and actual charges in each country.

53. The fact that using the weighted average column in table 2.6 eliminates Mexico from the list of most expensive countries reflects the high dispersion of fees in that country. According to figure 2.1, Mexico has some of the most expensive firms in Latin America, as well as some of the cheapest.

54. In these three countries, either the regulator or the law stipulates price ceilings. Price ceilings are also used in the Dominican Republic, Hungary, and Poland. In the first two countries, they have not resulted in the low fees observed in other countries (see table 2.8 and figures 2.3 and 2.4). Furthermore, as discussed in chapter 3, caps affect incentives to improve asset management quality.

55. The information for these countries is less recent: Hungary, December 2005; Poland, December 2006; and the Slovak Republic, February 2007.

56. Comparing the fees of pension funds in Eastern Europe and Latin America to those of mutual funds in the same countries would not be very relevant for a variety of reasons. Most important, pension funds benefit from a very large captive market, whereas the mutual fund industry targets a voluntary market and assets under management are relatively smaller. Thus, the U.S. mutual fund industry, with larger funds, is a more relevant indicator, albeit far from perfect.

57. Because pension funds in Latin America and Eastern Europe tend to be passive investors, fees would need to be smaller than the average fees charged by mutual funds of the same size in the United States. Moreover, the fees of U.S. mutual funds reflect large distribution fees associated with the provision of financial advice and other services, such as individual retirement planning, education, and tax returns.

58. The first adjustment is to exclude assets not required by the business, such as financial investments, investments in other firms, and investments in buildings that

can be rented. The second adjustment is to add the replacement cost of intangible assets, which by convention depreciate more quickly than what their actual economic life would suggest. The third adjustment is to add the expected cost of contingencies, such as the penalty for violating the floor to relative returns and the expected cost caused by unusual regulations such as excessive capital requirements and excessive stabilization reserve, after optimization.

59. Some of these policies were reversed with the April 2008 reform, and it is too early to assess the effect of such reversals.

60. The number of switches over contributors rose from a mere 0.5 percent in 2000 to about 18 percent in 2006.

61. *Yardstick competition* refers to takeovers, debt as a monitoring device, institutional investors, and so on.

62. See annex 2D for a review of the literature on switching costs.

63. This annex presents a brief literature survey on switching costs that draws heavily on Farrell and Klemperer (2006).

64. Switching costs are of particular importance when dominance leads to abuse. Particular caution needs to be exercised when investigating pricing abuses, and a dynamic perspective is necessary. Pricing below cost may not be predatory after follow-on sales have been taken into account, and seemingly high prices to locked-in customers may no longer appear excessive when intense competition before the customers were committed is taken into account. A dominant firm may also create switching costs that have the effect of foreclosing competitors from the market, through so-called loyalty rebates or exclusionary contracts. In these cases, the onus should be on the dominant firm to show that any pro-competitive benefits outweigh the potential exclusionary effects.

65. The no-switching outcome is sensible to the assumptions of the model, because switching costs are typically heterogeneous. For instance, assume a single-period market where one or more firms already has a customer base. If the switching cost is heterogeneous such that the cost is higher for some consumers than for others, then some switching may occur in equilibrium. In this scenario, prices and profits will still be higher than they would without switching costs.

66. This situation is useful to model cases where the market can be divided into a start-up phase, where competition for new customers is intense, and a mature phase, where most customers are already committed to a particular supplier (Klemperer 1987a, 1987c, 1995; Padilla 1992).

67. Because second-period profits are valuable, both firms are induced to compete aggressively in the first period. It may even be rational for the firms to price below cost in the first period, because they are able to price above marginal cost in the second period. In other words, because market share is valuable, there is competition for it. Firms "invest" in markets at an early stage in their development to be able to "reap" in later stages when consumers are locked in to the supplier they previously patronized. Prices are lower in the first period and higher in the second than would have been the case if no switching costs existed.

68. In an ideal world, firms and customers could contract for the whole life cycle of a product and specify future prices and qualities. Under such circumstances, the existence of switching costs would not lead to inefficiencies. Consumers would buy their whole lifetime's requirements from the lowest-cost supplier. However, in the vast majority of real-life circumstances, buyers and sellers are not able to contract for the complete life cycle of a product (Hart 1995).

69. Positive discount rates imply that agents prefer the present to the future.

70. The pricing decision a firm makes today influences how aggressive its competitors will be in the future.

71. The existence of switching costs makes it rational for customers to take into account expectations of future prices when making today's purchase decision.

72. For example, a customer switching an account from fund A to fund B may incur transaction costs (that is, filling in forms and transferring direct debits). In addition, the customer can incur search costs if he or she has to do research on the many alternative suppliers to identify which one offers the most suitable product. In some cases, search costs act as substitutes for switching costs. For example, with experience or credence goods, switching costs arise from imperfect information about products' or suppliers' characteristics. A consumer may spend time reading restaurant reviews in specialized guides and magazines (so incurring a search cost) or otherwise could just take the risk, go to a new restaurant, eat there, and experience the quality of food and service. Reading a restaurant's review in a magazine is costly for the consumer (it is time consuming, and the customer has to purchase the magazine), but it reduces the uncertainty cost incurred when changing to an unknown restaurant. In other cases, search costs and switching costs combine to increase further the cost of changing supplier. For example, in the pension fund industry, the customer typically has to first incur search costs to find out which alternative supplier offers the most appropriate product before incurring the actual transaction cost of switching supplier. When search and switching costs are both present, each reinforces the effect of the other on equilibrium switching and prices.

73. Although very high switching costs obviously will deter entry, a moderate level of switching costs may actually encourage entry for two reasons: (a) postentry profits are expected to be higher in a market with switching costs, thereby attracting entry, and (b) incumbents may price less aggressively in response to entry. Models showing these outcomes can be found in Beggs and Klemperer (1992), Farrell and Shapiro (1988), and Klemperer (1987b).

74. In general, the existence of switching costs has the effect of encouraging small-scale entry while discouraging large-scale entry. The reason relates to the fact that incumbents have an incentive to harvest their customer base, and therefore, new entrants have an incentive to design their strategies for attracting mainly new customers, which also reduces the likelihood of price retaliation by the incumbent. Models illustrating this concept can be found in Gelman and Salop (1983) and Yoffie and Kwak (2001).

75. In general, a growing market encourages new entry because the existence of new customers in each period means that new entrants are not reliant on winning the incumbents' locked-in customers. The presence of switching costs in a fast-growing market promotes contestability. The incumbent is worse off than in the absence of switching costs because the value of its customer base (and, therefore, of its harvesting strategy) is reduced. In the presence of switching costs, entry may be accompanied by price wars. Klemperer (1989) defines a *price war* as a period when prices fall and then subsequently rise in the absence of cost changes. Klemperer notes that price wars can happen both when switching costs are low and when switching costs are high. If switching costs are low, the incumbent has to reduce the price in response to entry. However, once the entrant has acquired a customer base, its prices will rise, which also permits a price rise from the incumbent. Because the entrant's price will always rise after it has acquired a customer base, Klemperer (1989) notes that the same pattern would also be expected in a market with high switching costs.

76. Moderate switching costs are generally conducive to at least small-scale entry, but not when strong economies of scale are present in the market. Economies of scale may mean that the incumbent's cost advantage is so great that it is able to price both substantially above its own cost and lower than a new entrant's cost. This situation is likely to deter entry. If per capita economies of scale are greater than per capita switching costs, then the incumbent can succeed in keeping the entrant out of the market, despite the entrant's willingness to price below its cost. These strong economies of scale combined with switching costs give rise to what is known as *network effects* (Farrell and Klemperer 2006).

References

Aguilera, Nelly, and César Velázquez. 2008. "Scale Economies in the Pension Fund Managers Industry in Mexico: A Semi Parametric Approach." *Well-Being and Social Policy* 4 (1): 55–72.

Antolin, Pablo, Sandra Blome, David Karim, Stéphanie Payet, Gerhard Scheuenstuhl, and Juan Yermo. 2009. "Investment Regulations and Defined Contribution Pensions." OECD Working Papers on Insurance and Private Pensions 37, Organisation for Economic Co-operation and Development, Paris.

Apella, Ignacio, and Daniel Maceira. 2006. "Economías de escala y barreras a la entrada en el mercado argentino de AFPJ." Paper presented at the 41st Reunión Anual de la Asociación Argentina de Economía Política, Salta, Argentina, November 15–17.

Arenas de Mesa, Alberto, David Bravo, Jere Behrman, Olivia S. Mitchell, and Petra Todd. 2008. "The Chilean Pension Reform Turns 25: Lessons from the Social Protection Survey." In *Lessons from Pension Reform in the Americas*, ed. Stephen J. Kay and Tapen Sinha, 23–58. Oxford, U.K.: Oxford University Press.

Armenta, Adriana. 2007. "Determinantes de los traspasos de los trabajadores en las administradoras del sistema de pensiones en México: 2000–2006." B.A. thesis, Instituto Tecnológico Autónomo de México, Mexico City.

Barber, Brad, and Terrance Odean. 2001. "Boys Will Be Boys: Gender, Overconfidence, and Common Stock Investment." *Quarterly Journal of Economics* 116 (1): 261–92.

Barberis, Nicholas, and Ming Huang. 2001. "Mental Accounting, Loss Aversion, and Individual Stock Returns." *Journal of Finance* 56 (4): 1247–92.

Barberis, Nicholas, Ming Huang, and Richard H. Thaler. 2006. "Individual Preferences, Monetary Gambles, and Stock Market Participation: A Case for Narrow Framing." *American Economic Review* 96 (4): 1069–90.

Barberis, Nicholas, and Richard H. Thaler. 2003. "A Survey of Behavioral Finance." In *Handbook of the Economics of Finance, Volume 1B: Financial Markets and Asset Pricing*, ed. George M. Constantinides, Milton Harris, and René M. Stulz, 1053–128. Amsterdam: Elsevier.

Barr, Nicholas, and Peter Diamond. 2008. *Reforming Pensions: Principles and Policy Choices*. New York: Oxford University Press.

Barrientos, Armando, and Aziz Boussofiane. 2001. "The Efficiency of Pension Fund Managers in Latin America." Centre on Regulation and Competition Working Paper 30696, Institute for Development Policy and Management, University of Manchester, Manchester, U.K.

Bateman, Hazel. 2000. "The Role of Specialized Financial Institutions in Pension Fund Administration." In *Policy Issues in Pension Reform: Proceedings of the Second APEC Regional Forum on Pension Fund Reform, Viña del Mar, Chile, 26–27 April 1999*, ed. Ministerio de Hacienda de Chile and Asian Development Bank, 121–47. Manila: Asian Development Bank.

Becht, Marco, Patrick Bolton, and Ailsa A. Röell. 2003. "Corporate Governance and Control." In *Handbook of the Economics of Finance, Volume 1A: Corporate Finance*, ed. George M. Constantinides, Milton Harris, and René M. Stulz, 1–109. Amsterdam: Elsevier.

Beggs, Alan, and Paul D. Klemperer. 1992. "Multi-period Competition with Switching Costs." *Econometrica* 60 (3): 651–66.

Bell, Elizabeth, and Robert I. Lerman. 2005. "Can Financial Literacy Enhance Asset Building?" Opportunity and Ownership Project 6, Urban Institute, Washington, DC.

Benartzi, Shlomo. 2001. "Excessive Extrapolation and the Allocation of 401(k) Accounts to Company Stock" *Journal of Finance* 56 (5): 1747–64.

Benartzi, Shlomo, and Richard H. Thaler. 1995. "Myopic Loss Aversion and the Equity Premium Puzzle." *Quarterly Journal of Economics* 110 (1): 73–92.

———. 1999. "Risk Aversion or Myopia? Choices in Repeated Gambles and Retirement Investments." *Management Science* 45 (3): 364–81.

———. 2001. "Naive Diversification Strategies in Defined Contribution Saving Plans." *American Economic Review* 91 (1): 79–98.

———. 2002. "How Much Is Investor Autonomy Worth?" *Journal of Finance* 57 (4): 1593–1616.

———. 2007. "Heuristics and Biases in Retirement Savings Behavior." *Journal of Economic Perspectives* 21 (3): 81–104.

Bernheim, B. Douglas, and Daniel M. Garrett. 2003. "The Effects of Financial Education in the Workplace: Evidence from a Survey of Households." *Journal of Public Economics* 87 (7–8): 1487–519.

Bernheim, B. Douglas, Daniel M. Garrett, and Dean M. Maki. 2001. "Education and Saving: The Long-Term Effects of High School Financial Curriculum Mandates." *Journal of Public Economics* 80 (3): 435–65.

Berstein, Solange, and Carolina Cabrita. 2007. "Los determinantes de la elección de AFP en Chile: Nueva evidencia a partir de datos individuales." *Estudios de Economía* 34 (1): 53–72.

Berstein, Solange, and Alejandro Micco. 2002. "Turnover and Regulation: The Chilean Pension Fund Industry." Working Paper 180, Central Bank of Chile, Santiago.

Berstein, Solange, and José Luis Ruiz. 2005. "Sensibilidad de la demanda con consumidores desinformados: El caso de las AFP en Chile." Working Paper 4, Superintendencia de Administradoras de Fondos de Pensiones de Chile, Santiago.

Calderón-Colín, Roberto, Enrique E. Domínguez, and Moisés J. Schwartz. 2008. "Consumer Confusion: The Choice of AFORE in Mexico." IMF Working Paper 08/177, International Monetary Fund, Washington, DC.

Caskey, John P. 2006. "Can Personal Financial Management Education Promote Asset Accumulation by the Poor?" Networks Financial Institute Policy Brief 2006-PB-06, Indiana State University, Indianapolis.

Cerda, Rodrigo. 2006. "Movilidad en la cartera de cotizantes por AFP: La importancia de ser primero en rentabilidad." IE-PUC Working Paper 309, Instituto de Economía, Pontificia Universidad Católica de Chile, Santiago.

Chan, Sewin, and Ann H. Stevens. 2004. "Do Changes in Pension Incentives Affect Retirement? A Longitudinal Study of Subjective Retirement Expectations." *Journal of Public Economics* 88 (7–8): 1307–33.

Chisari, Omar, Pedri Dal Bó, Lucía Quesada, Martin Rossi, and Salvador Valdés-Prieto. 1998. "Opciones estratégicas en la regulación de las AFJP: Modulo III— Costos, comisiones y organización industrial del régimen de capitalización." Instituto de Economía, Universidad Argentina de la Empresa, Buenos Aires.

Choi, James J., David Laibson, Brigitte Madrian, and Andrew Metrick. 2002. "Defined Contribution Pensions: Plan Rules, Participant Decisions, and the

Path of Least Resistance." In *Tax Policy and the Economy*, vol. 16, ed. James M. Poterba, 67–113. Cambridge, MA: MIT Press.

Comanor, William S., and Thomas A. Wilson. 1967. "Advertising, Market Structure, and Performance." *Review of Economics and Statistics* 49: 423–40.

Corvera, F. Javier, J. Mateo Lartigue, and David Madero. 2006. "Comparative Analysis of Administrative Fees of Pension Funds in Latin America." Comisión Nacional del Sistema Ahorro para Retiro, Mexico, City.

Dayoub, Mariam, and Esperanza Lasagabaster. 2008. "General Trends in Competition Policy and Investment Regulation in Mandatory Defined Contribution Markets in Latin America." Policy Research Working Paper 4720, World Bank, Washington, DC.

De Bondt, Werner F. 1998. "A Portrait of the Individual Investor." *European Economic Review* 42 (3–5): 831–44.

Dobrogonov, Anton, and Mamta Murthi. 2005. "Administrative Fees and Costs of Mandatory Private Pensions in Transition Economies." *Journal of Pension Economics and Finance* 4 (1): 31–55.

Farrell, Joseph, and Paul D. Klemperer. 2006. "Coordination and Lock-in: Competition with Switching Costs and Network Effects." CEPR Discussion Paper 5798, Centre for Economic Policy Research, London.

Farrell, Joseph, and Carl Shapiro. 1988. "Horizontal Mergers: An Equilibrium Analysis." Discussion Paper 17, Woodrow Wilson School, Princeton University, Princeton, NJ.

Ferro, Gustavo. 2003. "Regulación y costos variables endógenos en el mercado de fondos de jubilaciones y pensiones argentino." CEMA Working Paper 231, Universidad del Centro de Estudios Macroeconómicos de Argentina, Buenos Aires.

García-Huitrón, Manuel, and Tonatiuh Rodríguez. 2002. "La organización de mercado de ahorro para el retiro en México durante la etapa de acumulación." Instituto Tecnológico Autónomo de México, Mexico City.

Gelman, Judith, and Steven Salop. 1983. "Judo Economics: Capacity Limitation and Coupon Competition." *Bell Journal of Economics* 14 (2): 315–25.

Glennerster, Howard. 1991. "Quasi-Markets for Education?" *Economic Journal* 101 (408): 1268–76.

Gneezy, Uri, and Jan Potters. 1997. "An Experiment on Risk Taking and Evaluation Periods." *Quarterly Journal of Economics* 112 (2): 631–45.

Goetzmann, William N., and Alok Kumar. 2008. "Equity Portfolio Diversification." *Review of Finance* 12 (3): 433–63.

Gustman, Alan L., and Thomas L. Steinmeier. 2001a. "Imperfect Knowledge, Retirement, and Saving." NBER Working Paper 8406, National Bureau of Economic Research, Cambridge, MA.

———. 2001b. "What People Don't Know about Their Pensions and Social Security." In *Public Policies and Private Pensions*, ed. William G. Gale, John B. Shoven, and Mark J. Warshawsky, 57–119. Washington, DC: Brookings Institution.

Hart, Oliver. 1995. *Firms, Contracts, and Financial Structure*. Oxford, U.K.: Clarendon Press.

Hilgert, Marianne, Jeanne Hogarth, and Sondra Beverly. 2003. "Household Financial Management: The Connection between Knowledge and Behavior." *Federal Reserve Bulletin* (July): 309–22.

ICI (Investment Company Institute). 2006. "Fees and Expenses of Mutual Funds, 2005." *ICI Research Fundamentals* 15 (4): 1–8.

IFSL (International Financial Services London). 2006. "Fund Management." City Business Series, IFSL, London, August.

Impavido, Gregorio, and Roberto Rocha. 2006. "Competition and Performance in the Hungarian Second Pillar." Policy Research Working Paper 3876, World Bank, Washington, DC.

Kahneman, Daniel, and Amos Tversky. 1979. "Prospect Theory: An Analysis of Decision under Risk." *Econometrica* 47 (2): 263–91.

———. 1984. "Choices, Values, and Frames." *American Psychologist* 39 (4): 341–50.

———. 2000. *Choices, Values, and Frames.* Cambridge, MA: Russell Sage Foundation and Cambridge University Press.

Klemperer, Paul D. 1987a. "The Competitiveness of Markets with Switching Costs." *RAND Journal of Economics* 18 (1): 138–50.

———. 1987b. "Entry Deterrence in Markets with Consumer Switching Costs." *Economic Journal* 97 (388a): 99–117.

———. 1987c. "Markets with Consumer Switching Costs." *Quarterly Journal of Economics* 102 (2): 375–94.

———. 1989. "Price Wars Caused by Switching Costs." *Review of Economic Studies* 56 (3): 405–20.

———. 1995. "Competition When Consumers Have Switching Costs: An Overview with Applications to Industrial Organization, Macroeconomics, and International Trade." *Review of Economic Studies* 62 (4): 515–39.

Le Grand, Julian. 1991. "Quasi-Markets and Social Policy." *Economic Journal* 101 (408): 1256–67.

Le Grand, Julian, and Will Bartlett, eds. 1993. *Quasi-Markets and Social Policy.* London: Palgrave MacMillan.

Leibenstein, Harvey. 1966. "Allocative Efficiency vs. 'X-Efficiency.'" *American Economic Review* 56 (3): 392–415.

Luchak, Andrew, and Morley Gunderson. 2000. "What Do Employees Know about Their Pension Plan?" *Industrial Relations* 39 (4): 646–70.

Lusardi, Annamaria, and Olivia S. Mitchell. 2006. "Financial Literacy and Planning: Implications for Retirement Wellbeing." Pension Research Council Working Paper 2006-1, Wharton School, University of Pennsylvania, Philadelphia.

Madrian, Brigitte, and Dennis Shea. 2001. "The Power of Suggestion: Inertia in 401(k) Participation and Savings Behavior." *Quarterly Journal of Economics* 116 (4): 1149–87.

Marinovic, Iván, and Salvador Valdés-Prieto. 2004. "La demanda y los costos de las AFP chilenas, 1992–2002." Paper presented at the seminar Desafios del Sistema Chileno de Pensiones Competencia, Centro de Extensión Universidad Católica, Santiago, November 11–12.

Martin, Matthew. 2007. "A Literature Review on the Effectiveness of Financial Education." Federal Reserve Bank of Richmond Working Paper 07-03, Richmond, VA.

Masías, Lorena, and Elio Sánchez. 2006. "Competencia y reducción de comisiones en el sistema privado de pensiones: El caso peruano." *Revista de Temas Financieros* 3 (1).

Meléndez, Jorge. 2004. "La industria de la AFORE: Un análisis de su estructura y recomendaciones de política de competencia y regulación." In *Economic Competitiveness in Mexico*, ed. Comisión Federal de Competencia, 285–333. Mexico City: Editorial Porrúa.

Mitchell, Olivia S. 1988. "Worker Knowledge of Pension Provisions." *Journal of Labor Economics* 6 (1): 21–39.

Mitchell, Olivia S., and Stephen Utkus. 2004. "Lessons from Behavioral Finance for Retirement Plan Design." In *Pension Design and Structure: New Lessons from Behavioral Finance*, ed. Olivia Mitchell and Stephen Utkus, 3–42. Oxford, U.K.: Oxford University Press.

Odean, Terrance. 1998. "Are Investors Reluctant to Realize Their Losses?" *Journal of Finance* 53 (5): 1775–98.

OECD (Organisation for Economic Co-operation and Development). 2005. "Improving Financial Literacy: Analysis of Issues and Policies." OECD, Paris.

Padilla, A. Jorge. 1992. "Mixed Pricing in Oligopoly with Consumer Switching Costs." *International Journal of Industrial Organization* 10 (3): 393–411.

Palmer, Edward. 2004. "Sweden's New FDC Pension System." Paper presented at the seminar Desafíos del Sistema Chileno de Pensiones Competencia, Centro de Extensión Universidad Católica, Santiago, November 11–12.

———. 2006. "El nuevo sistema de pensiones sueco de cuentas individuales capitalizadas." Working Paper 15, Superintendencia de Administradoras de Fondos de Pensiones, Santiago. http://www.safp.cl/files/doctrab/DT00015.pdf.

Papke, Leslie. 2004. "Individual Financial Decisions in Retirement Saving Plans: The Role of Participant-Direction." *Journal of Public Economics* 88 (1–2): 39–61.

Rabin, Matthew, and Richard H. Thaler. 2001. "Anomalies: Risk Aversion." *Journal of Economic Perspectives* 15 (1): 219–32.

Rasmussen, Arne. 1952. "The Determination of Advertising Expenditure." *Journal of Marketing* 16 (4): 439–46.

Reyes, Gonzalo, and Rubén Castro. 2008. "Medidas pro-competencia de la reforma provisional." Working Paper 29, Superintendencia de Pensiones, Santiago. http://www.safp.cl/redirect/doctrab/showDoc.php.

Rofman, Rafael. 2007. "The Pension System in Argentina." In *Lessons from Pension Reforms in the Americas*, ed. Stephen J. Kay and Tapen Sinha, 379–402. Oxford, U.K.: Oxford University Press.

Rudolph, Heinz, and Roberto Rocha. 2007. *Competition and Performance in the Polish Second Pillar*. Washington, DC: World Bank.

Skog, Jeremy. 2006. "Who Knows What about Their Pensions? Financial Literacy in the Chilean Individual Account System." PARC Working Paper 12, Population Aging Research Center, Wharton School, University of Pennsylvania, Philadelphia.

Sutton, John. 1991. *Sunk Costs and Market Structure: Price Competition, Advertising, and the Evolution of Concentration*. Cambridge, MA: MIT Press.

Tapia, Waldo, and Juan Yermo. 2008. "Fees in Individual Account Pension Systems: A Cross-Country Comparison." OECD Working Paper on Insurance and Private Pensions 27, Organisation for Economic Co-operation and Development, Paris.

Thaler, Richard H. 1985. "Mental Accounting and Consumer Choice." *Marketing Science* 4 (3): 199–214.

————. 1999. "Mental Accounting Matters." *Journal of Behavioral Decision Making* 12 (3): 183–206.

Thaler, Richard H., and Cass Sunstein. 2003. "Libertarian Paternalism." *American Economic Review* 93 (2): 175–79.

Valdés-Prieto, Salvador. 2007. "State-Supported Defined Contribution Pensions: Quasi-Markets or Procurement?" Pontificia Universidad Católica de Chile, Santiago.

Valdés-Prieto, Salvador, and Iván Marinovic. 2005. "Contabilidad regulatoria: Las AFP chilenas 1993–2003." IE-PUC Working Paper 279, Instituto de Economía, Pontificia Universidad Católica de Chile, Santiago.

Yoffie, David B., and Mary Kwak. 2001. *Judo Strategy.* Boston: Harvard Business School Press.

3

Narrowly Focused Policies or Alternative Industrial Models?

Inaction is not an option for policy makers wishing to reduce the market power that pension firms enjoy as a consequence of consumers' inertia. Hence, different countries have introduced different ad hoc regulations or specific institutional arrangements aimed at reducing price distortions and fostering adequate redistribution of rents between pension firms and participants.[1]

The policy menu includes the following: (a) "soft" interventions such as the prohibition against charging different individuals different prices for the same services,[2] the reduction and simplification of fees that can be charged, and the bundling of pension services; (b) more draconian interventions, such as the imposition of price controls, restrictions, or bans on switches and informal acceptance of market agreements aimed at avoiding marketing wars; and (c) specific institutional arrangements such as the use of centralized agencies or auction mechanisms for certain pension services and the use of automatic assignment rules for undecided consumers.

This chapter discusses the policy trade-offs embedded in the use of ad hoc regulations and institutional arrangements commonly adopted in many jurisdictions. In particular, the next section discusses the trade-offs embedded in (a) restricting pension firm switching by participants, (b) requiring the use of uniform fee rates, (c) promoting simpler fee structures, (d) requiring the sale of multiple pension services in a single package, and (e) using price controls. Although price controls are becoming a popular tool among supervisors for redistributing rent to consumers, such controls are undesirable because they have serious drawbacks. The chapter later discusses ways to improve price regulation by linking it to the cost structure of pension firms. It also discusses the trade-offs policy makers face in using public procurement mechanisms and institutions as one form of industrial organization to address the consequences of consumer inertia. Policy conclusions follow in the last section.

From Light to Heavy-Handed Regulations

The continuum of ad hoc regulations and policy interventions aimed at reducing administrative fees in mandatory defined contribution (DC) pension quasi-markets is large. Most jurisdictions commonly use the examples discussed in this section.

These regulations have been justified by the paternalistic view that in a quasi-market with mandatory participation, the state has the obligation to reduce demand or supply distortions (efficiency and transparency objectives) and to ensure adequate redistribution of rents from pension firms to participants (equity objective). In other words, the performance of the mandatory pension industry is a matter of public interest.[3]

The ad hoc nature and narrow focus of these interventions implies that when the issue of concern is addressed, other distortions are created. Typically, measures that aim at increasing equity, transparency, or efficiency undermine one of the other two policy goals (and vice versa), and the magnitude of such trade-offs is usually proportional to the inertia of consumers.

In the discussion that follows, the chapter focuses on increasingly heavy-handed interventions: (a) uniform rate regulation (applied to heterogeneous fee bases), (b) simplification of fee structures and bundling of pension services, (c) switching restrictions, and (d) price regulation.

Uniform Rate Regulation

All jurisdictions require pension firms to charge the same price to participants. These prices are typically expressed as a percentage of the assets under management or the flow of contributions.[4] Uniform rates are considered more transparent and equitable. Other reasons for their use include lower incentives for tax evasion and the presence of disability and survivorship insurance (see box 3.1).

However, uniform rates reduce efficiency in supply,[5] whereas price discrimination would promote it (see box 3.2).[6] Therefore, a trade-off exists between (a) efficiency and transparency and (b) between efficiency and equity.

The trade-off between efficiency and transparency is better understood when one observes that individuals do not consume all the same services provided by pension firms. In addition, when they consume them, they do so to a different extent. If pension firms were allowed to charge consumers proportionally to the type of services and the extent to which they use them, efficiency in supply would increase. However, this outcome would be at the cost of transparency: participants would then need to compare a large menu of different prices across pension firms.

Box 3.1 Additional Motivations for Earnings- and Asset-Related Fee Bases

In addition to the equity and transparency rationale, earnings- and asset-related fee bases are traditionally thought to have other independent advantages. For instance, an earnings-related base is thought to spur pension firms to raise the density of contributions and reduce underreporting of taxable earnings. The rationale is that a pension firm may invest in improving collection of contributions and in detecting underreporting if this action allows it to earn higher revenues. In addition, positive externalities may arise from the use of an earnings-related base because more wage tax is collected and allocation of labor from the informal to formal market may improve. Unfortunately, no empirical evidence exists in favor of either claim. Regarding the first, this result is likely because the marginal cost of raising compliance is simply too large for administrators to profitably invest in it.

In the case of countries where pension firms also provide disability and survivorship insurance, an additional reason exists to use an earnings-related base. Insurance benefits and premiums are typically proportional to covered earnings, and an earnings-related fee would help achieve a more efficient resource allocation (if not, cross-subsidies would be large, and the incentive to capture those subsidies would induce pension firms to engage in actions that raise total costs, such as selection efforts).

Finally, an asset-related fee base has allegedly superior price information properties at the margin compared to an earnings-related base. That is, the former facilitates comparison of fees across pension funds. For instance, fees on assets can be directly subtracted from gross returns by consumers to compare pension firms across the single metric of net rates of return. This argument underpins the policy reform of 2007 in Mexico that aimed at promoting competition among pension firms based on net rates of return. Again, no empirical evidence supports this argument, notwithstanding its conceptual appeal.

The trade-off between efficiency and equity is better understood when one observes that uniform rates prevent price discrimination in proportional terms only (the proportional fee rate is the same for all customers), but not in absolute values (high-income or high-net-worth participants pay in absolute values more than low-income or low-net-worth participants while receiving the same quality of service). This redistributive objective has justified the adoption of uniform rate regulation, irrespective of the obvious inefficiency of this pricing scheme. However, the application of uniform rates to heterogeneous fee bases may have actually led

Box 3.2 Price Discrimination Promoting Efficiency in Supply

Efficiency in supply requires that a specialized fee cover the marginal cost of each service. Therefore, price discrimination would be more efficient than a uniform price covering all services consumed. In addition, some fees need to be either permanent or contingent, depending on the nature of the service. For instance, some services are permanently provided to participants once they are covered, regardless of whether individuals transit to or from the formal labor market. Such services include account updating and processing, distribution of quarterly or annual account statements, and passive asset management. In this first case, efficiency in supply requires a specialized fee levied on a permanent basis to cover the marginal cost. Other services either are contingent on formal labor force participation or are requested on a voluntary basis but still exhibit strong economies of scale. The typical example of the former type of service is the collection of contributions, which may justify the use of a fee on earnings. Examples of the latter type of service are advice on choosing a portfolio (investment profile), advice on retirement decisions, and processing of disability and survivorship claims. In this second case, efficiency in supply requires that a specialized fee be levied only when the service is provided.

to a redistribution that is against the totality of participants and in favor of pension firms, by encouraging firms to invest excessively in marketing and through this means to increase barriers to entry and market power (see box 3.3).

Finally, it is worth considering that inefficiency in supply associated with uniform rates likely worsens over time. Revenues grow with the expansion of assets and earnings bases over time, whereas pension fund costs have a strong fixed component. Thus, fee revenues can rise significantly above average costs over time, causing a strong redistribution against participants and in favor of pension firms. When the main fee is asset based, the critical vulnerability stems from trends in absolute returns and contribution rates.[7] When the main fee is contribution based, the critical vulnerability stems instead from trends in taxable earnings and contribution rates.[8] The trends in fee bases have prompted many jurisdictions to introduce price regulation in the form of arbitrary caps on fees, as discussed later in this section.

In summary, a pricing scheme based on uniform rates applied to heterogeneous fee bases is allegedly more transparent and more equitable—it aims at redistributing in favor of low-base participants—but it is not efficient. Hence, price distortions emerge, and they are reinforced by the incentive to invest in marketing. Additionally, earnings- and asset-related

---

Box 3.3 Who Really Benefits from Redistribution?

Whether uniform rates have actually been effective in subsidizing the participation of low-base consumers is unclear. Most likely, such rates have led to a redistribution that is against the totality of participants and in favor of pension firms, by promoting an increase in average prices as a consequence of marketing. This result is better understood when one observes that when uniform rates are applied to participants with different bases, different participants represent a different rent for pension firms. Therefore, the pension firm finds investment in marketing economically attractive whenever the marginal rent is larger than the marginal search or contact investment needed to attract that customer. The application of uniform rates to heterogeneous bases encourages firms to invest excessively in marketing and thus provides an explanation for the occurrence of marketing wars.

Notice that such a distortion, which stems exclusively from the pricing scheme adopted, is not eliminated when all customers are highly price sensitive. In fact, a higher average elasticity reduces the number of inert participants to warrant substantial investment in marketing (that is, higher elasticity reduces the productivity of the sales force and minimizes rents). However, even with a relatively smaller set of inert consumers, there is still justification for some (albeit smaller) marketing effort. Indeed, if all firms charge the same fee rate, but the average earnings base differs across firms, then the pension firm with the highest base will earn the largest rent, irrespective of demand elasticity.

---

fee bases grow over time, whereas pension firm costs are mainly fixed or proportional to the number of participants served. Thus, the aforementioned distortions are likely to become more severe over time.

These distortions would be greatly reduced (albeit not eliminated) if participants were not inert—that is, if the elasticity of demand to prices were high. Unfortunately, participants tend to be inert, which means that pension firms capture excessive rents at the expense of participants. These considerations prompted many jurisdictions to simplify fee structures (improve their transparency) as a way of increasing the elasticity of demand of participants and to introduce price regulation to compensate for the excessive market power of pension firms. The next two subsections discuss these issues in turn.

Simplification of Fee Structures and Bundling of Pension Services

The quest for transparency in fees has prompted many jurisdictions to adopt policies to simplify the choice that participants need to make, but such simplification has undermined the achievement of the efficiency objective. Two examples are the move toward a single fee base and the requirement for pension firms to offer all mandatory pension services as a single package.

Chapter 2 discussed how many jurisdictions allow pension firms to apply uniform rates simultaneously to more than one base. The more recent practice among regulators is the use of a single fee base because it allegedly simplifies price information and facilitates comparison and learning by participants—that is, it contributes to increasing demand elasticity.[9] Chile moved to fees on earnings only in the late 1980s and then to fees on assets only with the 2008 reform. Mexico, too, abandoned the use of a composite fee structure and moved to fees proportional to assets under management in 2007. However, if the fee bases currently used are per se inefficient (as previously argued), the change from a composite to a single fee base (motivated by the desire to simplify the fee structure) further increases the discrepancy between prices and marginal costs.

In addition, changes in the fee structure can be inequitable in that they may create intergenerational transfers. In general, a shift from an earnings-related base to an asset-related base creates an intergenerational redistribution in favor of the younger generation, and the converse shift favors the older generation. Older generations of participants, who already paid earnings-based fees in the past, will be forced to pay a higher pro rata share of total costs, now that their assets have grown, than they would have paid had earnings-based fees continued. In contrast, younger generations of participants will finance a smaller pro rata share of total costs in the coming years, while their assets remain relatively low, than they would have paid had earnings-based fees continued. The shift from an earnings-related base to an asset-related base may also constitute a nontrivial windfall gain for the industry of pension firms, depending on the level of the new fee rate, the prospects for increases in coverage, and the projected trends in the asset base relative to the earnings base.

Similar policy trade-offs exist in the case of bundling of pension services. Requiring pension firms to offer pension services in a single package spares consumers the search costs associated with choosing in several quasi-markets (one for each pension service) and at the same time reduces pension firms' marketing budgets. Hence, the belief is that price-cost margins would be reduced.

However, different pension services have different cost structures, and bundling can raise market concentration levels and, therefore, average prices. For instance, asset management has lower economies of scale than do customer services,[10] which are characterized by large sunk and fixed costs: When the two are bundled, the overall market concentration equilibrium is equal to the largest among the equilibriums that would occur in customer services and in asset management separately (in this specific case, customer services). Consequently, barriers to entry are artificially extended while market power and overall prices increase.[11]

In summary, regulations aimed at increasing transparency by simplifying fees and reducing search costs through bundling of pension services are likely to reduce efficiency and equity further. On the one hand, the desirability of increased price information and comparability (transparency objective) needs to be carefully weighed against the redistributive effects of a shift toward a single fee base (equity objective) and the overall effect on prices (efficiency objective). On the other hand, the alleged welfare gains associated with simplified choice through bundling (transparency objective) need to be carefully weighed against the adverse price impact stemming from the forcing of joint production of services with different cost functions (equity objective) and from the reduction in market contestability associated with higher barriers to entry (efficiency objective).

Switching Restrictions

Many governments have enforced regulations aimed at reducing the mobility of participants across pension firms as a way to curb socially unproductive marketing efforts.[12] Examples include (a) prohibitions against switching to a different firm if some criterion has not been met (traditionally, a minimum contribution period);[13] (b) imposition of financial penalties on participants who switch, as in some Latin American and European countries;[14] and (c) restrictions on the number and structure of the sales force to pension firms that want to expand, as in Argentina, Chile, or Poland at different times.[15]

Regulations aimed at controlling marketing expenses have been generally ineffective because they do not address the fundamental cause that justifies the marketing effort—namely, uniform rates applied to heterogeneous bases that encourage pension firms to selectively target high-rent individuals, as explained in the previous section.[16]

Indeed, a switching regulation[17] succeeds in eliminating marketing incentives when switches are completely banned. In this case, a firm with a captive clientele has no incentive to invest in marketing because it cannot attract new customers. However, a complete ban on switches encourages pension firms to increase prices so that a captive clientele cannot escape. When switches are only limited, the effect on marketing incentives is ambiguous. Lower elasticity both encourages firms to charge higher fees and increases the cost of marketing with an opposite effect on profits. In general, pension firms will still find investment in marketing profitable whenever the marginal profit from advertising is positive (see box 3.4 for a technical discussion).

In addition to having an ambiguous effect on the problem they attempt to solve, restrictions on transfers may affect asset management quality. The profit motive for investing in asset management quality is that a higher

---

Box 3.4 Switching Regulations That Do Not Eliminate Marketing Incentives

Generally, limited switches have an ambiguous effect on marketing incentives, because they simultaneously reduce the elasticity of demand perceived by the firm and increase the marginal costs of marketing.

On the one hand, the reduction in the effective elasticity of demand encourages firms to charge higher prices. This situation, in turn, increases both the marginal rent that can be extracted from new customers and the marginal profits from advertising, because a reduction in the effective elasticity of demand raises the equilibrium price charged at the margin, which increases revenues for the pension firms from the stock of customers. Clearly, higher prices will reduce the stock of customers in the future, because individuals will switch to cheaper funds. However, the future loss of profits caused by higher prices is further delayed when the restriction on transfers is strong. At the limit, with no transfers, an increase in prices has no negative impact on profits.

On the other hand, the increase in the marginal cost of advertising reduces marginal profits. Hence, the combined effect is ambiguous unless firms agree to collude in repressing the marketing effort.

---

return attracts more participants, which increases the value of the firm.[18] However, under a ban on transfers, a given increase in asset management quality results in much smaller net transfers. A similar effect to what was discussed before is now at work: incentives to invest in asset management are reduced because the lower switching rate raises the expected net present discounted value of the profits generated by the captive clientele.

The policy trade-offs associated with a restriction on switches are obvious. Restrictions on switches are introduced when observed marketing expenditures are excessive, because a large share of such expenditures is considered socially unproductive. However, low mobility is also costly for the industry because it impairs competition, and pressure mounts to relax regulations.

In some countries, pension firms have independently colluded to decrease marketing expenditures, reducing the trade-off. In other countries, and against all warnings from economic theory, the government has facilitated deals among firms to control marketing expenses. These forms of agreement are politically unstable and facilitate the possible capture of the regulator by the industry.[19]

In summary, the lesson from the history of mandatory DC pension quasi-markets is that restrictions on transfers address the symptoms but not the cause of the problem of socially costly marketing expenditures. In addition, equilibriums based on regulations or market agreements aimed at restricting transfers are likely to be welfare reducing compared to the second-best equilibrium of socially costly marketing expenditure.[20]

Price Regulation

Price controls have been a substantially more draconian policy intervention aimed at curbing the price distortions stemming from the excessive market power of pension firms. Many countries, especially in Eastern Europe, have adopted caps on administrative fees as a means of redistributing rents from pension firms to participants. Table 3.1 provides a summary of the key elements of price regulations introduced in selected countries.

From an economic perspective, the standard justification for price regulation is that it limits the price distortions generated by low demand elasticity and high barriers to entry. Low demand elasticity renders the clients of pension firms captive (unable to "vote with their feet" and to leave costly

Table 3.1 Price Regulation in Selected Countries, 2008

	Percentage of contributions[a]	Percentage of assets	Percentage of excess return over benchmark[b]
Bolivia	5	0.23	n.a.
Bulgaria	5	1.00	n.a.
Colombia	30	n.a.	n.a.
Costa Rica	4	n.a.	8.00
Dominican Republic	6	n.a.	30.00
El Salvador	13	n.a.	n.a.
Hungary	5	0.80	n.a.
Macedonia, FYR	6	0.50	n.a.
Poland	n.a.	0.54	0.05
Slovak Republic	1	0.07	n.a.

Source: Author calculations based on countries' regulations.

Note: n.a. = not applicable.

a. In many Latin America countries, caps are expressed as a percentage of earnings. In this table, those caps were divided by the contribution rate to express them as a function of the level of contributions.

b. In Costa Rica and Poland, the benchmark is zero, so the performance fee becomes a fee on nominal returns. In the Dominican Republic, the benchmark is close to the return on bank deposits, making the performance fee an asset management fee in disguise.

pension firms for more affordable pension firms). High barriers to entry also limit the extent to which new entrants can impose price discipline on incumbents. Hence, in mandatory DC quasi-markets, firms' ability to charge above-average costs is largely bounded by the credible threat of political interference (through the introduction of price caps) when markups become intolerably high.

That said, price caps also lead to distortions, so their economic case is indeed mixed. Possible drawbacks discussed here include (a) low-quality asset management, (b) discrimination among pension firms, (c) regulatory capture (or risk), and (d) de facto ineffectiveness to redistribute rents in favor of participants.

Price caps may discourage investment in asset management quality, which is a major issue for long-term savings schemes. For instance, annual underperformance of only 1 percent over the life cycle can reduce final cash balances by about 20 percent.[21] The reason caps may affect asset management quality is easy to understand. When caps are binding, they simply starve the asset management function of needed income. When caps are not binding, the effect on asset management quality takes place through a less obvious channel. Nonbinding price caps may mislead potential reformers into believing that current fees are acceptable just because they are capped. Hence, price caps discourage the adoption of policies that promote competition and healthy switching among pension firms, or they legitimize charges at the level of the cap irrespective of service quality.[22]

Price caps may discriminate against pension funds with a less valuable customer base because caps are applied to uniform rates and not to prices per unit of physical service. That is, a given cap provides less revenue per customer to pension firms with a lower average fee base. Consequently, price caps may encourage transactions with related parties with the objective of subsidizing capped revenues. For example, in Hungary, all pension firms outsource asset management, and caps apply to both contributions and asset management fees. Pension firms outsourcing to asset managers within the same financial group have an incentive to artificially inflate the asset management fee to offset forgone revenues resulting from caps on fees. This form of cross-subsidization (through transfer pricing) is not available to pension firms outside the financial group, which outsource asset management at lower market prices.[23]

Caps can expose regulators and supervisors to potential capture and firms to high regulatory risk. In the absence of a formal process to set caps that reflect the actual production costs of firms, pension firms rely on lobbying and related practices to make their point of view known when caps are set. In this case, regulatory capture by well-connected market players becomes likely. At the same time, pension firms are exposed to excessive regulatory risk if a populist administration decides to arbitrarily lower the caps.

Participants may not benefit from the introduction of caps after all, because caps can be easily evaded through fees charged on investment products offered by third parties and purchased by the pension firm (also known as *second-floor fees*). Second-floor fees do not yield additional revenues to pension firms, but they reduce net yields for participants. In Chile, for instance, the extensive use of mutual funds for foreign investment with an average fee of 100 basis points costs participants on average an extra 30 basis points on total assets. In other words, the use of third-party investment vehicles makes caps ineffective as a policy instrument for redistributing rents from firms to participants, and instead rents are redistributed from pension firms to third parties.

Finally, caps are not linked to the actual cost structure of firms and can easily become obsolete, given that factor prices, technology, and demand change over time. For instance, when the dispersion in the average fee base increases, caps become more discriminatory across firms, and when caps are decreased, they take away more revenue per customer in firms with high fee bases than in other firms, thus affecting incentives differently across pension firms. In other words, because of possible changes in fee bases, price caps are a less effective policy instrument for redistributing rents from firms to participants. Clearly, this result could be obviated by a schedule of cap revisions, as some countries have imposed. However, each new revision of caps is exposed to the drawbacks discussed earlier, in particular regulatory and political risks. Unfortunately, no government has yet adopted formal procedures for defining price caps that smoothly incorporate changes in factor prices, technology, and demand.

In summary, price regulation in the form of price caps is a substantially stronger form of policy intervention that is aimed at addressing the consequences of price distortions and redistributing rents in favor of participants. However, by not addressing the causes of price distortions, such regulation suffers from many drawbacks, as discussed previously. Most important, price caps could, in practice, redistribute rents in favor of pension firms' suppliers, instead of participants, through related-party transactions and could quickly become obsolete unless frequently changed. Irrespective of these drawbacks, price regulations are becoming very popular among supervisors because their mere introduction is perceived by the public as an effective rent redistributing tool.

Improving Pricing Schemes and Price Regulation

In the previous section, many of the distortions created by the use of uniform rates applied to heterogeneous fee bases were highlighted. This section suggests that flat fees and flat subsidies may be jointly more efficient and more equitable than are current pricing schemes. In addition, the section discusses how the design of price controls can be improved by linking them to the cost structure of pension firms.

Improving Current Pricing Schemes

Flat fees are a pricing scheme superior to uniform rates applied to heterogeneous bases, because flat fees increase efficiency in supply while avoiding price discrimination and because they eliminate marketing incentives.

The reason efficiency is increased is better understood when one observes that the production costs of many pension services provided by pension firms are not proportional to the earnings or asset bases on which fees are typically levied. Rather, they are fixed. Hence, a switch to the right combination of flat fees[24] would increase efficiency in supply. In addition, because every consumer is charged the same flat price per unit of service, price discrimination is avoided.

The reason marketing incentives would be reduced is better understood when one observes that with flat fees, all customers represent the same rent for pension firms. Hence, firms are not encouraged to engage in cream skimming or to invest in socially undesirable and excessive marketing.

However, flat fees are not equitable per se unless used in conjunction with a subsidy.[25] A flat subsidy can meet the equity objective to relieve low-base participants from the mandate to pay fees. For instance, an explicit tax on all covered earnings at a constant rate can be created, and the revenue from this tax can be used to pay each pension firm a flat subsidy per participant served per period, even if no contribution occurred in that period (the subsidy can also be paid to the participant's account). This tax-as-subsidy scheme redistributes more efficiently than the use of uniform rates applied to heterogeneous fee bases (that is, it is more equitable) because redistribution takes place over the whole covered population and not within each segment covered by any one pension firm.

New Zealand implemented this fee subsidy in the KiwiSaver program in 2007. Flat fees do not burden low earners in New Zealand, because the government also pays a flat subsidy to participants, advertised as support for paying fees and financed with redistributive general tax revenue. In New Zealand, the level of this subsidy was set slightly above the flat fee charged by firms and was advertised as a justification for firms to charge flat fees, thus encouraging their use (see table 3.2). Moreover, the fee subsidy is paid even when the participant does not contribute, thereby making it easier for firms to adopt flat fees.

Since 1997, Mexico has had a similar flat subsidy (called *cuota social*) equivalent to more than 90 percent of required contributions for very-low-income earners close to the minimum wage. The Mexican *cuota social* is advertised as the taxpayers' effort to raise the pensions of the poor (that is, as a noncontributory subsidy to the elderly poor, comparable to

Table 3.2 Fees Charged by KiwiSaver Default Providers, 2007

	Explicit[a,b]		Projected[c]			
Provider	Flat fee ($NZ per month)	Asset based (% per year)	Flat fee ($NZ per year)	Asset based (% per year)	Annual equivalent fee (2007 $NZ)[c,d]	Revenue from flat fee (%)
AMP	3.00	0.550	15.00	0.250	97.23	52
ASB	3.00	0.275	15.00	0.250	81.34	63
ING	2.75	0.470	15.00	0.250	89.61	54
Mercer	2.85	0.530	15.00	0.250	94.28	52
AXA	3.06	0.534	3.00	0.250	85.03	47
Tower	2.75	0.510	3.00	0.250	79.92	45
Average total fee ($NZ per year per account)					87.90	52
Fee subsidy ($NZ per year per account)					40.00	
Average fee (US$ per year per account)					64.30	

Source: Valdés-Prieto 2007.

a. Excludes mandatory employer fees announced in May 2007, after the auction.

b. Excludes second-floor fees.

c. See Valdés-Prieto (2007) for an explanation of the calculations performed and the assumptions used.

d. The exchange rate of May 2007 was $NZ 1 = US$0.7325.

minimum pension subsidies and universal flat noncontributory pensions). Mexico, however, does not allow pension firms to charge flat fees.

In summary, flat fees are more efficient than uniform rates applied to heterogeneous bases in both a high- and a low-demand elasticity environment because they limit the discrepancy between prices and marginal production costs. In addition, when used in conjunction with a flat subsidy, they create a more efficient redistributive mechanism than do fees based on uniform rates.

However, two important drawbacks need to be highlighted: (a) subsidies financed by the budget can be fiscally expensive, and (b) pension firms still enjoy considerable market power. The fiscal concern implies that flat subsidies may not be a practical tool after all, but this empirical issue is likely to differ from country to country. Market power implies that even if fees are flat, they are likely to be well above average costs in equilibrium, suggesting that the likelihood of political intervention on prices remains high. Therefore, unless alternative industrial organization structures are adopted, improved price regulation mechanisms are needed to reduce price distortions. The rest of this section analyzes the merits of an alternative price regulation design based on pension firms' cost structure. The next section discusses alternative industrial organization structures.

Improving the Design of Price Controls

As noted earlier, most of the distortion associated with the current design of price caps relates to the fact that they are not linked to the level and structure of pension firms' costs. The use of cost-based tariffs would reduce most of these distortions.

Clearly, a full dichotomy between price caps that are not linked to costs and cost-based tariffs that are linked to costs is impractical; some link to costs (even if implicit) is bound to exist even for price caps. For instance, in the KiwiSaver program in New Zealand, pension fees have been set through a process that reflects, albeit indirectly, the production costs of pension firms. An auction for default providers of undecided participants was used to make the market reveal the cost structure (and associated competitive markup) of allowable pension services. On the basis of these revealed costs, all pension funds were allowed to charge a flat fee per person per month.

One possible way to establish cost-based tariffs is through the use of a model firm, as is commonly done in the infrastructure sector for water and electricity distribution.[26] Basically, evidence on audited production costs would be used to estimate the cost function of a representative firm. Each real firm would then be allowed to receive income capped by the tariff to finance the costs of the model firm and could retain all savings from cutting costs below those of the model firm, thereby putting pressure on laggard firms to invest in cost savings. These tariffs are typically set for five years and allow for tariff indexation to inflation. The tariff formula often includes a parameter that is intended to estimate possible increases in total factor productivity resulting from technology changes.

An alternative regulatory approach used in the utility sector is the rate-of-return approach, which limits prices so that the regulated firm earns only a "fair" rate of return on its capital investment. Contrary to the cost-based tariff based on a model firm, rate-of-return regulation creates no incentives for reducing costs and increasing efficiency, and it can result in the regulated firm overinvesting in its capital stock (Guasch and Spiller 1999).[27]

For mandatory DC quasi-markets, the objective of the tariff-setting process would be to finance the long-term marginal production costs for each service that participants are mandated to consume and to raise sufficient revenues to finance nonproduction costs. Only permissible costs are considered in a model firm—that is, costs that must be incurred to produce the set of services expected from the model firm. Mandatory services typically include collection of contributions, record keeping, handling of transfers, benefit assessment, benefit payment, and passive asset management. Ideally, active asset management, which displays high and rapidly increasing marginal costs, would not be remunerated by the same tariff established for all other low-marginal-cost functions, but through a performance fee mechanism. Nonproduction costs typically include marketing and financial education.

The permissible costs should be periodically redefined because they depend on the industrial organization and the degree of subcontracting (vertical disintegration). For instance, some pension firms may subcontract record keeping, so a decision needs to be made whether record keeping costs should be included. Alternatively, if the government collects contributions centrally, such costs would not be included. Finally, the degree of common ownership between pension service providers and their suppliers also affects which costs should be considered. In short, the definition of *permissible costs* is a highly technical matter that cannot be determined in the law, because it requires periodic revisions.

In computing the costs of the model firm on the basis of information on real firms, one must pay attention to the costs recorded by firms belonging to large corporate groups. Price transfers can be used to artificially inflate costs within a group. Alternatively, inputs can be subsidized within a corporate group structure (again, record keeping, marketing, brokerage services, and so on), and the input price in transactions with related parties may be deliberately inflated to increase the final tariff of the model firm.

After the costs of the model firm are estimated, the question arises of how to raise revenues for pension firms. Earlier discussion indicated that a system of flat fees with flat subsidies would be more efficient and equitable than would current rates applied to heterogeneous fee bases, but such a system can be fiscally expensive. An alternative redistributive scheme could be engineered by leaving current fee structures unchanged and by setting fee rates to generate an average income from all pension firms equal to what is needed to finance the model firm. Overall revenues from this tariff would then be distributed among pension firms in the form of a monthly lump sum to cover fixed production costs plus a flat amount per participant to finance information and financial education (nonproduction costs).

This alternative scheme would achieve the same level of efficiency and equity as a system of flat fees and subsidies would accomplish but without raising fiscal concerns. The equity objective for low-base participants is achieved because participants continue to pay what amounts to a uniform rate on earnings or assets, but flat revenues for pension firms are totally financed by rates on participants' bases, thus mitigating the fiscal risk.[28] Moreover, because marketing expenditure is proportional to the churning rate,[29] the tariff model would, as discussed in the previous chapter, make it possible to raise sufficient revenues to target only a socially desirable churning rate. Finally, because firms cannot discriminate among participants on the basis of rents (their income is essentially flat), they are also discouraged from engaging in cream skimming.

The obvious challenge in the use of a model firm to establish tariffs is that costs need to be estimated very accurately, which requires a regulatory authority with very strong technical capacity and resources and the necessary independence to avoid capture by politicians, consumers, or firms. Estimating the cost structure of the model firm has proven costly and challenging for utility regulators (Guasch and Spiller 1999), especially in emerging markets, where regulatory authorities often have less capacity. Hence, the authorities in such markets have frequently invited international experts to help them define the cost model. Allowing pension regulatory authorities to define price ceilings introduces a new regulatory risk, which if mishandled or handled in a discretionary or unpredictable manner could adversely affect the development of the sector, as the experiences in the infrastructure area illustrate. In the infrastructure sector, an arbitration mechanism or a specialized court for appeals is commonly used to handle disputes on price regulation, given the complexity and technical nature of such regulation.

In summary, pricing schemes can be improved by the use of flat fees and flat subsidies. However, a flat subsidy can be fiscally expensive, and flat fees do not reduce per se the market power enjoyed by pension firms. Addressing the causes of the price distortions created by an inert customer base and high barriers to entry requires adoption of alternative industrial organization structures, which are further analyzed in the next section.

Alternative Industrial Organization Models

Alternative industrial organization models that directly address the causes of price distortion, such as consumers' inertia, are based on procurement. This section discusses the extreme case of pure procurement and the hybrid case where pure procurement is used in conjunction with a quasi-market.

Pure Procurement

Under pure procurement, each service provider that wins a board-designed procurement process is assigned a monopoly over a set of consumers. The essence of pure procurement is that consumers are not given the opportunity to choose the board; otherwise a quasi-market is re-created and consumer inertia regains significance. Examples of countries that have adopted this framework are Bolivia, Singapore, and the United States for the Thrift Savings Plan.

The merits of pure procurement arise directly from its primary objective, which is to deal in a radical manner with consumer inertia. When one demand block is granted to each of the firms that win the contest, provider incentive to spend on marketing to attract clients is removed. In addition, establishing competition *for* the market rather than *in* the market eliminates barriers to entry and rent extraction activities.

Nevertheless, pure procurement carries its own challenges for regulators, and, although superior in most aspects to price ceilings, it may not be a Pareto improvement in all cases for quasi-markets (that is, it is unclear that nobody is ever worse off). In particular, some form of supervision and monitoring needs to be imposed, especially on asset management quality.

In comparison to quasi-markets, two areas of concern exist with pure procurement boards. First, a procurement board is a centralized entity and, by definition, it has the power to influence the quality standards (often negatively) of pension firms.[30] This influence may lead to underinvestment in the adoption of innovations that would improve asset management quality. In addition, monitoring and evaluating the overall performance of the board is very difficult. Because the board is the only entity to assess, no valid performance benchmark can be used. Second, procurement boards are usually public offices in the sense that board members are designated by politicians, unions, employer associations, or large employers. Thus, there is a risk that political interference may reduce the ability of the board to maximize participants' welfare.[31]

Hybrid Systems

A hybrid industrial organizational model separates demand into two segments: procurement and quasi-market. In one segment, a public board selects the pension fund administrators, as in pure procurement, whereas in the other segment, participants choose their own provider, as in quasi-markets. In the most interesting types of hybrids, each participant is free to choose the segment, thus creating competition between organizational forms. Hybrids also differ in their treatment of undecided consumers. Consideration of hybrids is natural where the default for most of the undecided is the procured segment. Countries that have adopted hybrid industrial organization models include Argentina, Bulgaria, Chile, Hungary, Mexico, and New Zealand (KiwiSaver).

The KiwiSaver system, New Zealand's earnings-related system, began operations on July 1, 2007, following a procurement contest in 2006 to determine default providers. The Swedish Premium Pension System (Premiepensionsmyndigheten, or PPM) is also a hybrid, but it differs from the KiwiSaver because it has a state-owned monopoly provider in the "procured" segment, and the quasi-market firms are subject to very tight price ceilings. Mexico's rule to allocate undecided participants to the highest quartile of providers that operate in the quasi-market segment in terms of net returns is also a hybrid.[32] Similar rules are used in Bulgaria, Chile, and Hungary. The pension reform approved by Chile's National Congress in 2008 also establishes a hybrid system with an explicit procurement system.

The hybrid form has two potential economic advantages over pure procurement or a pure quasi-market. These advantages relate to the creation of a performance benchmark for the board and the creation of outside options for the board's suppliers.[33]

Pension firms in the quasi-market segment are the only adequate benchmark for evaluating the public procurement board. Such a well-tuned benchmark allows the political authorities and public opinion to better assess the performance of the public procurement board. By contrast, the absence of adequate peers for benchmarking in a pure procurement model impairs the ability of the public board to evaluate the quality of asset management.

The existence of a pension quasi-market with multiple providers improves the outside options for suppliers to the public procurement board. Underinvestment by suppliers in financial innovation and adaptation is therefore reduced relative to the pure procurement model. This reduction helps the procured segment attain returns as high as in the quasi-market.

A hybrid can also be superior to a pure quasi-market for other reasons. For instance, the welfare of undecided consumers increases when their choices are replaced by a technically qualified public board that compares prices while controlling asset management quality. In addition, if the allocation to the procured segment is reasonably targeted to inert participants, the share of active participants in the quasi-market segment increases. This increase raises the demand elasticity faced by firms in the quasi-market segment, which could result in lower prices and fewer marketing expenditures in that market. Finally, the "signaling effect" of establishing a procured segment may further increase public awareness about price differences among participants, thereby further raising price elasticity. For example, in Mexico, the allocation of the undecided led the press to intensify information on prices every time a new group of participants was assigned, which happened quarterly until December 2008.[34]

Policy considerations for well-functioning hybrid systems. The design of a well-functioning hybrid model needs to take into account several policy considerations, among which the following five appear critical.

First, a participant should not be allocated to a segment that does not maximize his or her expected future wealth, net of fees. The government should allocate participants to the procured segment only when it is arguably in their best interests. Given the volatility of equity returns and the direct effect of returns on pensions in a DC system, a government may face suits from individuals who find ex post that the government allocation materially reduced their pensions, even though this outcome could not be predicted ex ante. Thus, the allocation to the procured segment needs to be transparent and well reasoned, and individuals should be free to leave the procured choice if they consider it worse than the choices available in the quasi-market.

Second, the default allocation should be targeted to inert participants on the basis of objective rules. Involving the government in the business of finding the most suitable segment for an individual participant may lead to excessive interference, micromanagement, and legal liabilities. Possible objective rules include the simple requirement that the participant be undecided, in the sense that he or she does not choose a pension fund administrator. Alternatively (or in addition), rules could be based on the observable attributes of undecided participants, such as individuals with low assets. These attributes would be within a range that ensures that it is highly unlikely they will do materially worse in the default segment, if they choose to remain there.

Third, participants who recently chose a pension firm should be exempt from a default allocation. To be efficient, a hybrid model must limit duplication of search costs and switching costs. Consequently, excluding individuals who chose a provider relatively recently from the procured segment would be desirable.

Fourth, flat fees increase the stability of the hybrid model and should be an additional aspect to consider when selecting fee bases. This effect can be easily understood when one observes that differences in fee rates are driven by inequality in fee bases as well as cost differences. For instance, if the average base in the procured/undecided segment is lower than in the quasi-market/nondefault segment, providers to the undecided segment need a higher fee rate to collect the same fee income per period as providers to the nondefault segment. In other words, if the ratio between the average base in the procured segment and the average base in the quasi-market segment is low enough, then the fee rate obtained in the auction for the procured segment can be above the fee rate observed in the quasi-market segment. This outcome is possible even though the quasi-market must finance marketing costs and above-normal profits whereas the procured segment need not to do so. In that case, the best allocation rule for all undecided participants is the quasi-market (continuation in the last firm chosen, despite being undecided), and the procured segment is eliminated. The preceding suggests that, if inequalities in fee bases between the two segments are large enough, the potential welfare gains of a hybrid over the relevant extreme organizational form can be lost, and the former can be wiped out. This can happen with either asset-based[35] or contribution-based fees. By contrast, when flat fees are dominant, as in New Zealand, no inequality arises in fee bases, because the base is one unit of service per person per period. In other words, flat fees reduce the risk that the hybrid model will be eliminated.

Fifth, suppliers to the procured segment should be protected from cream skimming during the service period. Heterogeneity in fee bases and in fee restrictions creates sets of procured participants with large rents. Because cream skimming can be expected, bidders in the auction factor into their bid some amount to cover this loss of rents, leading them to offer higher fee rates. If these rates surpass those in the quasi-market segment, cream skimming unravels the procured segment and eliminates the hybrid organization form.[36] Again, because cream skimming is a consequence of the absence of flat fees, these last two considerations are obviously related, and they both provide an additional rationale for the use of flat fees.

Stock or flow design? Finally, one needs to consider what type of hybrid model should be adopted. Currently, a lively debate exists as to whether the stock design is superior to the flow design. With the stock design, providers in the procured segment are allowed to serve the full segment of participants (the inert customers) who would benefit from procurement. In addition, target participants can spend their whole working career in the procured segment, because they will be served by a sequence of providers selected through periodic procurement auctions. With the flow design, providers in the procured segment serve only a fraction of inert participants. In addition, no periodic auctions are held for the same target participant; once a participant is allocated to the procured segment, he or she will never be allocated to it again.

Generally, the stock design presents attractive characteristics, such as targeting all inert participants and protecting them from dynamic predatory pricing schedules. However, it may induce bidders to raise their prices if they fear that their clientele will be lost in a future auction, which is likely if a high degree of bundling is required from providers in the procured segment. Hence, the feasibility of the stock design is likely to be associated with a high degree of unbundling.[37]

In summary, pure procurement organizational models should be avoided in favor of hybrid models. However, several constraints must be addressed for a hybrid to be viable and efficient. Among others, these constraints affect the choice of fee bases: heterogeneity in fee bases is likely to make the hybrid model nonviable, further suggesting that increases in the flat component of current fees would be desirable. In addition, unbundling of pension services is likely to be desirable because it reduces the concentration equilibrium and, therefore, the incentives of firms to raise prices during the auctions.

Conclusions

A wide range of policy options has been used to attempt to lower administrative fees in mandatory DC pension quasi-markets. Typically, options attempt to achieve multiple objectives, such as improving transparency, efficiency, and equity, but they cannot be achieved simultaneously. Hence, most of these options entail marked trade-offs that policy makers should balance accordingly. The final resolution of such trade-offs is most likely country specific, because the final assessment depends on the current design of the pension market (status quo) and the degree of development of financial markets, among other idiosyncratic characteristics. This section concludes by reorganizing the policy interventions analyzed in this chapter according to the trade-offs they entail, emphasizing possible win-win solutions for policy makers.

Policies with Increasing Embedded Trade-Offs

Policies commonly used to contain administrative fees include the following: (a) prohibition against charging different customers different prices for the same services by requiring pension firms to use uniform fee rates, (b) simplification of fee structures, (c) bundling of pension services, (d) restrictions on transfers, and (e) price controls.

The desirable policy objective of subsidizing low-income or low-asset participants has favored the use of uniform rate regulation applied to heterogeneous fee bases. This pricing scheme is allegedly more transparent and more equitable, but it is less efficient, contributing to price distortions stemming from participants' inertia. In addition, it reinforces price distortions by encouraging excessive investment in marketing by pension firms. Moreover, earnings- and asset-related fee bases grow over time, whereas pension funds' costs are mainly fixed or proportional to the number of participants served. Hence, the distortion between prices and marginal costs is likely to become more severe over time.

The simplification of fees and the bundling of services are used to reduce participants' inertia, but trade-offs again exist among transparency, equity, and efficiency. The alleged welfare gains of increased price information and comparability through simplified fee structures need to be weighed carefully against the redistributive effects of a shift toward, and the inefficiency of, a single fee base. The alleged welfare gains associated with simplified choice through bundling need to be weighed against the price effect stemming from the joint production of services with different cost functions and the reduction in market contestability associated with higher barriers to entry. In both cases, increased transparency, aimed at reducing inertia, is likely to be offset by higher inefficiency, further increasing price distortions.

Experience indicates that restricting transfers of participants across pension firms, with the purpose of reducing socially unproductive marketing expenses, is not an effective policy tool. Such restrictions do not affect the fundamental incentive for firms to invest in marketing—namely, the presence of rent heterogeneity across consumers attributable to uniform fees applied to heterogeneous bases such as assets or earnings. In addition, policies may restrict transfers to protect participants from making systematic mistakes when choosing pension firms, but such policies decrease the effective elasticity of demand and increase barriers to entry. In other words, they increase the market power of the incumbent pension firms. Finally, alternative policies based on market agreements sponsored by regulators to restrict transfers are politically unstable and facilitate the possibility of regulatory capture by the industry. Hence, equilibriums based on regulations or market agreements aimed at restricting transfers are likely to be welfare decreasing when compared to socially costly marketing expenditures.

Many jurisdictions use price regulation, in the form of price caps, to reduce the consequences of price distortion and redistribute rents in favor of participants. However, price caps suffer from a series of drawbacks, including the fact that they are not linked to cost structures and, in practice, may not redistribute in favor of participants but in favor of third parties through related transactions with pension firms. Additionally, in a dynamic context, they quickly become obsolete unless frequently changed. If price controls are to be kept, their design can be vastly improved by linking them to the cost structure of pension firms. Techniques used in utility industries to design cost-based tariffs can be adapted to mandatory DC pension quasi-markets. Cost-based tariffs can be expected to be vastly superior to current caps on fees given the existing discrepancy between prices and costs. Nevertheless, allowing pension regulatory authorities to define price ceilings introduces a new regulatory risk, which, if mishandled or handled in a discretionary or unpredictable manner, could adversely affect the development of the sector.

Win-Win Interventions

A more aggressive use of flat fees and subsidies and hybrid industrial organizations, in conjunction with unbundling of pension services, appears to provide fewer policy trade-offs and should be pursued by policy makers in mandatory DC pensions to improve efficiency and equity and to reduce participants' inertia.

The efficiency objective is best achieved with the use of flat price schemes. These schemes greatly reduce price distortions because prices are based on one unit of service per person per period. In addition, flat prices radically eliminate cream-skimming marketing incentives and should be associated with lower barriers to entry.

The equity objective is best achieved by a separate subsidy. The subsidy may prove fiscally expensive, but it can be implemented in different ways to minimize the fiscal costs and achieve the socially desirable level of redistribution in the market.

However, flat fees do not address the problem of participants' inertia. This problem is best addressed by alternative industrial organization models involving some elements of procurement by a centralized public board. A pure procurement model can deal in a radical manner with consumer inertia: demand is assigned to providers through auctions. By establishing competition for the market rather than in the market, the pure procurement model eliminates barriers to entry and rent extraction activities. However, procurement boards have a monopsony power over pension firms, which may lead firms to underinvest in innovations to improve asset management quality. In addition, in the absence of a quasi-market, benchmarking the overall performance of the board is very difficult. Finally, the risk exists that political interference may reduce the ability of the board to maximize participants' welfare, by encouraging it to adopt very conservative strategies or to support investments that do not follow a purely commercial objective, especially if the country's governance framework is weak. Although pure procurement may not always be superior to quasi-markets, a hybrid model, with a combination of procurement and quasi-market, is likely to be.

Hybrids are organizational forms that separate participants into two segments: a procured segment for inert participants and a quasi-market segment for less inert participants. Hybrids can be superior to pure procurement because they provide a benchmark for the procurement boards' performance and outside options for the boards' suppliers. They can also be superior to a quasi-market because they replace the choices of undecided individuals with a technically qualified public board and increase demand elasticity in the quasi-market segment.

However, whether hybrids are indeed superior to either of the two extreme organizational forms of pure procurement or pure quasi-market depends on several issues being addressed. These issues include accurate targeting of inert participants for the procurement segment and protection of providers in the procured segment from cream skimming by providers in the quasi-market. Interestingly, if inequalities in fee bases between the two segments are large enough, the potential welfare gains of a hybrid over the two extreme organizational forms can be lost. Here the complementarities with the aforementioned options become evident: policies aimed at increasing efficiency by increasing the flat component in fees charged by pension firms would also promote the stability of hybrid industrial organizations and promote lower participant inertia.

Finally, there is an open debate on the relative superiority of the stock and flow hybrid designs. The stock design presents attractive characteristics, such as targeting all inert participants and protecting them from dynamic predatory pricing schedules. However, it may induce bidders to raise their prices if they fear their clientele will be lost in a future auction. This concern could be mitigated by lowering barriers to entry through the unbundling of pension services.

Annex 3A: Key Policy Concerns with Pure Procurement

Pure procurement raises two key policy concerns: (a) the possibility of underinvestment in financial innovation and (b) the possibility of undue political influence in asset management.

Underinvestment in Financial Innovation

Innovation of financial management techniques is an expensive sunk investment for pension providers, both for leading countries that innovate and for follower countries that adapt.[38] In both sets of countries, where a centralized board procures financial management technology from suppliers and where private domestic demand for financial products similar to those purchased by the procurement board is not well developed, underinvestment in financial technology may take place for at least three reasons: (a) the monopsony power of the board, (b) the lack of competition in procurement, and (c) the public good component of innovation.

Monopsony power of the board. According to Williamson (1971), underinvestment in adaptations that are specific to a customer (in this case the public board) emerges in any two-stage game situation in which the adapter invests in period 1 and expects to sell his adaptation in period 2.[39] In period 2, when the investments of the supplier are already sunk, the procurement board exercises its monopsony power to cut the marginal payment for quality. Looking ahead from period 1, the potential supplier realizes that the powerful purchaser will bargain away a portion of the sunk cost of producing quality—that is, part of the cost of quality is not expected to be fully remunerated. Thus, the supplier underinvests in period 1.

Lack of competition in procurement. Arrow (1962) developed a critical result for comparing public procurement boards with quasi-markets: the more purchasers compete in period 2, the smaller is the underinvestment in period 1. His model implies that a small pension firm that has zero profits in the output market (the quasi-market for DC pensions) has a higher willingness to pay for an increase in quality than a monopoly purchaser does for the same innovation. The rationale is straightforward: the small pension firm that purchases an innovation can gain by displacing its rivals, whereas a procurement board does not displace anybody else by improving quality because its market share is already 100 percent.

Public good component of innovation. No pension firm would finance research for financial innovations that cannot be kept proprietary, preferring to free-ride on public goods produced by others. Hence, investment in innovation will be undersupplied in both pure procurement and quasi-markets. Nevertheless, there are at least two reasons to believe that underinvestment incentives are larger under pure procurement. First, research contracts by public procurement boards are more prone to favoritism, capture, and collusion. Second, even if a public board engages in research contracts, it is subject to higher transparency constraints than is a private pension firm, which will likely lead to faster imitation. A private pension firm that hires an innovator can reap temporarily the benefits of that investment by using secrecy to slow down imitation by rivals.

Undue Political Interference

In addition to providing weak incentives for pension firms to invest in financial management innovation or adaptation, procurement by centralized public boards can result in low quality of asset management because of undue political interference. Procurement board members may respond to the needs of the politicians who designate them in ways that do not necessarily contribute to the welfare of participants.[40] In contrast, the members of the board of a private pension firm that competes in quasi-markets represent the owners of the firm and follow a profit motive.[41] This situation creates two scenarios of potentially increasing negative impact on performance. On the one hand, political principals face a technical difficulty in determining whether the public board is performing well in high-quality asset management, which can lead public boards to adopt safety-first strategies. On the other hand, board members are vulnerable to political demands to direct investments in a noncommercial way. In the following subsections, safety-first and socially responsible investment strategies are discussed in turn.

Safety-first strategies. In the absence of valid benchmarks, board members gain little on the upside when returns are large, but if asset management becomes obviously deficient, they suffer the burden of a loss of prestige.[42] Board members become overly averse to risk and adopt safety-first strategies, most of the time at the expense of the participants' expected returns.

Three types of safety-first strategies with an increasing level of severity follow:

- *Delaying the adoption of new asset management techniques until they are considered mainstream.* The most extreme form of this kind of herd behavior is to fully index all portfolios offered to participants. Indexing implies low fees that can be used to address the principal's political demands, but it often leads to lower gross yields. The U.S. Thrift Savings Plan represents a good example of this strategy and outcome.
- *Offloading asset management responsibilities onto participants.* Such offloading occurs despite the evidence of participants' inertia and inability to invest in a rational way, as discussed in chapter 2. The Swedish PPM does precisely this.
- *Leaving quality control of asset management services to external parties.* This strategy is more likely to be adopted when the public procurement board itself evaluates return performance. A public board may hire consultants to select the least defensible benchmarks that show the largest excess returns and the lowest tracking errors. When political principals and public opinion are tamed by performance statistics biased by self-selection, the public board can shirk on efforts to find the best asset managers.

Socially responsible strategies. In addition to safety-first strategies, public boards are vulnerable to various forms of interference in asset management. For example, two types of interference with increasing negative impact on performance are (a) what the literature refers to as "socially responsible investments" and (b) outright undue political interference in asset management to direct investments to development projects. Although socially responsible investments have proved to be somewhat compatible with participants' interests when canvassed in professionally and transparently designed strategic asset allocations, undue political interference can be substantially detrimental.

In general, political interference may lead a public procurement board to engage in a number of costly activities (see box 3A.1) that trade off participants' returns for political objectives. For instance, TIAA-CREF (2007) finds that over a six-year period, a socially responsible balanced portfolio did worse than its benchmark by 78 basis points per year. If this difference lasts the whole working life, the pension would be about 15 percent smaller. In countries where the social portfolio involves, for example, purchasing equity in state-owned companies that focus on maximizing employment, the loss can be much larger. Alternatively, Woidtke (2002) finds that pension funds that engage in politically influenced social investing in the United States pay lower returns to participants because they destroy value in the firms where they vote. Both participants of the pension fund and other company shareholders lose because of the destroyed value. Moreover, political interference weakens transparency and conflict-of-interest rules for the securities markets, while professionalism in asset management loses ground. However, some of these empirical studies face data limitations, especially about the timing of the interference.

Obviously, the size of the costs of political interference in a public procurement board depends on the quality of governance in the country, in general, and of the governance of the procurement board, in particular. For example, if general institutions ensure that political rivals, the national auditing office, and the press can easily observe the asset management quality achieved by the board, board behavior is likely to improve. However, in countries with weak governance frameworks, political influence in asset management can have serious negative consequences for participants.[43]

In summary, a series of drawbacks may offset the benefits of pure procurement in escaping participant inertia. These drawbacks include economic disincentives for asset management quality caused by the monopsony power of public boards over private suppliers of innovations and adaptations. In addition, the performance of centralized public procurement boards is difficult to assess because of the lack of valid benchmarks. This situation may encourage boards to adopt highly risk-averse strategies that may not benefit participants. Finally, centralized public procurement boards are vulnerable to political interference, which may lead to seriously

Box 3A.1 Political Influence in Asset Management

Investing Following the Principal's Agenda

This agenda involves instructions to buy and hold bonds and equities issued by state-controlled enterprises, government bonds with weak covenants and vulnerable to inflation, and bonds issued by foundations controlled by the dominant political parties. The experience of emerging countries with this type of social investing is long and disastrous (Mesa-Lago 1991). Alternatively, the board may instruct procured asset managers, either implicitly or explicitly, to sell blacklisted private securities, even if doing so sacrifices returns or security (Entine 2005).

Investing Following the Personal Agenda of Board Members

Some board members may push their own social agendas, with the support of aggressive publicity campaigns organized by outside activists, even against other board members and at a cost in terms of participants' welfare. Surveys of participants may be an efficient response to such pressures.[a]

Politicization of Proxy Voting

Pension funds can influence proxy voting in creditors' meetings for failing companies or in bondholders' meetings. Because some politicians may want to cater to electorates in districts where layoffs are concentrated, they may ask board members to lobby asset managers to favor less-than-efficient debt restructuring agreements. Alternatively, pension funds can influence proxy voting in the shareholders' meetings of companies whose shares are publicly traded. These meetings have to vote on sales of essential assets, selection of board members, and other issues important for politicians. Positions on the boards of large companies also allow influence over political donations for future campaigns.

Political Pressure That May Affect Activities Crucial to Achieving Liquidity

The liquidity of the investments of large pension funds depends on selling and buying in mergers, takeover battles, and public offerings of shares.

(continued)

Box 3A.1 Political Influence in Asset Management
(continued)

However, control over these proxy votes is also attractive for a politician seeking to promote a national champion, to protect political allies, or to win an election. Thus, a public board is vulnerable to political pressures in activities that are critical to achieving liquidity.

a. See Baue (2005) for a situation involving the appointment of a new director of social investing at the Teachers Insurance and Annuity Association–College Retirement Equities Fund (TIAA-CREF) and TIAA-CREF's (2006) response with surveys.

---

low-quality asset management in countries with weak governance. Clearly, the relative importance of these drawbacks depends on the specifics of each country.

Annex 3B: Alternative Policies to Discourage Cream Skimming

With a hybrid industrial organization model, cream skimming of the procured clientele could be prevented by the use of flat fees or additional policies, such as (a) prohibiting procured participants from leaving the procured segment, even if they become active and decide to search; (b) allowing exit fees, which are set ex ante; and (c) allowing ex post adjustment fees.

A major problem with imposing prohibitions is that they cannot last more than a few months. Otherwise, they would impair the freedom to choose a provider, which is essential for efficiency in an environment where prices are changing in response to changes in cost and demand. However, a limited duration simply delays cream skimming.

A second alternative is to allow the receiving firm to pay exit fees to the pension firm that was originally serving the customer. The exit fee would be the expected present value of rents until the end of the service period, so it would decline in size as the end of the service period comes closer. The allowed exit fee would be subject to a ceiling to prevent the creation of a captive clientele. The destination firm, however, would also take into account the possibility of losing the new customer to a third pension fund administrator. Fearing this second round of cream skimming, some pension firms would be unwilling to pay the exit fee in the first round.

A third alternative is an ex post adjustment fee. Each participant who was allocated to a procured pension fund administrator but subsequently left to join the quasi-market segment would originate a periodic payment to that procured pension firm, from the pension firm that served the participant during the previous month or quarter. The ex post nature of the adjustment fee implies that the first destination firm would stop paying when the customer moved to another firm in the quasi-market. The adjustment fee would be paid until the end of the procured service period on a flow basis and would be based on actual density and fee bases in the previous month or quarter (see Valdés-Prieto 2007). The complexity of such an adjustment fee raises concerns regarding its implementation.

Annex 3C: Types of Hybrid Design

This annex compares the advantages and costs of the major types of hybrid designs: the stock design and the flow design.

Stock Design

With the stock design, the full segment of participants (the inert customers) who would benefit from procurement is allowed to be served by providers in the procured segment. In addition, target participants can spend their whole working career in the procured segment because they will be served by a sequence of providers selected through periodic procurement auctions.

The most interesting example is the KiwiSaver scheme in New Zealand. The procured segment is made up of participants who, when switching jobs or joining a covered job for the first time in their lives, fail to decide between pension firms (undecided participants) and whose employer also fails to choose for them an active-choice provider (a firm in a quasi-market) or to offer an occupational plan (employer superannuation). Starting from July 1, 2007, the procured segment is being served for seven years by six default providers chosen in an auction.[44] Individual defaults are allocated randomly to one of the default providers. The New Zealand auctioneer required bidders to comply with asset management experience criteria and the use of brands that are also sold in voluntary markets. Default providers share the same investment profile, which creates a homogenous asset class and induces more intensive rate-of-return comparison and rivalry.

As mentioned at the beginning of the chapter, the KiwiSaver scheme reduces fee base heterogeneity by establishing a flat fee subsidy to participants, which is paid in both the quasi-market and the procured segments. This subsidy is estimated to amount to nearly half the revenue of default providers, and it encourages the use of flat fees. In addition, the use of flat fees is expected to reduce cream skimming.[45]

KiwiSaver default schemes charge on average US$65 for each of the 812,000 participants currently enrolled, which is much lower than the average fee charged by 401(k) plans in the United States. However, comparing fees charged in the KiwiSaver scheme with fees charged in other mandatory DC pension quasi-markets is difficult because, in New Zealand, the quasi-market is characterized by ease of entry (as shown by the presence of 20 conservative active-choice funds offered by 20 different firms) and small-scale providers in the active-choice segment. These characteristics would tend to make the New Zealand quasi-market more expensive than other quasi-markets. Additionally, the culling of undecided participants from the active-choice segment, achieved by the default allocation, is a factor that should increase the average sensitivity of demand to prices in the quasi-market segment and contribute to reductions in fees there relative to countries with a pure quasi-market. These differences prevent a simple extrapolation of the average price difference observed in New Zealand to other countries. In any case, as of September 2007, the median annual fee charged by 20 active-choice funds, with the same conservative investment direction as the default funds, was 23 percent above the median charge for the six default providers.[46]

In December 2008, Mexico moved to a stock design. Under the new regulation, if the undecided worker does not make an active choice to move to a different pension fund administrator during a two-year period, the worker will enter automatically into a new auction. This process can be recurrent for the entire accumulation period unless the worker takes control of the decisions.

Flow Design

With the flow design, providers in the procured segment serve only a fraction of inert participants. In addition, no periodic auctions take place for the same target participant; once a participant is allocated to the procured segment, he or she will never be allocated to it again.

Argentina and Mexico were the first countries to establish a flow design (with an implicit procurement) in 2001 and 2002, respectively. They both established regulations that assigned the flow of new participants who fail to choose a pension firm (that is, undecided) to the pension fund administrators that charge the lowest prices (rates). Hungary adopted the same rule recently, whereas Mexico moved to an allocation rule based on net returns in 2008 and, as mentioned previously, abandoned the flow design in favor of a stock design in December 2008. By contrast, the hybrid system approved in Chile in late 2007 has a formal procurement process. New participants to the DC system (the default segment) are assigned for a 24-month period to the pension fund administrator bidding the lowest fee.

Trade-off of the Stock and Flow Design

Currently, a large debate exists on the relative superiority of the stock and flow designs. Some authors (Larraín, Castañeda, and Castro 2006) consider the flow hybrid model more viable and less risky because the repeated auctions in the stock model imply that a large part of the clientele could be lost in the next auction, which could lead bidders to raise their bids significantly. This concern influenced the Chilean government's choice of a flow design in its 2008 reform. However, New Zealand's successful auction suggests that other parameters can compensate for sunk costs, such as the length of the service period. In addition, the flow design does not eliminate the risk of cream skimming of participants from the procured segment. Hence, both designs need to ensure an appropriate length of service for providers in the procured segment.

In addition, the flow design, by definition, does not target all inert participants, only new undecided participants. Nor does it raise the average sensitivity to price and return differences in the quasi-market segment, which would expose inert old participants to the payment of fees that are above production costs in the quasi-market segment. However, this issue is obviously more important in a mature quasi-market than in a younger system, where the covered population is small.

Finally, the flow design facilitates the exploitation of inert participants after the initial service period expires, because at that point the procured firm becomes free to raise fees. Only low-base participants, who tend to be characterized by high inertia, will not be cream skimmed by rivals after the service period ends. The unusually high inertia of the residual clientele means that fees charged on them could be high, thereby defeating the purpose of creating a procured segment.

In summary, the stock design presents attractive characteristics, such as targeting all inert participants and protecting them from dynamic predatory pricing schedules. However, in the absence of cream skimming, it may induce bidders to raise their prices if they fear that their clientele will be lost in a future auction. This scenario is likely to result if a high degree of bundling is required from providers in the procured segment, as discussed in the next section.

Stock and Flow Designs and the Level of Unbundling

A critical policy issue in the industrial organization design of the accumulation phase is to decide to which services bundling should apply and to which services a pure procurement, a quasi-market, or a hybrid model should apply.[47] In principle, any service can face a quasi-market, pure procurement, or a hybrid model. For instance, Mexican participants face a pure procurement for collection of contributions, provided by the Mexican Social Security Institute (Instituto Mexicano del Seguro Social) and Procesar, and for record keeping related to switching, provided by Procesar, but they face a flow hybrid model for all other services. Similarly, Hungarian participants face a pure procurement for collection of contributions provided by the Hungarian Tax and Financial Control Administration (Adó- és Pénzügyi Ellenörzési Hivatal) but a flow hybrid for all other services.

As mentioned earlier, requiring pension firms to provide bundled services increases sunk costs and barriers to entry. For the same reason, bundling raises the commercial risk faced by providers in the procured segment of a hybrid model of the stock design. However, when services are unbundled and only asset management is procured, the commercial risk decreases substantially. If the asset manager loses the contract in a future auction, it can move on to serve new customers at little loss of sunk costs (Valdés-Prieto 2005), as confirmed by the experiences of the AP7 manager in Sweden, the Thrift Savings Plan in the United States, and suppliers to the Australian pension industry funds.

In practice, most countries that use the hybrid model require a wider bundling of services. Bundling asset management with customer service and record keeping helps explain why, in New Zealand, default providers were appointed for seven years.[48] The experience with the KiwiSaver scheme demonstrates that a stock design is compatible with this particular bundling and low procured prices, provided that sunk assets are made small. Because Mexico exhibits the same degree of bundling as New Zealand, Mexico could use the stock design as well.[49]

When, as in Chile, the bundling of services also includes collection of contributions and disability insurance, the viability of a stock hybrid model becomes more problematic. Each Chilean pension firm is responsible for collecting contributions on its own. In practice, incumbent pension firms have already come together to collect jointly a majority of contributions through a subsidiary that is owned in common (Previred Ltd.). Contributions from high-cost small employers, however, are still collected separately. Until the 2007 pension reform, each Chilean pension firm had to provide disability insurance to its own participants. This requirement further increased entry costs because new firms did not know the rate of disability of their future clientele and had to pay large risk premiums to reinsurers.

The 2007 Chilean pension reform made progress in reducing the level of bundling: first, it separated disability insurance, and second, it permitted the purchase of benefit determination services from third-party providers. Separating the collection of contributions would have brought the Chilean degree of bundling in line with that observed in Mexico and New Zealand, but the authorities decided to create incentives for outsourcing the collection of contributions rather than establish a centralized portal for this purpose. Achieving costs as low as the AP7 in Sweden and the Thrift Savings Plan in the United States would require one more unbundling step: separating customer service and record keeping from asset management.

The Swedish system is a good example of the effects of unbundling on lowering costs.[50] Total charges were moderate in the initial years of operation and are expected to decline as the asset base expands; the total charge (the PPM administration fee and the manager's fees) was 60 basis points in 2005 and is projected to decline to less than 30 basis points in

2025 (Rocha and Hinz 2007). The PPM projects that its charge will fall to 10 and 4 basis points by 2015 and 2020, respectively. Initial costs were higher because of the small asset base and the fixed costs related to the development of information technology systems. The average fee for all funds (net of rebates) was 41 basis points in 2003, and it is projected to fall to about 24 basis points by 2020. The PPM designed a fee schedule for participating funds that is inversely related to the amount of assets held by fund managers, who can charge the fees they normally impose on similar products but pay a rebate, credited to the affiliates' accounts, to the PPM if the fees exceed the PPM benchmarks. Marketing expenditures by fund managers are modest.

The Swedish authorities have separated the administrative and investment management functions: the former is centralized and publicly managed, and the latter is open to private competition. The PPM was set up to administer the DC pillar, including maintenance of individual accounts, collection and information on participating funds, transfers, and provision of information services to workers. It relies on the Swedish tax administration authority to collect contributions, thereby allowing additional administrative savings. The sole responsibility of fund managers is to invest the funds during the accumulation phase, and they have no direct interaction with workers. In addition, the PPM will become the monopoly annuity provider during the decumulation phase.

The Swedish model is not easily replicable in countries with less developed institutional settings, particularly regarding financial markets.[51] Furthermore, it has not resolved the fundamental problem of the inertia of participants. The DC scheme was designed with free entry for fund managers with a price ceiling, and as a result, the number of funds is large. There are no restrictions on fund choices, and affiliates could place all their mandatory old-age savings in high-risk and poorly diversified portfolios. Critics have therefore called for limitations regarding fund choices and the lowering of the permissible risk exposure. The large number of alternatives has created a passive attitude among affiliates instead of promoting choice, because individuals have difficulty comparing investments to risk tolerance. This situation has resulted in (a) the lack of diversification of investments (there is a risk for home bias in the country one lives in or sector one works in) and (b) a risk that investment strategies do not change over time and, therefore, do not adapt to individuals' changing risk preference during their life cycle.

Notes

1. The previous chapter pointed out that an inelastic demand and a supply characterized by important barriers to entry yield considerable market power to pension firms. This market power enables firms to charge consumers prices in

excess of average costs; that is, pension firms enjoy a "rent" or a payment for a service, which is not necessarily an incentive for its production.

2. This practice is referred to as *price segmentation* in the economic literature.

3. The traditional "merit good" argument for compulsory social insurance is behind the paternalistic mandatory nature of demand. See Barr (1992) for a more detailed explanation.

4. In other words, pension firms are required to charge uniform rates typically as a percentage of an earnings- or asset-related fee base.

5. Uniform rates also encourage firms to invest excessively in marketing, as explained later in this section.

6. Efficiency in supply is an important policy objective because it allows the alignment of prices paid by consumers (administrative fees) with the structure of pension firms' costs. In other words, it contributes (together with a high elastic demand for pension services) to reducing supernatural profits (that is, revenues vastly in excess of operational costs because of lack of competition).

7. This logic implies that the regulatory decision made in Mexico in 2007, which prohibited flow-based fees and forced pension firms to rely on asset-based fees alone, is vulnerable to trends that increase assets under management.

8. Salaries, contribution rates, and matching rules are all variables subject to policy intervention for the most disparate reasons, which can unexpectedly create (or destroy) revenues for pension firms. For example, when New Zealand announced unexpectedly in May 2007 that it would mandate that employers match the contribution rate chosen by their employees, pension firms were unwittingly granted the opportunity to take more revenue or cut their commission rate. Another example occurred when Chile experienced fast growth in real salaries from 1986 to 1997: the pension firms were given the opportunity to combine taking more revenue and cutting rates. Most firms did both, and because total revenue increased substantially, a marketing war ensued in the mid-1990s.

9. On a similar note, Hastings and Tejeda-Ashton (2008) found experimental evidence in Mexico that when fees were presented in pesos instead of annual percentage rates, less financially literate workers would be more inclined to consider fees when choosing among investment funds (that is, they would be more likely to select funds with lower average fees).

10. Here one could include other services with high sunk costs such as record keeping or collection of contributions.

11. As argued later in this chapter, one way to mitigate this outcome is to promote unbundling of pension services and establish institutions for centralized production and procurement of services with high economies of scale (such as customer services or collection of contributions).

12. Such regulations have also been used as a complementary intervention to address information problems in mandatory DC quasi-markets. Because of informational problems, consumers make systematic mistakes when choosing pension firms. Hence, countries have been using switching regulations as a paternalistic effort to minimize the number of welfare-reducing switches from the consumer point of view. For instance, Mexico encouraged switches between 2003 and 2008. However, in 2008, switches were again made more difficult in response to increasing marketing efforts by firms, increasing transfer rates, and ambiguous evidence that individuals were not choosing pension firms optimally (see chapter 2 for a more detailed discussion).

13. For instance, the Mexican pension quasi-market started operations in 1997 with a switching ban, which attempted to prevent the marketing wars observed in Chile. The ban prohibited participants from switching before a year of residence in the previous firm. This regulation was in place from 1997 to 2003.

14. Poland allows firms to levy a flat exit fee of Zl 160 on switchers who have not completed 12 months of residence in the firm. The exit fee is paid out of pocket in cash. The fee falls to Zl 80 for switchers with residence between 13 and 24 months and to zero thereafter. These exit fees are equivalent to 12.3 percent and 6.1 percent of average net monthly earnings.

15. In Chile, independent brokers were banned in 1983, forcing pension firms to rely on direct agents. This regulation made entry costlier and slower. In Poland, each salesperson is prohibited from selling on behalf of a different pension firm for six months, counted from deregistration from the current firm. Therefore, an entrant firm cannot hire an expert salesperson with advance notice of less than six months. In Argentina, the regulator enacted some legislation to reduce the productivity of the sales force in November 1997. For a transfer to be legal, a participant needed to personally attend an office of its pension fund administrator (AFJP) and sign a release form. Prior to this regulation, it was only necessary to sign a release form and give it to the salesman.

16. This process is commonly known as *cream skimming*. The customers with the highest salaries or highest expected earning profiles (high-fee-base customers) are attractive to firms because rate uniformity regulations make them produce higher income than do low-fee-base customers.

17. The analytical framework needed to understand the effect of restrictions on switches is given by the literature on switching costs summarized in annex 2D of chapter 2.

18. The literature on mutual fund flows initiated by Ippolito (1992) has demonstrated that high returns in the past do attract significant volumes of new funds (see Chevalier and Ellison 1997). At the same time, a large body of evidence shows that high current performance (measured on past returns) has only modest persistence over time (for a recent work, see Ibbotson and Patel 2002). The profit motive operates even if performance persistence is modest, because new participants are attracted and pay more fees.

19. Valdés-Prieto (2007) explores in detail these collusive agreements and the role of the government in the cases of Chile, Hungary, and Uruguay.

20. This equilibrium is second best relative to a first-best equilibrium of a highly contestable pension market with high elasticity of demand to prices.

21. This rule of thumb holds for fairly standard assumptions, such as contribution rates and wage growth of 5 percent and a 40-year accumulation period. It is also robust to variations (albeit not too large) in these assumptions.

22. In some countries, price caps are extremely high and very difficult to lower. Colombia, for instance, has a cap of 30 percent of contributions, and the regulator is unable to force the industry to accept any reductions in the ceiling. It is fair to ask whether in such cases price controls effectively create a sense of appeasement simply because fees are capped.

23. Consequently, fees charged by asset managers on their pension funds within the financial group are on average 60 basis points higher than those charged on other pension funds. Some market players report that a few small funds outside financial groups even collude with outsourced asset managers to pay an asset management fee that is higher than market and receive back income from the asset manager to subsidize operational costs.

24. Although flat, fees would still be contingent or permanent, depending on the service provided, as discussed in box 3.2.

25. In the absence of a redistributive scheme, net returns can easily be negative for low-income earners and for new participants in the presence of flat fees.

26. The model firm is a hypothetical firm representative of the population of real firms in the industry being regulated. See Guasch and Spiller (1999) for a review of regulatory practices and challenges in the infrastructure sector in Latin

America, including lessons from member countries of the Organisation for Economic Co-operation and Development. See also Andres et al. (2008) and World Bank (1997).

27. This approach has been common in Canada, Japan, and the United States, although some states in the United States have moved over the years toward price caps based on cost-based tariffs through the use of a model firm. This rate-of-return approach usually has three components: the rate base, the rate level, and the rate structure. The *rate base* refers to the investments that are allowed to earn a rate of return, the *rate level* refers to the relation of overall revenues to costs, and the *rate structure* defines how individual prices are set for different services or customers (Guasch and Spiller 1999).

28. Indeed, this pricing scheme would provide the government with additional degrees of freedom to use the budget, should increased redistribution (to encourage participation, say) be deemed necessary.

29. The *churning rate* is the exit rate and entry rate of clients from the pension firm. It plays the role of a depreciation rate for the value of the clientele.

30. The economic literature refers to this influence as *monopsony power*.

31. Annex 3A provides analytical support for the concern that pure procurement models can lead to underinvestment in asset quality, and it discusses the concerns related to political interference.

32. In December 2008, the Mexican Congress passed a reform to the Pension Law that changed the design of the Mexican hybrid. The two main highlights for this chapter are that Mexico is moving from a flow hybrid to a stock hybrid (see later in this section for a definition of these two types of hybrid models) and that the regulator (the National Commission for the Pension System) is strengthening its implicit price control capabilities.

33. These advantages would mitigate the negative impact on asset management caused by the monopsony power of the public board and the lack of competition in procurement, as discussed in annex 3A.

34. With the December 2008 reform, the assignment occurs annually instead of quarterly.

35. The evidence from Mexico indicates that in the allocated segment, the average density of contribution starts at 40 percent and falls to 20 percent within 12 months, much smaller than the average density in the open quasi-market segment, which is about 60 percent. In addition, the average contribution amount in the allocated segment is about 60 percent of the average amount in the open quasi-market. If only contribution-based commissions were allowed, the commission rate in the allocated segment would have to be 3.3 times larger to collect the same revenue over the first year. However, Mexico switched in 2008 to asset-based-only revenues, which increases inequality between segments, because the average balance per participant in the assigned segment is US$30 compared to 10 times that in the quasi-market. The allocated segment does not need revenue to pay for marketing costs, but the point is that the effect of inequality in commission bases can be substantial.

36. Cream skimming is smaller when the share of flat fees in total revenues grows. This chapter has already described how the use of flat fees eliminates marketing incentives. Annex 3B lists additional policies that can be used to prevent cream skimming of the procured clientele.

37. Annex 3C presents country cases and discusses in detail the pros and cons of the stock and flow hybrid industrial organization models.

38. Why adaptation, like innovation, is characterized by sunk costs is less obvious. The following reasons suggest that sunk costs in adaptations are not negligible: (a) international adaptation in follower countries is more expensive and riskier than subnational adaptation in leading countries, and (b) the value of those

innovations in follower countries depends on careful customization to the local financial infrastructure, part of which may be weak or nonexistent.

39. Grout (1984) and Tirole (1986) proved the underinvestment result for the case of a single supplier that negotiates price with a single purchaser in period 2. Dasgupta (1990) extended this result for multiple suppliers who participate in a sealed-bid auction organized by the single purchaser in period 2.

40. In DC pensions, these principals are fairly interested in good pensions because good pensions can attract votes or may further other objectives; therefore, they are somewhat interested in achieving high-quality asset management.

41. Managers have compensation linked to pension firms' profits or to increases in brand value. These links can be explicit (profit sharing) or can be provided by the labor market for directors (board members), where the reputation of success boosts future expected compensation. Thus, the boards of private pension firms are willing to risk more when designing contracts for asset management, because they share in the upside to a much larger extent. Private pension firms have better incentives to adopt innovations that have not been fully tried if the expected payoff is large. Even though these risks sometimes turn out badly, this managerial risk is diversified away over a participant's lifetime, whereas the gain from well-motivated boards survives.

42. The situation is different for central banks, whose boards are also public. First, currency is a natural monopoly from the demand side because of externalities in the choice of a medium of exchange. In contrast, asset management is an activity in which innovation and product variety are desirable for participants. Second, the degree of participant inertia, which is the ultimate reason for centralized purchase, varies significantly, and some groups do not need it. Third, the world has at least a century of experience in measuring inflation, gross domestic product, and unemployment by independent statistical agencies. This experience makes performance evaluation of central bank boards by political principals and public opinion much easier than that of DC pension boards.

43. The literature on governance of public pension fund management is large, and good surveys as well as examples of good practices can be found in Impavido (2002, 2008); in Impavido, O'Connor, and Vittas (2008) and the papers referenced therein; and in Musalem and Palacios (2004).

44. Fees may be increased only at the end of years 3 and 5, and then only with a minister's approval.

45. The asset base of the KiwiSaver scheme is still very modest, and cream skimming may become more problematic in the future when assets grow.

46. See the fee comparator at http://www.gmk.co.nz. The comparison assumes an account balance of $NZ 5,780 and is limited to the funds with conservative investment direction.

47. See chapter 2, where bundling and unbundling of services was discussed.

48. Another advantage of infrequent procurement is that collusion among bidders is less likely.

49. Contribution collection is provided by the Treasury (pay-as-you-earn system) in New Zealand. Disability insurance is provided by other agencies in New Zealand and in Mexico.

50. In the 1990s, Sweden transformed its defined benefit pay-as-you-go (PAYG) scheme into a combination of a notional defined contribution PAYG scheme and a DC scheme with a defined benefit guarantee benefit level. Given the small size of the DC pillar, the authorities paid careful attention to its design and developed a structure in which funds could be managed efficiently at a low cost.

51. Major reforms, including structural reforms of the financial market in the 1980s, were important prerequisites of the new Swedish pension system (see Palmer 2008).

References

Andres, Luis A., J. Luis Guasch, Thomas Haven, and Vivien Foster. 2008. *The Impact of Private Sector Participation in Infrastructure: Lights, Shadows, and the Road Ahead.* Washington, DC: World Bank.

Arrow, Kenneth. 1962. "Economic Welfare and the Allocation of Resources for Inventions." In *The Rate and Direction of Inventive Activities*, ed. Richard Nelson, 609–25. Princeton, NJ: Princeton University Press.

Barr, Nicholas. 1992. "Economic Theory and the Welfare State: A Survey and Interpretation." *Journal of Economic Literature* 30 (2): 741–803.

Baue, William. 2005. "TIAA-CREF Creates New Director of Social Investing Post but Refrains from Some SRI Strategies," July 15. SRI World Group, Brattleboro, VT. http://www.socialfunds.com/news/article.cgi/article1756.html.

Chevalier, Judith, and Glenn Ellison. 1997. "Risk Taking by Mutual Funds as a Response to Incentives." *Journal of Political Economy* 105 (6): 1167–200.

Dasgupta, Sudipto. 1990. "Competition for Procurement Contracts and Underinvestment." *International Economic Review* 31 (4): 841–65.

Entine, Jon, ed. 2005. *Pension Fund Politics: The Dangers of Socially Responsible Investing.* Washington, DC: American Enterprise Institute Press.

Grout, Paul. 1984. "Investment and Wages in the Absence of Binding Contracts: A Nash Bargaining Approach." *Econometrica* 52 (2): 449–60.

Guasch, J. Luis, and Pablo Spiller. 1999. *Managing the Regulatory Process: Design, Concepts, Issues, and the Latin America and Caribbean Story.* Washington, DC: World Bank.

Hastings, Justine S., and Lydia Tejeda-Ashton. 2008. "Financial Literacy, Information, and Demand Elasticity: Survey and Experimental Evidence from Mexico." NBER Working Paper 14538, National Bureau of Economic Research, Cambridge, MA.

Ibbotson, Roger, and Amita Patel. 2002. "Do Winners Repeat with Style?" Yale ICF Working Paper 00-70, International Center for Finance, Yale School of Management, New Haven, CT.

Impavido, Gregorio. 2002. "Governance of Public Pension Fund Management: Preliminary Considerations." In *Financial Sector Governance: The Role of Public and Private Sectors*, ed. Robert Litan, Michael Pomerleano, and V. Sundararajan, 371–96. Washington, DC: Brookings Institution Press.

———. 2008. "Governance of Public Pension Plans: The Importance of Residual Claimants." In *Pension Fund Governance: A Global Perspective on Financial Regulation*, ed. John Evans, Michael Orszag, and John Piggott, 139–57. Cheltenham, U.K.: Edward Elgar Publishing.

Impavido, Gregorio, Ronan O'Connor, and Dmitri Vittas. 2008. "Improving the Investment Performance of Public Pension Funds: Lessons for the Social Insurance Fund of Cyprus from the Experience of Four OECD Countries." *Cyprus Economic Policy Review* 2 (2): 3–35.

Ippolito, Richard. 1992. "Consumer Reaction to Measures of Poor Quality: Evidence from the Mutual Fund Industry." *Journal of Law and Economics* 35 (1): 45–70.

Larraín, Guillermo, Pablo Castañeda, and Rubén Castro. 2006. "Licitaciones: Imprimiendo competencia al sistema de AFP." En Foco 62, Instituto de Políticas Públicas

Expansiva, Universidad Diego Portales, Santiago. http://www.expansivaudp.cl/media/en_foco/documentos/06032006130517.pdf.

Mesa-Lago, Carmelo. 1991. "Portfolio Performance of Selected Social Security Institutes in Latin America." Discussion Paper 139, World Bank, Washington, DC.

Musalem, Alberto R., and Robert Palacios, eds. 2004. *Public Pension Fund Management: Governance, Accountability, and Investment Policies.* Washington, DC: World Bank.

Palmer, Edward. 2008. "The Market for Retirement Products in Sweden." Policy Research Working Paper 4748, World Bank, Washington, DC.

Rocha, Roberto, and Richard Hinz. 2007. "Mandatory Private Pension Systems: Can They Meet Expectations?" Presented at the Financial and Private Development Forum *Finance and Markets for All: What, Why, When and How?* World Bank, April 25–26, Washington, DC.

TIAA-CREF (Teachers Insurance and Annuity Association–College Retirement Equities Fund). 2006. "TIAA-CREF Releases Participant Survey on Socially Responsible Investing." Press release, TIAA-CREF, New York, July 13. http://www.tiaa-cref.org/about/press/about_us/releases/pressrelease182.html.

———. 2007. "Socially Screened Investing: Combining Competitive Return Potential with Investors' Values." *Weekly Market Monitor*, March 5.

Tirole, Jean. 1986. "Procurement and Renegotiation." *Journal of Political Economy* 94 (2): 235–59.

Valdés-Prieto, Salvador. 2005. "Para aumentar la competencia entre las AFP." *Estudios Públicos* 98: 87–142. http://dialnet.unirioja.es/servlet/articulo?codigo=1250836.

———. 2007. "State-Supported Defined Contribution Pensions: Quasi-Markets or Procurement?" Pontificia Universidad Católica de Chile, Santiago.

Williamson, Oliver E. 1971. "The Vertical Integration of Production: Market Failure Considerations." *American Economic Review* 61 (2): 112–23.

Woidtke, Tracie. 2002. "Agents Watching Agents? Evidence from Pension Fund Ownership and Firm Value." *Journal of Financial Economics* 63 (1): 99–131.

World Bank. 1997. *The Private Sector in Infrastructure: Strategy, Regulation, and Risk.* Washington, DC: World Bank. http://www-wds.worldbank.org/external/default/WDSContentServer/WDSP/IB/1997/09/01/000009265_3980804143615/Rendered/PDF/multi0page.pdf.

4

Investment Choice and the Design of Investment Options

The financial turmoil of 2008 has brought to the fore the importance of investment regulations in mandatory defined contribution (DC) schemes. The crisis has shown that participants in DC pension schemes can be exposed to significant market risk. Even in more stable times, high participant inertia and the inadequate skills of participants to monitor portfolio management can easily lead to situations where participants hold their pension assets in suboptimal investment portfolios. This chapter analyzes policy issues related to the regulation of investment choice in mandatory DC schemes and the design of default options that allow inert participants to increase (gross) risk-adjusted expected rates of return over their lifetime.

In mandatory DC pensions, the investment risk is shared among the following: (a) the regulator, which defines the universe of allowable investments through investment regulation; (b) the asset manager, who makes the choice of asset allocations; and (c) the consumer, who chooses among alternative funds within or across pension firms. However, whereas the regulator and the asset manager bear mainly a reputational risk, the individual fully bears the investment risk associated with his or her choices, as well as the consequences of the actions of the regulator and the asset manager.

Participants' freedom to choose across pension firms and funds varies around the world, but in recent years, the general trend has been toward greater investment choice. Australia and Sweden, for example, grant individuals great freedom to choose among pension funds. By contrast, countries such as Hungary, Latvia, and the Slovak Republic in Eastern Europe; Chile, Mexico, and Peru in Latin America; and Hong Kong, China, in Asia tend to restrict the number of investment options. However, even the latter groups of countries increasingly recognize that individual participants and cohorts have different profiles requiring different investment strategies. Consequently, Hungary allowed limited investment choice in the mandatory

DC pension pillar starting in 2007, and the new system became compulsory for all pension providers in the mandatory system in 2009. Mexico first established investment choice in the mandatory DC pension system in 2004 and expanded available choices in 2008. Colombia enacted a multifund system in 2009 that became operational in 2010, and Bulgaria is planning to introduce some degree of choice in the voluntary pillar and subsequently in the mandatory one.

Yet empowering individuals with more choice poses new challenges, because individuals may still not take any action, as discussed in chapter 2. The presence of a large share of inactive participants has become a pervasive problem of mandatory DC systems worldwide. Even when participants do make choices, they often adopt simple rules of thumb to solve the investment problem, leading to systemic investment biases (see chapter 2 for a detailed discussion on the issue). Another issue of concern is that asset managers' investment incentives and participants' long-term retirement goals may be misaligned, because asset managers do not face a pension liability or an explicit long-term investment target.

Hence, a strong policy rationale appears to exist for designing investment regulations that address the problems emanating from (a) the large numbers of inert participants, (b) the systemic biases in investment behavior, and (c) the misalignment of the incentives of asset managers with the long-term retirement targets of participants.

The rest of this chapter is organized as follows. The first section reviews the regulations applying to investment choice and default investment options in several Latin American countries that pioneered the use of multifunds and life-cycle funds in mandatory DC pensions, in contrast to the more extensive freedom of choice granted in more mature financial markets such as Australia and Sweden. It also explains the theoretical reasoning behind the life-cycle fund model presented in Blake, Cairns, and Dowd (2008). The second section then reviews the effect of the financial crisis on mandatory DC pension schemes, with a special emphasis on the performance of those that follow a life-cycle fund framework. The third section identifies weaknesses in the current design of multifunds and life-cycle funds and presents evidence from Raddatz and Schmukler (2008) of gaps in the behavior of pension fund managers in Chile. The fourth section, also drawing extensively from Blake, Cairns, and Dowd (2008), presents a conceptual framework for reforming the design of investment default options so that they better align the incentives of asset managers with the long-term retirement goals of participants. Policy recommendations follow in the last section.

Investment Choice and Default Options

The regulation of investment choice and the design of default options for inert participants vary from country to country. Broadly speaking, they tend to be more restrictive in emerging markets, relative to countries with more mature financial systems,[1] but even the former are starting to allow greater choice. Thus, countries such as Australia and Sweden give participants a great deal of freedom in selecting their portfolios and pay little attention to the investment portfolio to which undecided participants are assigned by default. Despite regulatory trends allowing greater individual choice, the high level of inert participants seems to be an issue in most countries with mandatory DC systems, thus designing well the default investment options is of paramount importance.

Sweden

In the Swedish Premium Pension System (Premiepensionsmyndigheten, or PPM), 86 fund managers had been licensed by the end of 2007, with 785 funds registered. Each manager can register up to 25 funds among four broad categories: (a) equity funds, (b) balanced funds, (c) fixed-income funds, and (d) life-cycle funds. Individual choice is restricted to up to five funds, with no restrictions on the number of switches per year (PPM 2007). Undecided individuals are assigned to a default option that replicates the average asset allocation observed before individuals were allowed to select their own portfolios. The default portfolio has an 80 percent equity exposure, reflecting the fact that the PPM represents a small component of the whole mandatory pension system, collecting only 2.5 percent of wages in contributions.

The large number of funds seems to be discouraging rather than stimulating rational choices. Since the first round of fund choices in 2000, very few individuals have changed their asset allocation, and those who have made changes have displayed a strong home bias (Palme 2005).

Australia

In Australia, participants in the superannuation system, which constitutes the country's main mandatory DC retirement scheme, have potentially even more freedom than in Sweden, especially in the retail segment. At the end of 2007, about 575 pension firms (superannuation entities) with at least four members existed, and 63 percent of them offered on average 38 alternative funds (table 4.1). Not all entities are required to offer a default investment option, but when offered, it contains on average a 55 percent share of equities, as shown in table 4.2.

Countries in Eastern Europe and Latin America

Traditionally, participants in mandatory DC plans in Eastern Europe and Latin America could choose among pension firms, but they had no investment fund choice; pension firms could offer only one investment fund subject to tight investment restrictions. Starting in the early 2000s, a few emerging

Table 4.1 Investment Choices in the Australian Superannuation System

Date	Corporate	Industry	Public sector	Retail	Average
Share of entities offering investment choice[a] (%)					
June 2007	55	85	65	66	63
June 2006	48	85	67	66	56
Average number of investment choices per entity[b]					
June 2007	6	10	8	97	38
June 2006	6	10	7	88	34

Sources: APRA 2006, 2007.
a. Number of entities with at least four members.
b. Average calculated on the share of entities actually offering choice.

Table 4.2 Asset Allocation of Default Investment Options in the Australian Superannuation System

Instruments[a]	Corporate entities	Industry entities	Public sector entities	Retail entities	Average
Australian shares	40	33	29	26	31
International shares	23	26	24	20	24
Listed property	4	2	4	4	4
Unlisted property	3	9	7	2	6
Australian fixed interest	12	6	10	22	11
International fixed interest	6	6	9	5	7
Cash	5	4	8	15	8
Other	7	14	8	6	10
Total	100	100	100	100	100

Source: APRA 2007.
a. Not all superannuation entities are required to have a default investment strategy. If there is no default strategy, the strategy of the largest option is reported or the fund strategy as a whole.

markets began to recognize differences in the preferences and needs of participants, and they opened the system to some investment choice, although choice remains more restricted than in Australia or Sweden. In light of high participant inertia, the design of appropriate default investment options became critical. This design generally follows the concept of life-cycle funds, which seek to maximize risk-adjusted rates of return by diversifying risk over a participant's lifetime. They stand on two key premises: (a) investing in risky assets such as equities is optimal, and (b) doing so early in one's working life is better. The theoretical underpinnings of life-cycle funds are presented in box 4.1.

Box 4.1 Life-Cycle Funds: Theoretical Underpinnings

The design of life-cycle funds and age-dependent default investment options seeks to maximize risk-adjusted rates of return (on a gross basis) by diversifying risk over a participant's lifetime. It stands on two key premises: (a) investing in risky assets is optimal, and (b) doing so over time is less optimal. Several factors must be considered to determine the optimal asset allocation for a portfolio. The three most critical are (a) adequately measuring risk aversion and the risk premium associated with the risky assets and their evolution, (b) measuring the evolution of investment opportunities, and (c) adequately measuring the level and changes in human capital. These three aspects are further discussed below.

The risk premium is the extra return on a risky asset (above the return on the risk-free asset) that investors demand as compensation for absorbing risk. The premium is generally a function of the volatility of the return of the risky asset and the investor's risk aversion. The higher the volatility and the lower the risk tolerance are, the higher is the risk premium for investing in the risky asset. Investors with different attitudes to risk will have different holdings of risky assets such as equities. Risk-averse investors will be prepared to forgo some of the upside potential of equities when investment conditions turn out to be favorable to avoid some of the losses on equities when conditions turn out to be unfavorable.

The relationship between holdings of risky assets, risk aversion, and risk premium is best understood in the simplest case with a two-asset portfolio (a risk-free asset and a risky asset such as equities) and a single-period investment framework. In such a setup, Campbell and Viceira (2002) show that, given the level of equity risk premium (assuming equity is the risky asset), the only parameter that is important to determine the member's optimal portfolio allocation to equities is his or her risk aversion and the volatility of equity returns. In a multiperiod investment framework, Merton (1969, 1971); Mossin (1968); and Samuelson (1969) show that if investors have constant risk aversion and asset returns are not predictable, the results do not change. Optimal portfolio choice in each investment period would depend on risk aversion and the volatility of equity returns. In other words, if attitude to risk does not change with age and if equity returns are unpredictable, then investors are better off by assuming that each investment period is the last period before

(continued)

Box 4.1 Life-Cycle Funds: Theoretical Underpinnings
(continued)

retirement. This finding implies that the share of the portfolio allocated to the risky and risk-free asset would not change over time.[a]

However, substantial evidence shows that equity returns tend to be mean reverting or predictable, which implies that investment opportunities and the optimal portfolio allocation should vary with time. (The empirical evidence is not unequivocal, but it generally supports mean reversion.) If equity returns are mean reverting or predictable, then an unexpectedly high return today will be offset by lower expected returns in the future. Investing in equities over long periods is therefore beneficial, because it reduces the long-run volatility or variance of the equity returns, a benefit known as *time diversification*. This finding suggests that the portfolio of young investors with a long investment horizon should have higher equity exposure than that of investors closer to retirement who face a shorter investment horizon.

The presence of decreasing human capital over a participant's lifetime also suggests that the weights of the investment portfolio should vary with time. When human capital (or the present value of lifetime labor income) is taken into account, the total long-term assets of a participant in a DC plan comprise both financial assets and human capital. Overall, the inclusion of human capital in the long-term portfolio has the effect of increasing the portfolio weights of the risky financial assets (equity) relative to the less risky financial assets. This effect is straightforward to understand when labor income is considered riskless. The introduction of a riskless investment in any portfolio causes the weights on risky investments to increase to rebalance the portfolio to make it compatible with the desired level of risk aversion.

Labor income, however, is not without risk and is correlated with returns on financial assets, but the correlation is not perfect. Hence, investors can compensate or hedge wage risk by adjusting equity holdings. Furthermore, younger individuals should invest proportionally more in equities than older individuals, because the ratio of human capital to financial assets is higher at the beginning of the working career and they face a greater need to hedge the human capital risk. When other assets, such as housing, are considered, the strategic asset allocation of mandatory DC plans would need to be further rebalanced in favor of risky financial assets such as equities.

In summary, designing life-cycle funds on the premises that investing in risky assets is optimal and less so over time broadly follows the normative implications of the literature and, as such, life-cycle funds should be welfare improving. That is, the predictability of equity returns in the long

(continued)

Box 4.1 Life-Cycle Funds: Theoretical Underpinnings
(continued)

run (that is, mean reversion); the opportunity to hedge labor income risk with equities; and the declining human capital relative to financial wealth over an individual's lifetime suggest that optimal portfolio allocations vary over time and point to a higher equity exposure at the beginning of the working career.

Source: Box 4.1 draws from Blake, Cairns, and Dowd (2008), which was written as a background paper for this book. See annex 4B for a more detailed discussion.

a. In a multiasset framework, when the portfolio includes more than one risky asset, it is necessary to estimate the variance-covariance matrix of the returns on the risky assets (or excess returns over the risk-free asset).

In 2002, Chile became the first country in Latin America to introduce investment choice for participants, and Peru and Mexico followed in 2003 and 2004, respectively. Pension fund administrators in Chile and Mexico offer five funds each; those in Peru offer only three. Chile is the only country that allows participants to allocate their account balances to two funds, creating, in practice, a wider set of investment options.[2,3] The funds differ with respect to the quantitative limits defined by asset class.[4] The more aggressive funds in Chile and Peru can hold up to 80 percent of the portfolio in equity, and the most conservative ones can hold up to 0 percent in Chile and 10 percent in Peru (table 4.3). By contrast, the transition to investment choice in Mexico has been more gradual, with the more aggressive funds limited to a 30 percent equity exposure and the most conservative to zero. The ceiling on foreign investment allocations was also raised to 30 percent in Chile and to 20 percent in Peru.[5] Besides having different quantitative restrictions by asset class, Mexico's multifunds are subject to value-at-risk (VaR)[6] limits, which are measured daily on the basis of historical data (annex 4A and table 4.3). This daily risk measure, however, is not linked to the long-term risks and performance of the funds and thus had to be temporarily suspended at the peak of the financial turmoil in late 2008.[7] Otherwise, funds would have been forced to sell assets at distressed prices and at a loss to participants.

All three countries have instituted a life-cycle fund model as the default option, as illustrated in tables 4.4, 4.5, and 4.6. Participants who do not choose a fund are automatically placed in a default fund (shaded dark gray in the tables) according to their age; they are then moved to another fund with less equity exposure as their age increases and the time span to

Table 4.3 Maximum Equity Investment Limits for Multifunds in Chile, Mexico, and Peru

	Percentage of portfolio				
Country	Fund A	Fund B	Fund C	Fund D	Fund E
Chile	80	60	40	20	0
Mexico[a]	30	25	20	15	0
Peru	80	45	10	n.a.	n.a.

Sources: Data for Chile are from the Superintendencia de Pensiones; data for Mexico are from the Comisión Nacional del Sistema de Ahorro para el Retiro; and data for Peru are from the Superintendencia de Banca, Seguros y AFP.

Note: n.a. = not applicable. a. In Mexico, Funds A to E are legally referred to as Siefores 5 to 1.

Table 4.4 Age-Dependent Default Options in Chile

	Men ≤ 35 years Women ≤ 35 years	Men > 35 and ≤ 55 years Women >35 and ≤ 50 years	Men > 55 years Women > 50 years
Fund A			Not allowed
Fund B	Default		
Fund C		Default	
Fund D			Default
Fund E			

Source: Data are from the Superintendencia de Pensiones.

Table 4.5 Age-Dependent Default Options in Mexico

	X ≤ 26 years	X > 26 and ≤ 37 years	X > 37 and ≤ 45 years	X > 45 and ≤ 55 years	X > 55 years
Fund A	Default	Not allowed	Not allowed	Not allowed	Not allowed
Fund B		Default	Not allowed	Not allowed	Not allowed
Fund C			Default	Not allowed	Not allowed
Fund D				Default	Not allowed
Fund E					Default

Source: Data are from the Comisión Nacional del Sistema de Ahorro para el Retiro.
Note: Funds A to E in Mexico are called Siefore Básica 5 to 1, respectively.

Table 4.6 Age-Dependent Default Options in Peru

	X ≤ 60 years	X > 60 years
Fund A		Not allowed
Fund B	Default	Not allowed
Fund C		Default

Source: Data are from the Superintendencia de Banca, Seguros y AFP.
Note: Funds A, B, and C in Peru are called Funds 3, 2, and 1, respectively.

retirement decreases. In Chile, no more than 20 percent of the balance is switched to another fund within a given year. By contrast, switches in Mexico need to be completed within six months regardless of market conditions, which is too quick.[8]

Participants can move to another fund if they so choose (shaded light gray in the tables). In the cases of Mexico and Peru, a participant can switch only to funds that are more conservative than the default fund selected for his or her age. In Chile, a participant can switch to more or less volatile funds than the default fund, with the exception of participants close to retirement, who cannot select the most aggressive fund (Fund A). The number of investment options in Peru is limited, and participants close to retirement (that is, 5 to 10 years away) can be exposed to significant equity risk (up to 80 percent). Other emerging markets have implemented or are in the process of implementing variations of these three models. Estonia and Hungary have already implemented them, and Bulgaria and Colombia are in the process of doing so.

Severe participant inertia highlights the importance of designing the default option well. Only a small share of participants has exploited the greater investment choice under the multifund framework. In Chile, for example, more than 65 percent of participants were automatically assigned to their age-dependent default option by August 2008.

Effect of the Financial Crisis on Mandatory Pension Funds

The financial turmoil of 2008 significantly affected pension funds worldwide with some very limited exceptions (table 4.7).[9] By October 2008, total assets of pension funds in countries of the Organisation for Economic Co-operation and Development (OECD) had declined by more than US$4 trillion, or more than 20 percent relative to December 2007.[10] In emerging markets, mandatory DC pension systems that were heavily exposed to equity (table 4.8); for example, Chile and Peru in Latin America and Bulgaria, Croatia, and Estonia in Eastern Europe

Table 4.7 Mandatory DC Pension Assets in Selected Emerging Markets

Country	Percentage of gross domestic product		
	December 2007	*December 2008*	*March 2009*
Latin America			
Chile	64.4	52.8	57.8
Colombia	14.7	16.0	15.1
Costa Rica	5.1	5.3	6.2
Dominican Republic	2.4	3.5	3.8
El Salvador	21.2	24.0	25.2
Mexico[a]	8.5	7.7	7.8
Peru	18.5	13.8	13.7
Uruguay	15.7	9.6	10.1
Eastern Europe			
Bulgaria	2.17	2.18	2.34
Croatia	6.44	6.60	6.91
Estonia	4.60	4.59	4.99
Hungary	7.79	7.02	7.08

Sources: Asociación Internacional de Organismos de Supervisión de Fondos de Pensiones and staff calculations on supervisory data.

a. Excludes PensionISSSTE.

also experienced negative real rates of return in the double digits in 2008 (table 4.9). However, and as expected by the temporary nature of the shock, the performance of these pension funds had already started to recover by mid-2009 along with the recovery in financial markets.

Despite the severity of the global financial turmoil, preliminary data suggest that life-cycle funds in Chile and Mexico have shielded individuals close to retirement from the severe shock. Average investments in variable-income instruments in these two countries at the end of 2008 were close to 14 percent and 6 percent, respectively, but investments in the most conservative funds were zero in both countries. The most conservative funds in Chile and Mexico reported an annual real rate of return of –0.9 percent and –0.1, respectively, in 2008, compared to an average decline for the system of –20 percent and –6.5 percent, respectively (tables 4.9 and 4.10). By June 2009, the real rate of return of the two most conservative funds in Chile and Mexico was already positive.

Table 4.8 Equity Shares in Total Pension Portfolio

Country	December 2007 (%)	December 2008 (%)	March 2009 (%)
Latin America			
Chile	14.5	13.8	13.6
Colombia	22.3	20.0	20.5
Costa Rica	0.4	0.6	0.3
Dominican Republic	0.0	0.0	0.0
El Salvador	0.0	0.0	0.0
Mexico	3.8	5.9	5.1
Peru	41.2	25.3	26.3
Uruguay	0.1	0.2	0.2
Eastern Europe			
Bulgaria	28.3	14.5	12.7
Croatia	18.0	13.3	11.4
Hungary[a]	32.8	39.1	41.7

Sources: Asociación Internacional de Organismos de Supervisión de Fondos de Pensiones and staff calculations on supervisory data.
a. Equities and mutual funds.

By contrast, from December 2007 to December 2008, the most conservative funds in Peru reported a more severe decline of –10.2 percent in real terms, comparable to the performance of the most aggressive funds in Mexico (table 4.10). This loss is explained to a large degree by the funds' exposure to variable assets and the peak in inflation, which reached 7 percent in 2008.[11] However, by June 2009, the real rate of return accumulated over the past year and the past three years was equal to 3.1 percent and 16.3 percent, respectively.

Assessing the performance of the current design of default options in mandatory DC systems is difficult for various reasons. First, their introduction is very recent. Second, the benchmarks to use for measuring performance are unclear, given that the current design lacks any connection with the retirement phase—that is, the final objective for accumulating savings. However, the preliminary evidence discussed previously suggests that if equities are not included in the default option of participants close to retirement, individuals are likely to be shielded from major asset price shocks such as the one observed in 2008.

Regarding the effect of multifunds on intertemporal diversification, some preliminary evidence exists, but only for Chile.[12] Cheyre (2006)

Table 4.9 Performance of Mandatory Defined Contribution Pension Systems in Selected Emerging Markets

	Real rate of return over previous 12 months (%)		
Country	December 2007	December 2008	March 2009
Latin America			
Chile	5.5	–20.0	–15.1
Colombia	0.9	–2.7	7.5
Costa Rica	–0.7	–9.0	–7.6
Dominican Republic	–0.4	8.0	11.4
El Salvador	1.4	–2.3	0.3
Mexico	2.5	–6.5	–6.3
Peru	21.6	–26.2	–22.7
Uruguay	0.5	–21.5	–21.9
Eastern Europe			
Bulgaria	4.2	–26.8	18.1
Croatia	0.9	–15.8	–14.7
Estonia	–0.5	–41.7	–32.4
Hungary	0.5	–6.1	0.2

Sources: Asociación Internacional de Organismos de Supervisión de Fondos de Pensiones and staff calculations on supervisory data.

reports that the introduction of multifunds led to an increase of 244 basis points in the average performance of all funds between September 2002 and December 2005.[13] This exceptional performance, if continued over time, would increase average replacement rates by 80 percent. Yet less than 35 percent of participants have exploited the increased investment choice provided by the multifunds system—confirming high participant inertia, as discussed in chapter 2.

Gaps in the Current Design of Multifunds

Although current multifunds generally follow the normative implication of the literature by exposing younger investors to higher levels of equity risk, their design presents several gaps that need to be addressed. Some of these gaps are minor, but others, such as the absence of a long-term investment target for investors and the lack of an explicit consideration of some

Table 4.10 Performance of Multifunds' Investment Options in Latin America

Type of fund	Real rate of return over previous 12 months (%)		
	December 2007	December 2008	June 2009
Chile			
(More) conservative	2.9	–0.9	4.5
Conservative (default)	3.3	–9.7	9.1
Balanced (default)	5.0	–18.9	–6.6
Aggressive (default)	7.5	–30.1	–14.1
More aggressive (no default)	10.1	–40.3	–22.2
Mexico (simple average)			
(More) conservative (default)	4.5	–0.1	4.5
Conservative (default)	5.2	–4.9	1.6
Balanced (default)	n.a.	–6.4	1.1
Aggressive (default)	n.a.	–8.0	0.2
(More) aggressive (default)	n.a.	–9.3	–0.6
Peru			
Conservative (default)	6.4	–10.2	3.1
Balanced (default)	20.2	–26.7	–12.0
Aggressive	38.0	–41.7	–24.0

Source: Authors' estimates based on data from respective supervisory authorities.
Note: n.a. = not applicable.

key risks faced by participants, have more serious implications and involve a deeper rethinking of the current design of multifunds.

Rigidities in the Investment Rules of Current Multifunds

The first set of limitations of the current design of multifunds involves (a) the restrictions on the investment universe of pension funds, (b) the small number of funds available, and (c) the stepwise rules for rebalancing assets across default options.

The investment rules of current multifunds in Latin America appear to place excessive restrictions on the investment universe of pension funds, preventing the construction of efficient portfolios. For instance, all three Latin American countries surveyed severely limit investment in foreign assets, thus reducing the scope for geographic diversification. In addition, exposure to equity is severely constrained in Mexico, thereby affecting intertemporal risk diversification.[14] Even the most aggressive fund in Chile and Peru, which allows equity investments up to 80 percent of the total portfolio,[15] does not constitute a default option for the youngest cohorts in the system.[16]

Even assuming that the underlying investment rules span the investment universe, countries such as Mexico and Peru do not let individuals allocate their cash balances to more than one fund, thereby preventing them from constructing portfolios that better match their own degree of risk aversion.

Investment rules often allow considerable discretion to asset managers. However, whether asset managers are using this discretion in the long-term interests of participants is unclear, because they lack a long-term investment target. For example, the equity weight in the most aggressive Chilean fund can vary between 40 percent and 80 percent of the total portfolio. Such considerable discretion could lead to situations where pension fund managers over- or underinvest in equities relative to the optimal strategic allocation suggested by the literature (see box 4.1). The lack of a long-term investment target and the risks it poses are discussed further below.

Moreover, the rules for rebalancing assets across default portfolios (also known as the *glide paths*) and the low number of funds cause individuals to remain in static default portfolios for long periods until they reach the trigger age to be switched to a more conservative default option. Rebalancing rules need to be more continuous. The problem is most severe in Peru, where participants can remain in the same default portfolio for more than 40 years. Even in Mexico, when a participant reaches the trigger age, DC account balances automatically have to be switched to a more conservative portfolio within six months,[17] regardless of market conditions. If market conditions are very unfavorable, as in late 2008, this rule would force participants to realize the losses instead of weathering the market volatility and transferring balances more gradually over time.[18]

These observations suggest that there is scope for improving risk-adjusted expected rates of return over the life cycle in different ways in different countries by making minor improvements to current designs. In general, welfare gains could be achieved as follows: (a) by expanding the set of investment options to enable fund managers to construct more efficient portfolios, (b) by making equity funds a default option for young cohorts, (c) by requiring more gradual glide paths for default options, and (d) by allowing a richer combination of investment options through increasing the number of funds or by allowing cash balances to be allocated to more than one fund.

Introducing Annuitization Risk and Nonfinancial Assets

Another problem that affects the current design of multifunds is the lack of attention to risks originating outside the management of pension financial assets. The most important are annuitization and labor income risks. However, accounting for other important asset risks, such as housing, will also affect the optimal portfolio composition.

Annuitization risk. Annuitization risk is an important risk that the current design of multifunds and associated default options fails to consider. The risk arises from the physical separation between the accumulation and retirement phases and the timing of the conversion of the accumulated assets into annuities.[19,20]

The decision of when to transform accumulated assets into retirement income is crucial, because the specific conditions of the capital market in which a given cohort retires determine the lifetime income of that cohort. This decision is affected by risk aversion, the bequest motive, and the difference between the implicit rate of return on the annuity and the rate of return on equities. Ignoring risk aversion and bequest motives, annuitization is optimal when the implicit rate of return on the annuity is higher than the rate of return on equities (Milevsky and Young 2002). When risk aversion is considered, Milevsky and Young (2007b) show that higher levels of risk aversion lead to lower annuitization ages because individuals have a lower tolerance for investment risk.[21] However, for many participants in mandatory DC systems, especially when the DC pillar constitutes the main pillar of the mandatory retirement system, policy makers are likely to drive this decision. Concerned about the risk of retirees outliving their assets, policy makers typically set (a) the annuitization age at the mandatory retirement age (although in a few countries, such as the United Kingdom, participants can postpone annuitization for a few years) and (b) the minimum annuitization level.

Labor income risk. The key consequence of explicitly considering human capital or labor income risk in the long-term strategic asset allocation is that the hedging demand for equities should be even stronger than that explained by mean reversion alone (box 4.1). In principle, because labor income is risky and imperfectly correlated with other assets such as equities, young investors should leverage their positions to invest more than 100 percent of the portfolio in equities. This proposition of literally leveraging pension assets is unrealistic in most jurisdictions, because incomplete financial markets do not allow individuals to borrow outside the pension system to leverage their pension asset positions. In addition, tax rules in all jurisdictions prevent individuals from saving excessively in tax-preferred accounts. Notwithstanding the preceding, one can safely argue that labor income risk was not explicitly considered in the design of default investment options in the three countries surveyed.

What would be the optimal equity risk levels for younger investors when accounting for human capital or labor income risks? The answer to this question is likely to be country specific. Higher-income countries with greater experience in asset management and sufficiently deep and liquid capital markets would find default options for younger participants with high levels of equity risk exposure easier to design. In addition, countries with a diversified financing source of retirement benefits would find it optimal, all other things being equal, to expose young participants to higher levels of equity risk than would countries where the provision of retirement income is concentrated in only DC arrangements.[22]

Finally, the financial turmoil of 2008 has raised the perception that a trade-off exists between the need to hedge wage risk with equities, on the one hand, and the need to avoid short-term volatility of portfolios, on the other. The trade-off is only apparent, however. In fact, pension assets are illiquid investments for pension participants until retirement, and short-term volatility does not necessarily affect long-term performance. Indeed, policy makers in countries with a more financially educated workforce will have an easier time communicating the short-term and cyclical nature of increased volatility in asset returns that will stem from larger holdings of risky assets. Therefore, investing in financial education is likely to remain a priority for most jurisdictions in the long term.

Housing risk. Clearly, other risks might influence the optimal investment strategy for a pension plan participant, in particular the housing risk. A house is an illiquid asset that can provide rental services in addition to being an investment asset, the value of which is often highly correlated with inflation.

When the return on nonfinancial assets is imperfectly correlated with equity returns, it is likely to induce an increase in the weight of equities within financial wealth. This outcome reflects a diversification benefit: homeowners can use housing wealth to hedge equity and labor income risks.[23] Thus, when home ownership is considered, the strategic asset allocation of mandatory DC plans would need to be further rebalanced in favor of risky assets.

When housing is considered and reverse mortgages (or housing-equity release plans) are available, Sun, Triest, and Webb (2007) show that the optimal investment of financial wealth in equities further increases, and less financial wealth would need to be annuitized at any point in time. The intuition is straightforward: the reverse mortgage provides a long-term coupon to the retiree, very similar to an annuity. In addition, the bond nature of a reverse mortgage will prompt a rebalancing of the financial wealth portfolio toward risky assets for a given level of risk aversion.

In sum, the long-term strategic asset allocation of mandatory DC plans clearly needs to take a holistic view of the key risks that participants face. An explicit consideration of labor income and annuitization risks is likely to generate the largest welfare gains for participants. Countries with more sophisticated financial sectors, however, might also want to consider the risks of other important assets, such as housing.

Evidence of Gaps in Asset Manager Behavior in Chile

The empirical literature on the misalignment of incentives between asset managers and pension participants is extremely scarce. The scarcity of empirical studies relates to the difficulty in defining the long-term preferences of pension participants. Raddatz and Schmukler (2008) conducted one of the few empirical studies of this nature. It analyzes the investment decision of Chilean pension firms during 1996–2005 and reaches a broad conclusion that pension fund asset management behavior may not have been consistent with the long-term preferences of pension participants.

The system of multifunds in Chile exhibits some clearly identifiable trends. Since the introduction of the multifund system in 2002, Fund C (the balanced fund) has had the largest relative share of assets in the system, mainly because it constitutes the default option for middle-age workers. Nevertheless, the shares of Fund A and Fund B (the two most aggressive) have also increased substantially, because of active choice in the former case and a combination of active choice and automatic assignment in the latter (figure 4.1).[24]

Overall asset allocation across types of fund has been generally consistent with investment regulations (annex 4A). At the end of 2008, Fund A had invested about 75 percent of assets in equities[25] and 15 percent in bank deposits. At the other extreme, Fund E had no investments in equities (by

Figure 4.1 Chile Pension System Holdings as a Share of Gross Domestic Product, 1996–2008

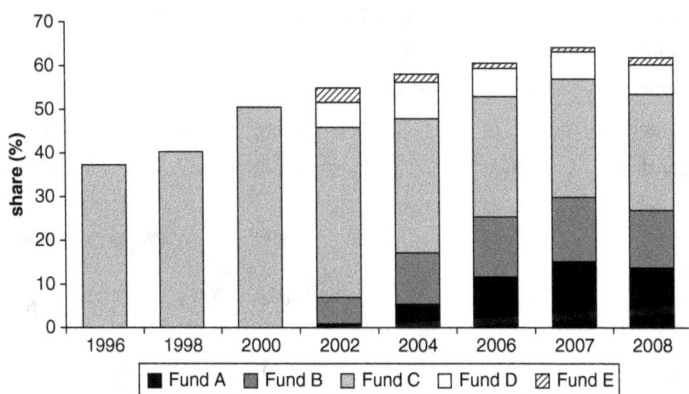

Source: Authors' estimates based on data from the Superintendencia de Pensiones.

design), about 65 percent of assets in fixed income, and around 35 percent of assets in bank deposits (table 4.11). Consistent with the rationale of multifunds, the Chilean system appears to be moving individuals from equities to bonds over their careers until retirement.

However, pension funds seem to be holding a disproportionate amount of liquid assets, particularly cash and fixed-income securities. For instance, all funds held on average 20 percent and 13 percent of assets in bank deposits at the end of 2008 and end-July 2009, respectively. Fund A had only 15 percent and 7 percent of assets, respectively, in bank deposits during the same dates, which is much higher than the 3.5 percent average weighting in "cash" of U.S. equity mutual funds. In addition, fixed-income holdings are skewed toward shorter-term issues. For example, during 1996–2005, on average, 45 percent of fixed-income securities were held in instruments with less than three years to maturity and 24 percent in instruments with less than one year. The bias is even more severe for Fund A than for Fund E.

The large holdings of liquid assets suggests that pension firms are forgoing the illiquidity premium embedded in long-term illiquid assets in

Table 4.11 Asset Allocation by Type of Fund in Chile, December 2008

	Allocation (%)				
	Fund A (most aggressive)	Fund B	Fund C	Fund D	Fund E (most conservative)
Domestic assets	43.1	59.5	77.2	87.9	98.0
Variable income	23.3	20.6	17.0	9.4	0.1
Public debt	2.1	7.8	15.6	21.7	35.3
Private debt	9.0	15.1	23.7	27.5	22.9
Mortgage bonds	1.24	2.42	4.49	5.29	3.61
Certificates of deposit	14.9	18.4	18.5	24.6	35.6
Foreign assets	56.9	40.1	22.8	12.1	2.0
Variable income	52.1	38.1	19.6	8.4	0.1
Public debt	4.7	2.1	3.2	3.7	1.9

Source: Data are from the Superintendencia de Pensiones.

favor of holdings that allow rapid changes in tactical asset allocation. In addition, the high concentration of bank deposits and short-term fixed-income securities in Fund E suggests that Chilean retirees are exposed to high annuitization risk.

Setting aside these strategic asset allocation issues, the tactical asset allocation of Chilean pension funds appears to be inconsistent with the long-term objectives of the system's participants. In particular, Raddatz and Schmukler (2008) find evidence of both contemporaneous and dynamic herding, as well as evidence that pension funds follow momentum investment strategies, but they find no evidence of active asset management.

Contemporaneous herding takes place when all pension funds buy and sell similar assets at the same time, and dynamic herding takes place when asset classes bought at any given point in time are also bought in subsequent periods. Evidence of contemporaneous herding is found for all funds in domestic corporate bonds and quotas of domestic and foreign mutual funds. For the other assets, herding seems to occur only among the largest pension funds. Evidence of dynamic herding exists for domestic equities and foreign mutual funds. On average, the economic magnitude of herding is close to the evidence reported for mutual funds in developed countries but is significantly higher in some asset classes. The fact that different pension funds arrive independently at the same conclusions regarding the optimal timing for trades that will maximize the long-term welfare of participants can explain the high degree of herding. However, they more likely follow each other's investment strategies, in particular given the need to comply with a relative rate of return guarantee.[26]

In addition, Chilean pension funds follow momentum investment strategies. In particular, they tend to buy government bonds, former pension system bonds, and quotas of foreign mutual funds when lagged returns are positive. However, they tend to buy domestic equity when lagged returns are negative. In other words, they follow a contrarian strategy for this asset class. This strategy may relate to some degree of mean reversion in domestic equities.

Finally, Chilean pension funds are not active asset managers—generally, they buy and hold securities. Pension funds tend to change only about 10 percent of their portfolio every month, but this share varies substantially according to fund type: Fund A and Fund E display the highest degree of turnover, whereas Fund C and Fund B display the lowest degree of turnover. The findings are compatible with the fact that the highest degrees of turnover are observed for domestic government bonds (largely held by Fund E) and for quotas of foreign mutual funds (largely held by Fund A). On average, however, pension funds buy fixed-income instruments and hold them until maturity, not trading them on the secondary market.

Reconnecting the Accumulation
and Retirement Phases

Although the earlier section proposed some changes to the current framework of multifund rules that could result in welfare gains to participants, more substantial adjustments are necessary to link the incentives of fund managers to the long-term retirement objectives of participants. Requiring funds managers to offer investment products, which can be called *target annuitization funds*, could help link the accumulation and retirement phases.

Target annuitization funds are DC products with a target maturity (for example, the retirement date) and a long-term financial target that drives construction of the investment portfolio. The retail pension management industry in some OECD countries has already made these investment products available, and they present some similarities to the multifund products currently offered by pension firms in Eastern European and Latin American countries, which should allay concerns related to their eventual implementation. However, they differ in three key aspects:

- First, they target a retirement benefit within a confidence interval, whereas current multifunds do not have a specific target.
- Second, the optimal (strategic) asset allocation of these funds is not deterministic (that is, it is not based on static rules) but is derived from stochastic programming techniques[27] that take into account the main risks faced by contributors during the accumulation phase, including labor income or human capital.
- Third, target annuitization funds' long-term financial target allows policy makers or regulators to better track the performance of pension fund managers throughout the entire accumulation phase of participants. However, this target also implies that contributions may become endogenous. That is, participants may need to make additional individual contributions if the target appears unlikely to be achieved.

Although these key features are discussed in more detail later, one must understand from the outset that the target is only probabilistic. Thus, the asset manager has no liability, and pension funds are not expected to start giving annuities, which should continue to be purchased from insurance companies.

Identifying the Long-Term Investment Target

A target annuitization fund would seek to achieve—within a confidence interval—a long-term financial target deemed sufficient to finance a desired consumption profile during retirement. Because of its probabilistic nature, the target would not create a liability that fund managers need to meet, and therefore, it would remain compatible with the DC nature of the pension plans under discussion.

The target can be expressed as a minimum cash balance or a replacement rate (that is, a percentage of the participants' average salary during the accumulation phase). Different ways of expressing the target have different implications. For instance, a replacement rate target has the advantage of creating an explicit connection between the accumulation and retirement phases, encouraging managers to hedge annuitization risk as participants approach retirement age. However, a cash balance target with specific investment rules aimed at smoothing the interest risk associated with the transformation of cash balances into annuities could probably be a valid alternative.

Irrespective of how the long-term financial target is expressed (which is likely to be country specific), its definition involves estimating the consumption path of reference cohorts[28] during retirement and thus requires the development of accurate mortality tables. Unfortunately, accurate mortality tables are not available in many emerging countries.

The Construction of Target-Driven Investment Strategies

When the long-term investment target has been identified, the strategic asset allocation of the default investment options during the accumulation phase needs to be designed. Stochastic programming solutions have been used for numerous financial products, and because they allow for the uncertainty facing agents in the context of asset-liability management, they are commonly used in defined benefit (DB) plans to implement liability-driven investment strategies. That said, these models are solved through numerical optimization, which requires that the probability distributions governing the data be known or be possible to estimate. In many cases, uncertainties might be approximated by a scenario tree with a finite number of states of the world for each period. In other words, some modeling risk exists, and the models are data intensive.

The literature suggests the optimal strategic allocations can probably be constructed with three or four funds that would serve to hedge the main risks faced by participants (see annex 4C for a more detailed discussion): a bond fund, an equity fund, and a cash fund, and possibly a deferred annuity fund where feasible. The funds would be dominated by a main asset class (that is, the equity fund by equities), but each would contain some of the other assets to hedge interest rate volatility and intertemporal shift in investment opportunities.

As discussed in box 4.1, the purpose of the equity is to hedge human capital or labor income risk and benefit from the equity risk premium. Equity holdings in the strategic allocation would be very high at the beginning, when the ratio of human capital to financial wealth is very high. Then, they would gradually decrease to zero toward retirement (assuming no bequest motive).[29] The cash or money market fund could be used to hedge the inflation risk in labor income.[30]

The purpose of the bond fund is to hedge the interest rate risk and the annuitization risk (for which the deferred annuity fund can also be used). Its weight would be high for young participants, because of the need to hedge interest rates that vary over time. It would decrease rapidly but rise again toward retirement to hedge the annuitization risk. The annuitization risk could be hedged by investing in long-term bonds with a duration similar to that of the annuity that individuals would be required to purchase after retirement.[31] The price sensitivity of the annuities and long-term bonds to interest rates would be similar, thus mitigating the risks of any changes in interest rates. By contrast, the investment rules of the current multifunds do not include long-term bonds (with durations similar to the annuities to be acquired) for those close to retirement to mitigate the annuitization risk. The annuitization risk could also be addressed through an annuity fund.[32] The purpose of the cash fund is first to finance the initial very high leveraged positions in equities and bonds, so its weight is highly negative, and then to hedge the inflation risk in labor income, when its weight becomes positive.[33]

Variable Contributions and Short-Term Performance Evaluation

The proposed concept of a target annuitization fund implicitly assumes that individuals have a "funded position" to protect that is akin to the funded position of a DB plan. This assumption has two implications: (a) it requires some variability in individuals' contributions, and (b) it creates a useful benchmark for monitoring asset managers' performance, as explained in the rest of this section.

First, target annuitization funds imply variable contribution rates. This implication is best understood by noticing that any target-driven fund implicitly assumes that the future states of the world are known ex ante, when the strategic asset allocation is designed. However, when new information arrives, as it does in reality, contingency plans need to be ready. In a classical DB plan, this situation implies a modification of the investment strategy or the level of contribution of the sponsor (which assumes the DB liability). In the target annuitization fund, new information implies a modification of the investment strategy or the level of contribution of the individual (consistent with the DC nature of the funding mechanism).

How much volatility in contribution levels should be introduced? The answer is likely to be country specific. In fact, because the target of the investment strategy in an annuitization fund is only probabilistic, a change in the individuals' contribution rates following new information does not need to be mandatory. In other words, individuals should be allowed to choose whether to change their contribution levels or to live with a modified probability of reaching their investment target at retirement.[34] Notwithstanding these considerations, a well-functioning system of target annuitization funds clearly involves the following: (a) periodic estimations of the individuals' funded positions, (b) a process for communicating to individuals the effect of market events on the probability of reaching their investment target, (c) a process for communicating to individuals the effect of market events on the level of contributions that is expected to reach their investment target, and (d) a close integration of the system of voluntary individual accounts—which many countries have also introduced—with the system of mandatory individual accounts.

Second, target annuitization funds create an additional benchmark for monitoring manager's performance. The extent to which individual funded positions can be used as a short-term performance evaluation benchmark depends on the adequacy with which assets and liabilities are evaluated. Given the model risk associated with such an exercise, short-term performance evaluation obviously would also need to rely on other short-term benchmarks such as asset benchmarks or minimum return benchmarks.

Conclusions

The financial turmoil of 2008 highlighted the importance of investment options in mandatory DC systems—in particular, of default investment options. Their design is critical to achieving adequate replacement rates during retirement. In general, the design of multifunds in Chile, Hungary, Mexico, Peru, and soon Bulgaria and Colombia constitutes an improvement over the single-fund system formerly available. This design broadly follows the normative implications of the literature on strategic asset allocation, attempting to achieve welfare gains by diversifying risk intertemporally. Preliminary evidence for Chile and Mexico also indicates that these funds have succeeded in protecting individuals close to retirement from the financial turmoil of 2008.

Notwithstanding the improvements over single funds, multifunds continue to present a number of weaknesses. These weaknesses include restrictions on the investment universe, an insufficient number of portfolio options, the need for smoother rebalancing of portfolios over time, and—most important—the lack of an explicit consideration of labor income and annuitization risks. Additional welfare gains can be achieved easily by modifying some of the features of the current rule-based multifunds. More substantial gains will be possible only within a risk-based framework, but these frameworks will be achieved only in developed countries and in emerging markets with deeper and more liquid capital markets and robust technical capacity on the part of pension firms and supervisors.

This chapter therefore concludes with a summary of policy recommendations for improving the current rule-based multifunds and implementing
risk-based investment products.

Policy Recommendations for Rule-Based Frameworks

A number of welfare improvements can be attained within the rule-based
framework of current multifunds—in particular, changes that would better (a) accommodate differences in the profile of the covered population,
(b) smooth the transition among funds, and (c) mitigate the annuitization
risk. First, the universe of permissible investments needs to be expanded,
and the number of default options currently available in countries such as
Peru (and soon Hungary) needs to be increased to accommodate the needs
of different cohorts. Second, individuals could be allowed to allocate their
cash balances to more than one fund to construct a greater variety of portfolios and smooth the transition among funds. Third, the annuitization
risk in the current multifund design can be reduced by requiring default
funds for participants close to retirement to be invested in deferred annuities or long-term (inflation-indexed) bonds. The price of such instruments
is sensitive to changes in interest rates, making them a good hedge. That
is, if interest rates fall at the time of retirement or annuitization, the price
of these instruments increases, and so does the value of the annuities to be
acquired by the retiring participant. Finally, countries with a single fund
should seriously consider moving toward a multifund framework while
taking into account the preceding suggestions.

Policy Recommendations for Risk-Based Frameworks

Although the outlined changes could be welfare enhancing, the achievement
of further improvements would require pension firms to actively manage important risks faced by participants, such as annuitization and labor
income risks. This change entails a gradual move from the current rule-
based framework to a risk-based framework, where policy makers define
minimum criteria and monitor their implementation, while fund managers
design investment products in accordance with those criteria. In particular,
the introduction of target annuitization funds would provide a stronger basis
for reconnecting the accumulation and retirement phases without reintroducing liabilities for pension firms. In other words, they would minimize the
risk associated with DC systems (namely, the risk of volatile replacement
rates) and maximize the benefits of DB systems (namely, pension stability,
albeit only in probabilistic terms). The retail pension management industry
in some OECD countries already offers such products.

Target annuitization funds are essentially funds with a target maturity
date (that is, the retirement date) and an investment portfolio whose construction is driven by a consumption target at retirement. The latter can
be defined as a cash balance or replacement rate.

The optimal strategic asset allocation of the target annuitization fund is constructed with the aid of stochastic programming techniques. Such techniques help define the paths for rebalancing the portfolios over time and can account for key risks faced by participants, including human capital and annuitization risks, which the current rule-based framework does not. These techniques are complex and information intensive and thus can be safely implemented only in developed markets or in emerging markets with a minimum degree of capital market development and strong technical capacity on the part of pension supervisors and pension firms. When such conditions are not present, following more deterministic (rule-based) models for defining the optimal strategic asset allocation and rebalancing portfolios over time may be preferable—but incorporating the aforementioned suggestions.

The use of three or four funds (a cash fund, an equity fund, a bond fund, and possibly a deferred annuity fund) appears sufficient to formally consider and hedge such risks.

The identification of a long-term investment target (defined as a cash balance or replacement rate) will not represent a liability for the pension firm, but will allow policy makers to monitor fund management performance throughout the accumulation phase by tracking the level of individual funded positions relative to the defined target. However, when an unexpected negative shock to asset returns occurs, the likelihood of achieving the long-term financial target will be impaired, thus raising the need to adjust investment portfolios as well as to increase contribution rates.

The latter raises a key policy trade-off: should contribution rates become endogenous to the mandatory DC plan, or should policy makers rely on participants to meet the financial shortfall by increasing contributions to voluntary plans? The answer will depend on the degree of contribution volatility that participants will be willing to accept vis-à-vis the extent to which policy makers will be willing to minimize the potential fiscal cost of any implicit or explicit pension guarantees. For instance, some individuals might not welcome volatile contributions into the mandatory pension plan because they would automatically imply a more volatile consumption pattern during the accumulation phase. However, in the presence of unexpected shocks to asset prices and no adjustments to contributions, participants might face bigger sacrifices in consumption at retirement. This outcome might lead to a less optimal consumption pattern over their lifetime.

The Key Policy Compromise of Target Annuitization Funds

The policy compromise embedded in the use of target annuitization funds should now be clear to the reader. On the one hand, a pure DC financing mechanism minimizes the volatility of consumption during the accumulation phase by fixing the contribution rate, but it considers only indirectly the desired level of consumption at retirement through the DC rate. The consumption pattern at retirement remains volatile depending on the portfolio performance during the accumulation phase. On the other hand, a pure DB financing mechanism minimizes the volatility of consumption during retirement by fixing benefits, but it does not consider the volatility of the funding mechanism during the accumulation phase.

The target annuitization fund, which defines long-term investment targets, represents a compromise between the two aforementioned financing mechanisms. On the one hand, similar to a DB mechanism, it seeks to smooth replacement rates over time and, therefore, to minimize volatility of consumption during retirement. On the other hand, similar to a DC mechanism, it does not impose a liability on the sponsor or asset manager. Hence, it continues to promote diversification of risks among providers, consumers, and future generations of taxpayers.

Annex 4A: Investment Limits for Multifunds

Table 4A.1 shows the key maximum investment limits for Chilean funds. The limits for Mexican and Peruvian funds are shown in tables 4A.2 and 4A.3, respectively.

Annex 4B: Rationale and Assumptions for Current Rules and Designs of Life-Cycle Funds

The design of age-dependent default investment options discussed in the first section seeks to maximize long-term expected rates of return by diversifying risk over a participant's lifetime. It stands on two key premises: (a) it is optimal to invest in risky assets, and (b) it is less optimal to do so over time. Several factors must be considered to determine the specific parameters of the optimal asset allocation underlying life-cycle funds. The three most critical are (a) the adequate measurement of the risk premium and the risk penalty (that is, the attitude to risk) associated with the risky assets and their evolution, (b) the measurement of the evolution of investment opportunities, and (c) the adequate measurement of the level and changes in human capital. The following sections discuss these three aspects in detail.

The Role of Risk Premium

The risk premium for an individual to invest in the risky asset is generally a function of the volatility of the return on risky assets and the individual's risk aversion. In a mean-variance framework, volatility is measured by the variance of the return on the risky asset and, more generally, participants'

(continued on page 137)

Table 4A.1 Key Maximum Investment Limits for Chilean Multifunds, 2009

Instruments[a]	Investment limit (%)				
	Fund A	Fund B	Fund C	Fund D	Fund E
Limits per instrument					
Government paper	40	40	50	70	80
Time deposits, bonds, other financial institutions	40	40	50	70	80
Letters of credit	40	40	50	60	70
Bonds of public and private companies	30	30	40	50	60
Bonds convertible to shares (sublimit)	No sublimit	No sublimit	10	5	Not eligible
Open private limited company shares and real estate private limited company shares	60	50	30	15	Not eligible
Investment and mutual fund shares + committed payments	40	30	20	10	Not eligible
Mutual fund shares (sublimit)	5	5	5	5	Not eligible
Commercial paper	10	10	10	20	30
Foreign (superlimit across all funds)			30		
Other authorized by the Central Bank of Chile	1–5	1–5	1–5	1–5	1–5
Risk-hedging operations	Investment of the fund in instruments being hedged				
Foreign currency without exchange coverage	37	22	18	13	9
Financial loan	15	10	5	5	5

(continued)

Table 4A.1 Key Maximum Investment Limits for Chilean Multifunds, 2009 (continued)

Instruments[a]	Investment limit (%)				
	Fund A	Fund B	Fund C	Fund D	Fund E
Limits per group of instruments					
a. Equities					
Equities					
Maximum	80	60	40	20	Not eligible
Minimum	40	25	15	5	Not eligible
Freely available equities	3	3	1	1	Not eligible
Low-liquidity shares	10	8	5	2	Not eligible
Freely available foreign shares traded on the local stock exchange	1	1	1	1	Not eligible
b. Fixed income					
Debt BBB and N-3	10	10	10	5	5
c. Fixed-income and equities					
Equities + debt BBB and N-3 + bonds that are exchangeable for shares	No limit	No limit	45	22	Not eligible
Issuers with a history of less than 3 years	10	10	10	8	5
Restricted (low liquidity; freely available and traded on local stock exchange; issuers with a history of less than 3 years; debt BBB and N-3)	20	20	20	15	Not eligible

Source: Data are from the Superintendencia de Pensiones.

a. All limits are expressed as a percentage of assets per fund unless otherwise noted.

Table 4A.2 Key Maximum Investment Limits for Mexican Multifunds, 2009

	Instruments[a]	Siefore básica investment limit (%)				
		1	2	3	4	5
Market risk	Historical VaR (1-alpha = 95%, daily)	0.6	1.0	1.3	1.6	2.0
	Equities (only through indexes)	0.0	15.0	20.0	25.0	30.0
	Foreign currency	30.0	30.0	30.0	30.0	30.0
	Derivatives	Yes	Yes	Yes	Yes	Yes
Credit risk	Fixed-income AAA[b] and government securities	100.0	100.0	100.0	100.0	100.0
	Fixed-income AA–	50.0	50.0	50.0	50.0	50.0
	Fixed-income A–	20.0	20.0	20.0	20.0	20.0
Concentration or counterparty risk — Local	Mexican instruments AAA in single issuer or counterpart	5.0	5.0	5.0	5.0	5.0
	Mexican instruments AA in single issuer or counterpart	3.0	3.0	3.0	3.0	3.0
	Mexican instruments A in single issuer or counterpart	1.0	1.0	1.0	1.0	1.0
	Mexican foreign exchange instruments BBB+ in single issuer or counterpart	5.0	5.0	5.0	5.0	5.0
	Mexican foreign exchange instruments BBB– in single issuer or counterpart	3.0	3.0	3.0	3.0	3.0
Concentration or counterparty risk — International	Foreign instruments A in single issuer or counterpart	5.0	5.0	5.0	5.0	5.0

(continued)

Table 4A.2 Key Maximum Investment Limits for Mexican Multifunds, 2009 (*continued*)

Instruments[a]	Siefore básica investment limit (%)				
	1	2	3	4	5
Other limits					
In any single issue[c]	20.0	20.0	20.0	20.0	20.0
Foreign instruments (minimum A– for fixed income)	20.0	20.0	20.0	20.0	20.0
Securitized instruments[d]	10.0	15.0	20.0	30.0	40.0
Structured securities[d]	0.0	5.0	10.0	10.0	10.0
Real estate investment trusts[e]	0.0	5.0	5.0	10.0	10.0
Inflation protection	Yes (minimum 51)	No	No	No	No
Related parties					
Related parties investments	15.0	15.0	15.0	15.0	15.0
Related parties with participation in AFORE's capital[f]	5.0	5.0	5.0	5.0	5.0

Sources: Data are from Comisión Nacional del Sistema de Ahorro para el Retiro (http://www.consar.gob.mx/limite_inversion/limite_inversion.shtml and Circular 15–23, August 3, 2009).

a. All limits are ceilings based on assets under management of each Siefore, with the exception of inflation protection, which is a floor.

b. Ratings are local for domestic instruments and international for foreign instruments.

c. Percentage of the total amount stated in the prospectus, adjusted by future amortizations and repurchases. For structured securities, the limit is 35 percent.

d. Issued by Mexican nationals.

e. Real estate, infrastructure in Mexican territory, and bank trusts or leasing.

f. In cases where a related party is a financial entity, the limit is 0 percent.

Table 4A.3 Key Maximum Investment Limits for Peruvian Multifunds, 2009

Instruments	Investment limit (%)		
	Fund 1	*Fund 2*	*Fund 3*
Variable income	10	45	80
Fixed income	100	75	80
Derivatives (hedging only)	10	10	20
Cash	40	30	30
Foreign investments[a]	20	20	20

Source: Data from Superintendencia de Banca, Seguros y AFP.
a. Applied to total net assets in the three funds with no specific limit per fund.

Annex 4B: Rationale and Assumptions for Current Rules and Designs of Life-Cycle Funds (continued from page 132)

Box 4B.1 Individuals' Attitude to Risk

Individuals' attitude to risk is conventionally measured by the coefficient of relative risk aversion, which is defined as the wealth elasticity of the marginal utility of wealth:

$$\gamma = -W \frac{U''(W)}{U'(W)}$$

where the participant's pension wealth is denoted by W, the utility of (or welfare derived from) pension wealth is denoted by $U(W)$; the marginal utility of pension wealth (that is, the change in utility if pension wealth changes by US\$1) is denoted by $U'(W)$; and the degree of curvature of the utility function of pension wealth (which measures the rate at which marginal utility changes if pension wealth changes by US\$1) is denoted by $U''(W)$. For all investors, $U'(W) > 0$, utility increases with wealth; that is, more wealth means higher utility. For risk-averse investors, $U''(W) < 0$. Hence, their utility functions are positive but concave functions of wealth, which implies that a US\$1 increase in wealth increases utility by less than a US\$1 reduction in wealth reduces utility. The greater the curvature of the utility function is, or the more negative is $U''(W)$, the greater is the degree of risk aversion.

---

attitude to risk is conventionally measured by the coefficient of relative risk aversion (box 4B.1). The higher the volatility and the lower the risk tolerance are, the higher is the risk premium for investing in the risky asset. The risk premium is the extra return on a risky asset (above the return on the risk-free asset) that investors demand as compensation for absorbing risk. All things being equal, the optimal holdings of risky assets are positively correlated with the risk premium and negatively correlated with the risk penalty. Box 4B.2 summarizes the literature on the risk premium puzzle of U.S. equities, or why that premium appears to have been so high.

Box 4B.2 Equity Risk Premium in the United States

The issue of what explains equity risk premium and the puzzle of why it seems to have been so high in the United States has been the subject of a large debate in the economic literature.

Mehra and Prescott (1985) suggest that the very high estimated equity premium in the United States of 7.43 percent could be explained only if individuals had implausibly high coefficients of relative risk aversion. Kurz and Beltratti (1996) explain the size of the equity premium using a rational belief equilibrium model where price uncertainty is endogenously propagated, and this uncertainty is the predominant source of volatility in asset returns. Risk-averse investors need to be compensated for this volatility, and using the same parameters as in Mehra and Prescott (1985), Kurz and Beltratti (1996) are able to generate the historically observed equity premium in the United States. Constantinides, Donaldson, and Mehra (2002) and Kogan, Makarov, and Uppal (2007) explain the size of the equity premium in terms of borrowing constraints. Constrained, young individuals cannot invest as they would like in the stock market, and this constraint reduces demand and raises the return on equities above the risk-free rate sufficiently to generate the observed equity premium. Rietz (1988) argues that the size of the equity premium can be explained by low-probability disasters—that is, the possibility that the economy and hence the stock market could be subjected to an extreme negative shock, even if this possibility has a very low probability. Barro (2005) also supports this view and argues that a 1 percent annual probability of a 50 percent fall in gross domestic product (GDP) and the physical capital stock would be sufficient to produce the observed premium as well as the low long-run real return on risk-free government bonds. However, Julliard and Ghosh (2008) argue that the rare-event hypothesis is incompatible with the consumption capital asset pricing model and, therefore, cannot by itself explain historical levels of equity premium, and Jorion and Goetzmann (1999) and Ross, Brown, and Goetzmann (1995) explain the size of the equity premium in terms of survivorship bias, with the observed equity premium being upward biased because of the long-term survival of the markets from which they are measured. Faugère and Van Erlach (2006) argue that the U.S. long-run equity premium is

(continued)

Box 4B.2 Equity Risk Premium in the United States
(continued)

consistent with U.S. GDP growth. Fama and French (2002) explain the high equity premium in the second half of the twentieth century in terms of an unanticipated decline in discount rates. This decline led to a fall in the dividend-price ratio, which, in turn, caused a substantial, but unanticipated, capital gain increase. The high observed equity premium is merely the realization of this gain.

In short, whether or not a genuine equity premium puzzle exists is unclear. Most recent studies (Fama and French 2002; Jagannathan, McGrattan, and Scherbina 2000; Poterba et al. 2006; Siegel 1999) have used much lower estimates for the future U.S. equity premium of about 3.5 percent compared with the historical average between 1951 and 2000 of 7.43 percent. The 3.5 percent figure lies roughly midway between 2.55 percent (Fama and French's [2002] estimate of the equity risk premium based on long-run dividend growth rates) and 4.32 percent (their estimate based on long-run earnings growth rates).

Investors with different attitudes to risk will have different holdings of risky assets. Investors who are more risk averse will tend to have lower holdings of risky assets than do risk-seeking investors. Risky assets, such as equities, have higher returns in boom conditions than do conservative assets, such as bonds, but lower returns in slump conditions. Therefore, risk-averse investors are prepared to forgo some of the upside potential of equities if the investment conditions turn out to be favorable so they can avoid some of the downside losses on equities if investment conditions turn out to be unfavorable.

The relationship between holdings of risky assets, risk aversion, and risk premium is best understood in the simplest case of a single-period portfolio choice with one risky and one risk-free asset. In such a setup, Campbell and Viceira (2002, equations 2.46 and 2.25) show that the optimal weight of the portfolio in the risky asset is equal to the ratio of the risk premium on the risky asset to the risk penalty on the risky asset.[35]

In a multiperiod portfolio choice, Merton (1969, 1971); Mossin (1968); and Samuelson (1969) show that if investors have a constant relative risk aversion and asset returns are unpredictable, results do not change. In other words, given the level of equity risk premium (if equity is the risky asset), the only parameter that is important to determine the member's optimal portfolio allocation to equities is the risk penalty: that is, the plan member's degree of relative risk aversion to equities and the volatility of the returns on the risky asset. If attitude to risk does not change with age, then investors are better off investing in a myopic way (that is, by assuming that each period is the last period before retirement), which implies constant portfolio weights over time. In a multiasset framework, when the portfolio includes more than one risky asset, estimating the variance-covariance matrix of the returns on the risky assets (or excess returns over the risk-free asset) is also necessary.

In summary, risk aversion, volatility of returns, and risk premium are key in determining the optimal portfolio allocation at any given point. Assuming that risk does not change with age and the return on the risky asset is unpredictable, then portfolio weights would not vary with time. However, substantial evidence indicates that equity returns are mean reverting or predictable, which would suggest time-varying investment opportunities. The presence of decreasing human capital (net present value of labor income) also suggests that portfolio weights should vary with time.

The Role of Time-Varying Investment Opportunities

In the real world, the risk-free rate, the excess returns on risky assets, the variances of the returns on risky assets, and the covariances between the excess returns on risky assets are all time varying or stochastic (Campbell and Viceira 2002). A stochastic investment opportunity set creates intertemporal hedging demands for specific assets that are capable of hedging against adverse movements in the investment portfolio (Merton 1973). This situation calls for time-varying portfolio weights for specific assets, as opposed to strategic asset allocations with static or myopic weights.

For instance, the presence of time-varying interest rates creates demand for long-term bonds as a hedging instrument. A fall in interest rates reduces the income generated by the portfolio, but the bond price increase associated with the interest rate fall can compensate for this reduction. By contrast, the prices of short-term instruments change very little when interest rates fluctuate, exposing investors to refinancing risk attributable to the short maturities. In addition, in the presence of substantial inflation risk, an inflation-indexed long-term bond is actually less risky than short-term instruments as well as long-term nominal bonds.

Substantial evidence shows that equity returns are mean reverting and, therefore, predictable. If equity returns are mean reverting, then an unexpectedly high return today will be offset by lower expected returns in the future. Therefore, investing in equities over long periods is beneficial because such an investment pattern reduces total variance—a benefit known as time diversification (or the horizon effect). Time diversification is the equivalent of risk sharing with the future, because it implies that risk compounds less than linearly with time, as shown in figure 4B.1.

Above all, mean reversion of equity returns implies that one would expect a hedging demand for this asset class that increases with the time horizon of investments. For instance, Barberis (2000) estimates significant mean reversion in U.S. stock returns[36] and shows that the optimal hedging demand for

Figure 4B.1 Mean Reversion and Variability of Returns in the United States, 1980–98

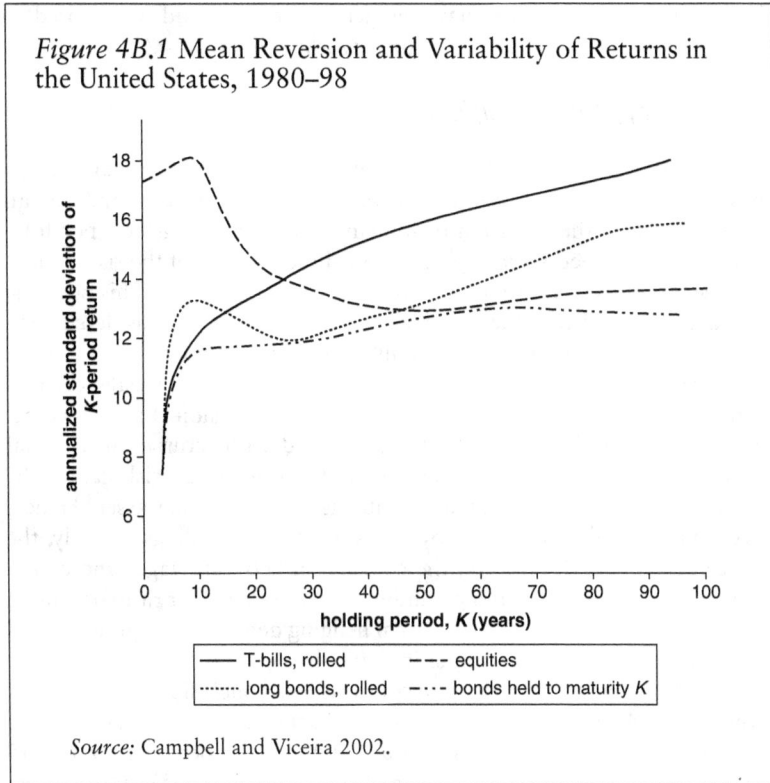

Source: Campbell and Viceira 2002.

equities for investors with a 10-year horizon is 40 percent of the portfolio without predictability and reaches 100 percent with predictability.[37] Thus, in the presence of mean reversion, younger investors should skew their portfolios toward riskier assets, even if they have a high level of risk aversion.

Notwithstanding the preceding, the predictability of equity returns is not unequivocally supported by the theoretical literature. In fact, evidence also indicates that the volatility of returns is also time varying or stochastic (Ghysels, Harvey, and Renault 1996). Contrary to mean reversion, where bad news on returns today is also good news for the investment opportunity set in the future, stochastic volatility means that bad news today can be associated with other bad news tomorrow. Chacko and Viceira (2005) show that with stochastic volatility of equity returns, younger investors should reduce (and not increase) their exposure to equities and select safer portfolios. Yet they also find that stock return volatility does not seem variable or persistent enough.

In other words, despite the less than unequivocal support of the theoretical literature, most research suggests that equity returns tend to be predictable, which implies that younger investors should be exposed to equity risk in the initial phases of their working lives.

The Role of Human Capital

When human capital (or the net present value of labor income) is taken into account, total long-term assets comprise financial assets and human capital. Overall, the inclusion of human capital in a long-term portfolio choice has the effect of increasing the portfolio weights of the risky financial assets (equity) relative to the less risky financial assets.[38] This outcome is straightforward to understand when labor income is considered riskless. The introduction of a riskless investment in any portfolio causes the weights on risky investments to increase so the portfolio is rebalanced and again compatible with the desired level of risk aversion. Labor income, however, is *not* without risk and is correlated with returns on financial assets, but correlation is not perfect. In addition, wage risk cannot be hedged directly because human capital is a nontradable asset. Hence, investors can hedge wage risk by adjusting equity holdings. Clearly, the degree of hedging depends on the correlation between wages and equity returns. Finally, because younger individuals have a higher ratio of human capital to financial wealth, the optimal hedging demand for equities would be higher for them than for older individuals.

Indeed, the empirical literature confirms this conclusion. For instance, Gomes and Michaelides (2005) show that in the presence of labor income and with borrowing constraints, young individuals (between 20 and 35 years of age) with even a high degree of risk aversion ($g = 5$) should invest 100 percent of their financial assets in equities. Equity weights should gradually decrease to about 40 percent at the age of 65 when the ratio between human capital and financial wealth decreases.

In addition, the features of mandatory DC plans should consider the individual's gender and occupation, because salary profiles vary for these factors and will affect the final pension. Although specific profiles vary across countries, low-skilled workers generally have the highest average salary relative to final salary, and the salary of women generally peaks much earlier in their careers than does the salary of men. For illustrative purposes, see figures 4B.2 and 4B.3, which depict the career salary profiles for male and female workers in the United Kingdom, respectively.[39]

The higher the average salary is relative to final salary and the earlier the salary peaks, the longer is the time frame for contributions to compound. Consequently, the difference between the final pension and the final salary will be higher on average for women relative to men and higher on average for low-skilled workers. Blake, Cairns, and Dowd (2007) estimate this difference for the United Kingdom and show that, in the case of an equity-only investment strategy, the largest median pension-to-final salary difference between occupations is 34 percent for men and 38 percent for women

Figure 4B.2 Career Salary Profiles for Male Workers in the United Kingdom, Mid-1990s

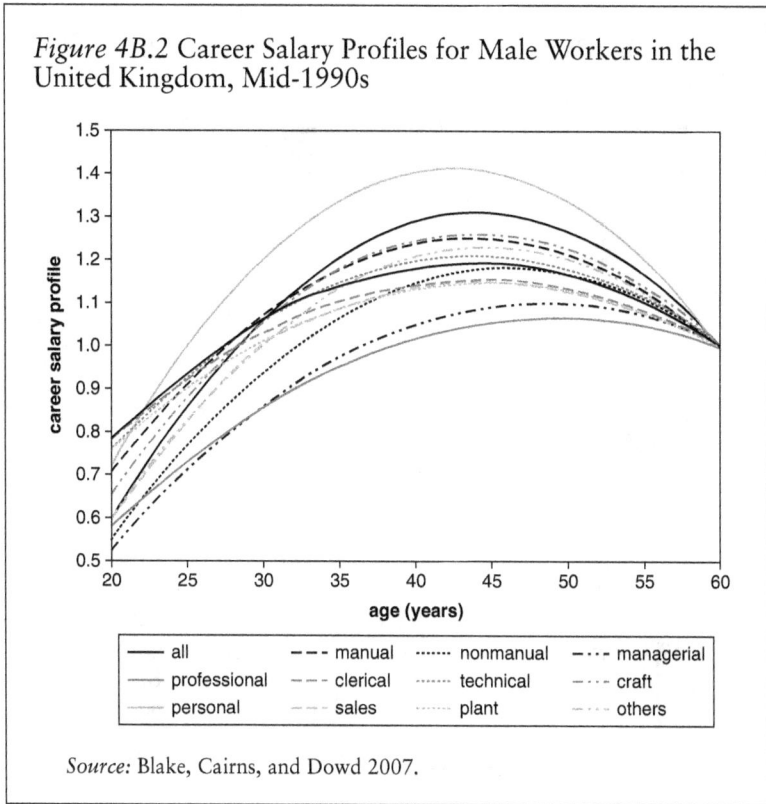

Source: Blake, Cairns, and Dowd 2007.

for the same contribution rate. This finding suggests that key features of a DC pension plan should be occupation and gender specific.

In summary, this annex shows that the regulation of investment choice and the design of associated default options known as *life-cycle funds* broadly follow the normative implications of the literature briefly surveyed, and as such, they should be welfare improving. This conclusion stems from the following considerations. First, equities have a place in the myopic investment strategy because they exhibit a risk premium. Second, time-varying returns create an intertemporal hedging demand for securities that do well when the investment set deteriorates. Third, equity returns are predictable in the long run because they are mean reverting. Hence, investing in equities over long periods reduces total variance, a benefit known as *time diversification*, and it is optimal to expose younger investors to higher levels of equity risk. Fourth, equities can be used to offset labor income risk because the two are not perfectly correlated. Fifth, younger individuals should invest proportionally more in equities than do older individuals because the ratio of human capital to financial assets is

Figure 4B.3 Career Salary Profiles for Female Workers in the United Kingdom, Mid-1990s

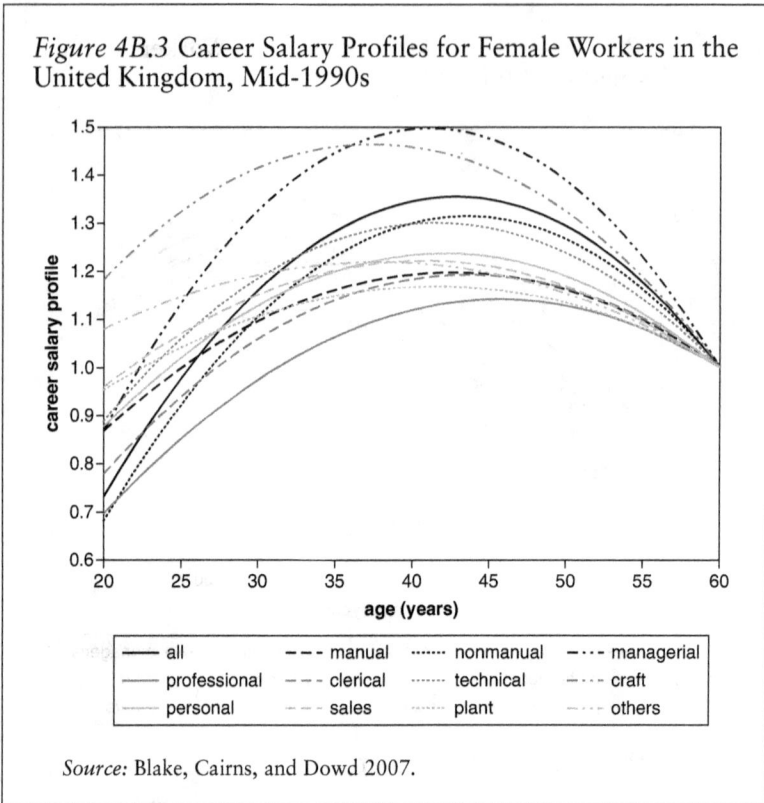

Source: Blake, Cairns, and Dowd 2007.

higher at the beginning of the working career and younger individuals face a greater need to hedge the human capital risk.[40]

Annex 4C: The Construction of Liability-Driven Investment Strategies

Once the long-term investment target is identified, the strategic asset allocation of the default investment options during the accumulation phase needs to be designed. Stochastic programming solutions have been applied in numerous commercial applications because they allow an account of the uncertainty facing agents in the context of asset-liability management. That said, these models are solved through numerical optimization, which in most cases requires that uncertainties be approximated by a scenario tree with a finite number of states of the world for each time period. In other words, there is some modeling risk.

Cairns, Blake, and Dowd (2006) give an application of stochastic programming that addresses the weaknesses of the current multifund design and allows for labor income and annuitization risks. They show that a strategic asset allocation based on three funds would be sufficient to hedge intertemporal shifts in investment opportunities, interest rate risk, and human capital risk. The three funds are dominated by equities, bonds, and cash, respectively, but each fund contains some of the other assets to hedge intertemporal shifts in investment opportunities, interest rate volatility, and correlation with labor income. For example, the equity fund is an efficient portfolio of primarily equities plus bonds and cash, with the weights of the risky assets depending on the ratios of the assets' risk premium to return variance in the standard fashion. Over time, weights are adjusted to account for variations in the correlation between asset returns and labor income.

The purpose of the equity fund is to hedge labor income risk and to benefit from the equity risk premium. As shown in figure 4C.1, equity holdings in the strategic asset allocation are highly leveraged at the beginning, when the ratio of human capital to financial wealth is very high. Then, they gradually decrease to zero toward retirement when the aforementioned ratio becomes zero. The purpose of the bond fund is to hedge interest rate risk and annuitization risk. Its weight is also very high at the beginning of the career because of the hedging demand caused by time-varying interest rates. It decreases very rapidly but rises again toward retirement to hedge the annuitization risk. The purpose of the cash fund is first to finance the initial very high leveraged positions in equities and bonds, so its weight is highly negative, and then to hedge the inflation risk in labor income, when its weight becomes positive (figure 4C.1).[41]

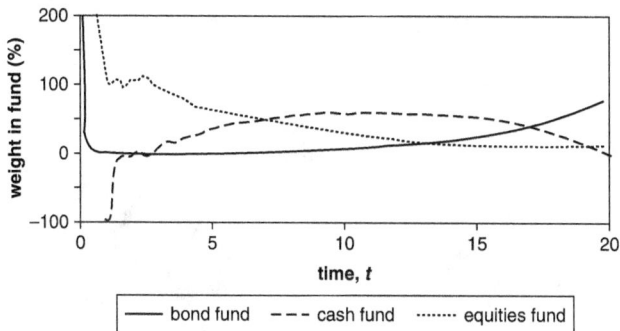

Figure 4C.1 Lifestyling without Deferred Annuities

Source: Cairns, Blake, and Dowd 2006.

Booth and Yakoubov (2000) and Howie and Davies (2002) have already suggested that the use of long-term bonds before retirement would be effective in hedging annuitization risk. This use is straightforward and stems from the observation that the price of annuities is inversely related to the interest rate. Ideally, the duration of the bond portfolio to be annuitized at any given point should be close to the duration of the annuity being purchased. Neither the long-term bonds nor the duration requirements are contained in the investment rules of the current default options of those close to retirement.

Horneff, Maurer, and Stamos (2008) suggest that a more effective way to hedge the same risk is to annuitize gradually over time rather than at retirement; in this way, bonds can be used to hedge other risks, such as the bequest risk. The optimality of gradual annuitization stems from the trade-off between the illiquidity of annuities and the longevity risk insurance they provide. Although longevity insurance is valuable, the purchase of an annuity is irreversible, making it a very illiquid asset. The option value from waiting is valuable at younger ages, explaining why gradual annuitization is preferable.[42]

Another application of stochastic programming that explicitly considers bequest motives is given by Horneff, Maurer, and Stamos (2006). With no bequest motive, they show that it is optimal to begin to annuitize from as early as age 20. The rising value of the longevity risk insurance crowds out bonds (at around age 50) and eventually equities (by age 79) as shown in figure 4C.2. With a bequest motive, bonds and equities are never crowded out, and their weights remain high to accumulate bequeathable

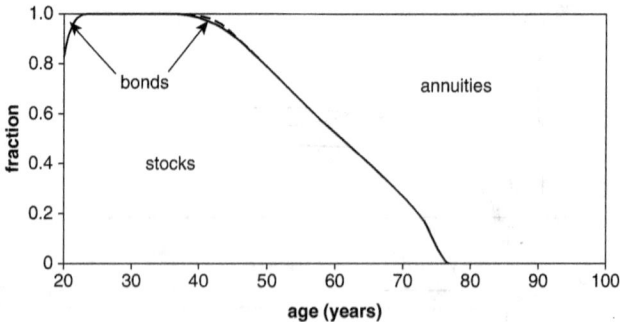

Figure 4C.2 Lifestyling with Deferred Annuities, No Bequest Motive

Source: Horneff, Maurer, and Stamos 2006.

assets. In fact, individuals start buying annuities only at age 60, and these annuities are crowded out by bonds at age 80 as the bequest motive dominates the value of the longevity risk insurance (figure 4C.3). The switch into bonds is justified by the opportunity to exploit time-varying interest rates and to meet a bequest motive at the end of the life cycle.

Reveiz and León (2008) and Reveiz et al. (2008) provide a third interesting application of stochastic programming for the case of Colombia. Their framework moves away from the mean-variance framework implicit in the previous examples and defines *risk* as the maximum shortfall that individuals are ready to withstand in any given period.[43] This framework is an example of a practical way of targeting a replacement rate. For such targeting to be possible, one need only (a) allow a wide set of instruments for all multifunds and (b) determine for each an investment horizon to maximize wealth given a maximum shortfall for a given period (say, 0, 2, 5, 10, and 20 percent per year for funds A, B, C, D, and E, respectively, at a given confidence interval) that would be consistent with the target replacement rate. Asset limits could be used mainly for instruments that are highly complex or difficult to price fairly in the markets (joint ventures or infrastructure projects). Each fund then determines the appropriate combination of assets (benchmarks) that does not surpass these shortfall constraints, and the regulator can verify that the resulting risk exposures of the fund are aligned with the objectives of each fund.[44] These allocations are then determined as a benchmark and can be modified only two times every three years to avoid fund synchronization (macroeconomic volatility) and ensure stability. Active management,

Figure 4C.3 Lifestyling with Deferred Annuities, Bequest Motive

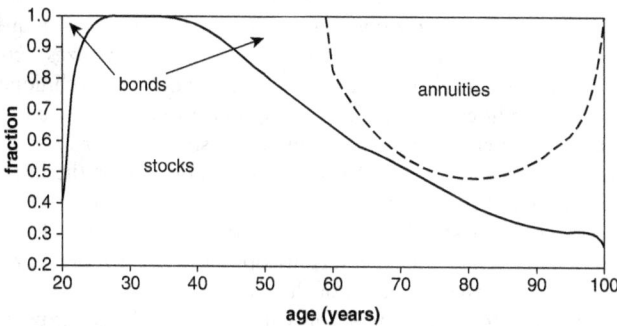

Source: Horneff, Maurer, and Stamos 2006.

determined as a tracking error deviation, can be authorized as a deviation of these benchmarks for the managers to take opportunistic bets or decrease the overall risk of the portfolio if important changes on risk aversion are expected.

The preceding are presented as illustrative examples of how to calibrate optimal investment strategies through stochastic simulations that take into account a series of background risks such as labor income and annuitization. They yield paths for the optimal rebalancing of portfolios over time that are far superior to the stepwise deterministic rules for rebalancing assets across funds, which are characteristic of multifund design today. However, these techniques are very complex, and their stochastic nature makes them very information intensive, constantly requiring updating information about factors such as labor income, human capital, and other background risks. Hence, they are difficult to implement, and many countries would need to consider simpler (deterministic) strategies that are easier to carry out.

Finally, in addition to issues related to the construction of portfolios, consideration should be given to what techniques plan managers should be allowed to use to implement over time the strategic asset allocation. The discussion on this point is limited to box 4C.1, but it is an issue worth further analysis in the future.

Box 4C.1 Liability-Driven Investment Strategies: How Are They Implemented?

Various definitions of liability-driven investment strategies exist, but they all essentially involve managing assets in a way to hedge the duration and convexity risk of assets and liabilities or the surplus stemming from the difference between assets and liabilities.

A traditional way to implement a liability-driven investment strategy is through *surplus optimization*. Pure target maturity date techniques for allocating assets produce an efficient frontier that maximizes expected return for a given level of total expected risk, and such techniques are unaware of liabilities. Instead, surplus optimization techniques produce an efficient frontier that maximizes expected surplus return for a given level of expected surplus risk. *Surplus return* is defined as the difference between the liability return and the return on assets, and the *surplus risk* is defined as the standard deviation of the surplus return. The target maturity date frontier and the surplus optimization frontier portfolios are very similar at the beginning of the working career of an individual. If anything, portfolios on the surplus frontier have larger exposure to

(continued)

Box 4C.1 Liability-Driven Investment Strategies: How Are They Implemented? *(continued)*

equity, given the longer-term horizon under consideration. However, they are very different toward retirement, when portfolios on the surplus optimization frontier would include a larger proportion of inflation indexed long-term bonds.

A more recent way to implement a liability-driven investment strategy involves separating assets between a *liability-matching portfolio* and a *performance-generation portfolio*. This approach can be thought of as the combination of two separate strategies: (a) investing in immunization (for risk management) and (b) investing in standard asset management (for performance generation). When leverage is involved, the immunization portfolio would include the use of derivatives (typically, interest rate or inflation swaps, or both) in the liability-matching portfolio. This approach allows more potential for performance generation. Under this general class of strategies are constant proportion portfolio insurance (CPPI) strategies, which are designed to prevent final terminal wealth from falling below a specific threshold, and extended CPPI strategies (or dynamic core-satellite strategies), which are designed to protect asset value from falling below a prespecified fraction of the benchmark value given by the liability portfolio.

Notes

1. Hong Kong, China, which restricts choice, is a notable exception within the set of countries with mature financial systems.

2. Mexico introduced a two-fund system (a fixed-income fund and a balanced fund allowing both fixed-income and equity) in 2004 and expanded it to five funds in early 2008. At the same time, investment rules were amended to allow three new asset classes: real estate investment trusts; mortgage-backed securities; and structured securities linked to private equity, venture capital, and project finance. Investments in private capital and infrastructure are possible through trusts and structured notes, but investments in real estate are limited to trusts. The new asset classes present a low degree of correlation with other allowed assets and therefore offer an excellent opportunity to reduce risk through asset diversification.

3. In Peru, investment choice was first enacted in 2003 and subsequently modified in 2005. It became effective in July 2005, with participants having six months to elect a fund. Pension firms are required to offer at least the two more conservative funds among the three allowed funds: Fund 1 (Fund C in table 4.6) is a capital preservation fund with low volatility, Fund 2 (Fund B in table 4.6) is a balanced fund with average volatility, and Fund 3 (Fund A in table 4.6) is a capital appreciation fund with higher volatility.

4. See annex 4A for detailed information on investment limits for Chilean, Mexican, and Peruvian multifunds.

5. In Mexico, the limit for foreign investment has been 20 percent since this type of investment was approved.

6. VaR is defined as an absolute threshold expressed in local currency units such that the probability that the mark-to-market loss on the portfolio over a given time horizon (in Mexico the time horizon is one day) exceeds the threshold (assuming normal markets and no trading in the portfolio) is equal to a given level (typically 1 percent or 5 percent). Under normal market behavior, this measure has allowed pension funds to hold portfolios with weighted average maturity exceeding 10 years and equity exposure of 12 percent.

7. All market risk measures increased during the financial turmoil, not only the daily VaR. In response, Comisión Nacional del Sistema de Ahorro para el Retiro (Mexico's National Retirement Savings Commission, or CONSAR) allowed pension funds to exceed their VaR limits on a temporary basis, as long as the pension fund administrator's portfolio managers communicated to the regulator why they exceeded the risk limit and how and when they were planning to return to levels below the limit. The number of observations was increased from 500 to 1,000 to reduce the particular weight on specific shocks (such as the failure of Lehman Brothers, which severely affected the risk factors).

8. Transfers of resources in kind can be made to avoid liquidity risk. When disorderly market conditions prevail, the transfers can be postponed at the discretion of CONSAR, as happened at the end of 2008.

9. The Dominican Republic was one of the exceptions, with no equity exposure, no foreign diversification, and relatively limited volatility in local markets through most of 2008.

10. When individual retirement accounts are included, the loss increases to more than US$5 trillion.

11. In Peru, fund exposures at the beginning of 2008 even surpassed the 10 percent limit established in the investment regulations because the Superintendencia de Banca, Seguros y AFP (Superintendency of Banking, Insurance, and Pension Funds) had given the pension fund administrators a transitory period to adapt to the investment rules.

12. Other systems, such as in Mexico and Peru in Latin America and in Estonia in Eastern Europe, were introduced very recently, and not enough information has been accumulated on them.

13. However, this result may capture improved macroeconomic and financial conditions over the same period.

14. Notwithstanding this limitation, portfolio diversification in Mexico greatly improved under the multifund structure compared to the single-fund structure previously available. In 2000, for example, fixed-income instruments represented 93 percent of overall assets whereas this share was only 67 percent in 2007. In addition, longer-term maturities (more than 10 years) represented about 22 percent of total assets.

15. In Chile, the most aggressive fund also has an equity investment floor of 40 percent.

16. An 80 percent equity limit would not even suffice in the view of authors such as Barberis (2000), who argue for a very strong hedging demand for equities.

17. However, the National Retirement Savings Commission can relax these constraints, as explained in note 8.

18. The losses would be commensurate to the difference in the equity limits between sending and receiving funds.

19. A *life annuity* is an insurance product by which a life insurance company commits to a series of payments in the future to the buyer (until his or her death) in exchange for the immediate payment of a lump sum (single-payment annuity) or a series of regular payments (regular-payment annuity), prior to the onset of the annuity.

20. The other important dimension of annuitization risk is how much to annuitize. On this point, the literature shows that the optimal degree of annuitization is reduced if (a) retirement income from other sources is high (Bernheim 1991); (b) risk pooling within the family is efficient (Brown and Poterba 2000; Kotlikoff and Spivak 1981); (c) risk aversion is low (Milevsky and Young 2002, 2007b); (d) the equity premium is sufficiently high (Horneff, Maurer, and Stamos 2006); (e) investment volatility is low (Milevsky and Young 2007a); (f) availability of housing and other social welfare (health) is low (Milevsky and Young 2002); and (g) the bequest motive is high (Bernheim 1991). However, most mandatory DC systems determine the minimum annuitization level to mitigate the risk of participants' outliving their assets.

21. Higher bequest motives would lead to a preference for annuitization at higher ages.

22. Earlier, the chapter showed how Sweden allows very aggressive investment options, given the relatively small (but definitely not trivial) role of the mandatory DC system in financing total replacement rates.

23. Yao and Zhang (2005) find that homeowners hold a lower average proportion of equities in their total net worth holdings (that is, bonds, equities, and housing), a reflection of the substitution effect of housing wealth for risky equities, but hold a higher equity weighting in their financial wealth portfolio (that is, bonds and equities).

24. Fund B constitutes the default option for participants under 35 years of age.

25. Foreign mutual funds are considered equity mutual funds, irrespective of their asset composition. Considerable evidence indicates that the vast majority of foreign mutual funds are indeed equity funds. In fact, Chilean pension funds achieve equity exposure through foreign mutual funds and fixed-income exposure through the domestic market. This situation is partly explained by competition rules, because fees charged by foreign mutual funds are not considered among the fees charged by pension firms to participants.

26. Some emerging economies have imposed regulations on minimum rates of return, relative to the industry average, on investments made by pension fund administrators. In the case of Chile, each administrator must guarantee that the average real rate of return in the previous 36 months is not lower than the lesser of the following: (a) the average real return of each fund, minus 2 percentage points for funds C, D, and E and 4 percentage points for funds A and B; or (b) 50 percent of the average real return of all the funds.

27. *Stochastic* (or *dynamic*) *programming* is a framework for modeling optimization that involves uncertainty. By contrast, deterministic optimization is formulated with known parameters. Although Basu, Byrne, and Drew (2009) show that deterministic switching rules produce inferior wealth outcomes for the investor than do strategies that dynamically alter asset allocation, stochastic programming requires that the probability distributions governing the data be known or can be estimated. Hence, they increase model risk.

28. An obvious criticism of the new investment product proposed is that its production costs can be high. High costs are indeed likely if these products are defined at the individual level. However, costs could be contained if individuals are lumped in a limited number of cohorts. Clearly, this issue merits further empirical investigation.

29. Horneff, Maurer, and Stamos (2006) show that with a bequest motive, bonds and equities are never crowded out, and their weights remain high to accumulate bequeathable assets (see annex 4C).

30. In addition to productivity improvements and career progression, labor income increases with inflationary expectations. The return on cash adjusts to reflect inflation expectations.

31. The duration of a financial asset measures the sensitivity of the asset's price to changes in interest rates.

32. Horneff, Maurer, and Stamos (2008) suggest that a more effective way to hedge the same risk is to annuitize gradually over time rather than at retirement; in this case, bonds can be used to hedge other risks, such as the bequest risk. The optimality of gradual annuitization stems from the trade-off between the illiquidity of annuities and the longevity risk insurance they provide (see annex 4C).

33. In addition to productivity improvements and career progression, labor income increases with inflation expectations. The return on cash adjusts to reflect inflation expectations.

34. Making endogenous contribution rates mandatory is likely to be suboptimal for many individuals. For instance, individuals with a low intertemporal elasticity of substitution in consumption (these are individuals who prefer more stable contribution patterns during the accumulation phase but potentially lower consumption patterns in the future) would not find increased volatility of contributions optimal.

35. The risk penalty, in turn, is proportional to the volatility of the returns on the risky asset and the degree of risk aversion.

36. Similar conclusions are reached by Balvers, Wu, and Gilliland (2000); Fama and French (1988); and Poterba and Summers (1988).

37. For investors with a risk aversion of 10 (that is, extremely conservative).

38. Most literature favors the view that human capital is similar to bonds. Although generally true for employees, this view may not always be the case. In the United States, for example, the compensation is often linked to shares. But more important, labor reforms that increase temporary work and self-employment may result in equity-linked profiles.

39. See also IMSS (1998) for the case of Mexico City, which also validates the salary profile of women at an earlier age. Broadly speaking, the same applies to low-skilled occupations. This analysis was subsequently conducted for another 21 cities in Mexico, generally confirming similar findings.

40. See Campbell and Viceira (2002) for a more formal treatment of this topic.

41. In addition to productivity improvements and career progression, labor income increases with inflation expectations. The return on cash adjusts to reflect inflation expectations.

42. Clearly, the presence of transaction costs will reduce the extent to which gradual annuitization can be implemented. In the presence of large transaction costs, annuitization may be feasible only at a few moments in time.

43. Reveiz and León (2008) and Reveiz et al. (2008) justify this approach by arguing that in most emerging markets pension assets are likely to be the only financial asset for individuals; therefore, asset management should have as an objective the minimization of shortfalls in individuals' cash balances.

44. The composition of the portfolio is not relevant for the regulators, who should focus only on the risk exposure; the strategic asset allocation is the responsibility of the manager.

References

APRA (Australian Prudential Regulation Authority). 2006. *Annual Superannuation Bulletin*. Sydney: APRA. http://www.apra.gov.au/Statistics/Annual-Superannuation-Publication.cfm.

———. 2007. *Annual Superannuation Bulletin*. Sydney: APRA. http://www.apra.gov.au/Statistics/Annual-Superannuation-Publication.cfm.

Balvers, Ronald, Yangru Wu, and Erik Gilliland. 2000. "Mean Reversion across National Stock Markets and Parametric Contrarian Investment Strategies." *Journal of Finance* 55 (2): 745–72.

Barberis, Nicholas. 2000. "Investing for the Long Run When Returns Are Predictable." *Journal of Finance* 55 (1): 225–64.

Barro, Robert J. 2005. "Rare Events and the Equity Premium." NBER Working Paper 11310, National Bureau of Economic Research, Cambridge, MA.

Basu, Anup, Alistair Byrne, and Michael E. Drew. 2009. "Dynamic Lifecycle Strategies for Target Date Retirement Funds." Discussion Paper in Finance 2009-02, Griffith University, Brisbane, Australia. http://ssrn.com/abstract=1302586.

Bernheim, B. Douglas. 1991. "How Strong Are Bequest Motives? Evidence Based on Estimates of the Demand for Life Insurance and Annuities." *Journal of Political Economics* 99 (5): 899–927.

Blake, David, Andrew J. G. Cairns, and Kevin Dowd. 2007. "The Impact of Occupation and Gender on the Pensions from Defined Contribution Plans." *Geneva Papers on Risk and Insurance* 32 (4): 458–82.

———. 2008. "Turning Pension Plans into Pension Planes: What Investment Strategy Designers of Defined Contribution Pension Plans Can Learn from Commercial Aircraft Designers." Discussion Paper PI-0806, Pensions Institute, Cass Business School, City University, London. http://www.pensions-institute.org/workingpapers/wp0806.pdf.

Booth, Philip, and Yakoub Yakoubov. 2000. "Investment Policy for Defined-Contribution Scheme Members Close to Retirement: An Analysis of the 'Lifestyle' Concept." *North American Actuarial Journal* 4 (2): 1–19.

Brown, Jeffrey, and James Poterba. 2000. "Joint Life Annuities and Annuity Demand by Married Couples." *Journal of Risk and Insurance* 67 (4): 527–54.

Cairns, Andrew J. G., David Blake, and Kevin Dowd. 2006. "Stochastic Lifestyling: Optimal Dynamic Asset Allocation for Defined Contribution Pension Plans." *Journal of Economic Dynamics and Control* 30 (5): 843–77.

Campbell John Y., and Luis M. Viceira. 2002. *Strategic Asset Allocation: Portfolio Choice for Long-Term Investors*. New York: Oxford University Press.

Chacko, George, and Luis M. Viceira. 2005. "Dynamic Consumption and Portfolio Choice with Stochastic Volatility in Incomplete Markets." *Review of Financial Studies* 18 (4): 1369–402.

Cheyre, Hernán. 2006. "El desafío de fortalecer el sistema privado de pensiones." Presentation to the Comisión de la Reforma de Pensiones, Santiago, May 2. http://www.consejoreformaprevisional.cl/documentos/audiencias/02-05-2006-econsult.pdf.

Constantinides, George, John Donaldson, and Rajnish Mehra. 2002. "Junior Can't Borrow: A New Perspective on the Equity Premium Puzzle." *Quarterly Journal of Economics* 117 (1): 269–96.

Fama, Eugene, and Kenneth French. 1988. "Permanent and Temporary Components of Stock Prices." *Journal of Political Economy* 96 (2): 246–73.

———. 2002. "The Equity Premium." *Journal of Finance* 57 (2): 637–59.

Faugère, Christophe, and Julian Van Erlach. 2006. "The Equity Premium: Consistent with GDP Growth and Portfolio Insurance." *Financial Review* 41 (4): 547–64.

Ghysels, Eric, Andrew C. Harvey, and Eric Renault. 1996. "Stochastic Volatility." In *Handbook of Statistics, Volume 14: Statistical Methods in Finance*, ed. G. S. Maddala and C. Radhakrishna Rao, 119–91. Amsterdam: North-Holland.

Gomes, Francisco, and Alexander Michaelides. 2005. "Optimal Life-Cycle Asset Allocation: Understanding the Empirical Evidence." *Journal of Finance* 60 (2): 869–904.

Horneff, Wolfram J., Raimond Maurer, and Michael Z. Stamos. 2006. "Life-Cycle Asset Allocation with Annuity Markets: Is Longevity Insurance a Good Deal?" Working Paper 146, Michigan Retirement Research Center, University of Michigan, Ann Arbor.

———. 2008. "Optimal Gradual Annuitization: Quantifying the Costs of Switching to Annuities." *Journal of Risk and Insurance* 75 (4): 1019–38.

Howie, Robert, and Helen Davies. 2002. "Setting Investment Strategy for the Long Term: A Closer Look at Defined Contribution Investment Strategy." Presented at the Finance and Investment Conference, Bracknell, U.K., June 28. http://www.actuaries.org.uk/__data/assets/pdf_file/0003/19479/howie.pdf.

IMSS (Instituto Mexicano del Seguro Social). 1998. *Estudio Demográfico, Laboral y Económico en Grandes Ciudades.* Mexico City: IMSS.

Jagannathan, Ravi, Ellen R. McGrattan, and Anna Scherbina. 2000. "The Declining U.S. Equity Premium." *Federal Reserve Bank of Minneapolis Quarterly Review* 24 (4): 3–19.

Jorion, Philippe, and William Goetzmann. 1999. "Global Stock Markets in the Twentieth Century." *Journal of Finance* 54 (3): 953–80.

Julliard, Christian, and Anisha Ghosh. 2008. "Can Rare Events Explain the Equity Premium Puzzle?" London School of Economics and Political Science, London. http://papers.ssrn.com/sol3/papers.cfm?abstract_id=1104760.

Kogan, Leonid, Igor Makarov, and Raman Uppal. 2007. "The Equity Risk Premium and the Riskfree Rate in an Economy with Borrowing Constraints." *Mathematics and Financial Economics* 1 (1): 1–19.

Kotlikoff, Laurence J., and Avia Spivak. 1981. "The Family as an Incomplete Annuities Market." *Journal of Political Economy* 89 (2): 372–91.

Kurz, Mordecai, and Andrea Beltratti. 1996. "The Equity Premium Is No Puzzle." Working Paper 96-004, Department of Economics, Stanford University, Palo Alto, CA.

Mehra, Rajnish, and Edward C. Prescott. 1985. "The Equity Premium: A Puzzle." *Journal of Monetary Economics* 15 (2): 145–61.

Merton, Robert C. 1969. "Lifetime Portfolio Selection under Uncertainty: The Continuous Time Case." *Review of Economics and Statistics* 51 (3): 247–57.

———. 1971. "Optimum Consumption and Portfolio Rules in a Continuous Time Model." *Journal of Economic Theory* 3 (4): 373–413.

———. 1973. "An Intertemporal Capital Asset Pricing Model." *Econometrica* 41 (5): 867–87.

Milevsky, Moshe, and Virginia R. Young. 2002. "Optimal Asset Allocation and the Real Option to Delay Annuitization: It's Not Now-or-Never." Working Paper, Schulich School of Business, York University, Toronto. http://www.ifid.ca/research.htm.

———. 2007a. "Annuitization and Asset Allocation." *Journal of Economic Dynamics and Control* 31 (9): 3138–77.

———. 2007b. "The Timing of Annuitization: Investment Dominance and Mortality Risk." *Insurance: Mathematics and Economics* 40 (1): 135–44.

Mossin, Jan. 1968. "Optimal Multiperiod Portfolio Policies." *Journal of Business* 41 (2): 215–29.

Palme, Joakim. 2005. "Features of the Swedish Pension Reform." *Japanese Journal of Social Security Policy* 4 (1): 42–53.

Poterba, James, Joshua Rauh, Steven Venti, and David Wise. 2006. "Lifecycle Asset Allocation Strategies and the Distribution of 401(k) Retirement Wealth." NBER Working Paper 11974, National Bureau of Economic Research, Cambridge, MA.

Poterba, James, and Lawrence Summers. 1988. "Mean Reversion in Stock Prices: Evidence and Implications." *Journal of Financial Economics* 22 (1): 27–59.

PPM (Premiepensionsmyndigheten). 2007. *Annual Report 2007.* Stockholm: PPM. http://www.pensionsmyndigheten.se/download/18.55d850a012569f73994800 017985/Annual+Report+PPM+2007.pdf.

Raddatz, Claudio, and Sergio Schmukler. 2008. "Pension Funds and Capital Market Development: How Much Bang for the Buck?" Policy Research Working Paper 4787, World Bank, Washington, DC.

Reveiz, Alejandro, and Carlos León. 2008. "Efficient Portfolio Optimization in the Wealth Creation and Maximum Drawdown Space." Borradores de Economía 520, Banco de la República de Colombia, Bogotá. http://www.banrep.gov.co/ docum/ftp/borra520.pdf.

Reveiz, Alejandro, Carlos León, Juan M. Laserna, and Ivonne Martínez. 2008. "Recomendaciones para la modificación del régimen de pensiones obligatorias de Colombia." *Ensayos sobre Política Económica* 26 (56): 78–113.

Rietz, Thomas. 1988. "The Equity Risk Premium: A Solution." *Journal of Monetary Economics* 22 (1): 117–31.

Ross, Stephen, Stephen Brown, and William Goetzmann. 1995. "Survival." *Journal of Finance* 50 (3): 853–73.

Samuelson, Paul A. 1969. "Lifetime Portfolio Selection by Dynamic Stochastic Programming." *Review of Economics and Statistics* 51 (3): 239–46.

Siegel, Jeremy. 1999. "The Shrinking Equity Premium." *Journal of Portfolio Management* 26 (1): 10–17.

Sun, Wei, Robert K. Triest, and Anthony Webb. 2007. "Optimal Retirement Asset Decumulation Strategies: The Impact of Housing Wealth." Public Policy Discussion Paper 07-2, Federal Reserve Bank of Boston, Boston.

Yao, Rui, and Harold H. Zhang. 2005. "Optimal Consumption and Portfolio Choices with Risky Housing and Borrowing Constraints." *Review of Financial Studies* 18 (1): 197–239.

5

Conclusions

This book focuses on the following two interrelated policy challenges in mandatory defined contribution (DC) pensions:

- Pension firms enjoy considerable market power because of the characteristics of the supply and demand of pension services. Mainly, the supply is characterized by important economies of scale, and the demand is highly inelastic to prices (consumers are inert). Hence, pension firms tend to treat their clientele as captive and to charge high administrative fees that finance excessive marketing activity or translate into supernormal profits.
- The recent financial crisis has reignited the debate on whether DC pension participants, especially those close to retirement, bear excessive investment risk that is not adequately compensated with higher expected risk-adjusted gross rates of return over the life cycle.

Individual consumers must address these challenges because they can jointly translate into increased costs of financial intermediation measured by lower risk-adjusted expected net rates of return. Addressing these challenges is also critical for the political economy of pension system design because policies aimed at either lowering fees or increasing risk-adjusted expected returns will inevitably strengthen the rationale for introducing mandatory DC pensions as a key element of a pension system.

These policy challenges are interrelated because they both stem (among other causes) from the limited capacity of individuals to choose what is best for them. Limited capacity, in turn, stems from a combination of inadequate financial education, bounded rationality, and use of simplistic rules of thumb in the decision-making process that introduces systematic biases into individuals' decisions.

This book endorses the broad consensus on the usefulness of financial literacy and acknowledges the importance of identifying the most relevant content and delivery mechanisms to influence behavior, which are topics that merit further research. However, it is more concerned with institutional designs in the areas of industrial organizations and default investment options. In particular, it focuses on ways to exploit the systematic biases of individuals' decision-making processes (rather than correcting them) to yield improved risk-adjusted expected replacement rates.

The key conclusion on the first policy challenge is that policies focusing on participants' inertia are likely to be far more effective than those aimed at lowering barriers to entry. In particular, this book contends that jurisdictions should (a) make more use of flat fees to increase price efficiency and reduce incentives for cream skimming, (b) introduce fiscally responsible and transparent flat subsidies from the budget to pursue equity policy objectives, and (c) make more use of hybrid industrial organization models and unbundling of pension services to exploit individuals' inertia.

The key conclusion on the second policy challenge is that all jurisdictions with mandatory DC pensions should introduce life-cycle default investment options. However, to effectively protect individuals close to retirement from excessive annuitization risk and to improve risk diversification over the life cycle, such default options must be well designed. In particular, this book contends that jurisdictions should (a) review investment rules to promote the use of deferred annuities and long-duration bonds towards retirement, and (b) where feasible, introduce investment products that reconnect the accumulation phase with the decumulation phase without reintroducing liabilities for asset managers.

The remaining conclusions expand on the rationale for the preceding key conclusions and are structured as follows: the next two sections summarize the analysis conducted on policies linked to administrative fees, while the following two sections summarize the analysis conducted on policies linked to risk-adjusted expected long-term gross performance.

Current Policies Focusing on Administrative Fees

Chapter 3 focuses on the trade-offs related to policy interventions aimed at reducing administrative fees. These policies include the following: (a) the use of a uniform rate applied to heterogeneous fee bases, (b) the simplification of fee structures, (c) the bundling of pension services, (d) restrictions on transfers, and (e) price controls in the form of price caps.

These interventions are defined as ad hoc because they either attempt to achieve multiple policy objectives or target only the consequences (and not the causes) of participants' inertia. Hence, they generate unsatisfactory compromises, inevitably reinforcing market power and, therefore, price distortions. The following subsections and table 5.1 briefly summarize the main conclusions drawn from the discussion on the use of such policies.

Table 5.1 Ad Hoc Interventions with Increasing Trade-Offs

Policy	Pros	Cons
Uniform fee rates	They are more transparent and equitable.	They are inefficient because they imply a divergence between fees and marginal costs across pension services, and they encourage excessive investment in marketing and cream skimming. Their redistributive power is limited because they redistribute only across the members of a single pension firm. Finally, price distortions increase over time because fees are vulnerable to trends in the fee bases, and the production function of most pension services has a large fixed-cost component.
Simplification of fee structures	It increases transparency and reduces participants' inertia.	It further increases the discrepancy between fees (prices) and marginal costs. In addition, it produces intergenerational transfers in favor of younger or older cohorts.
Bundling of pension services	It increases transparency and reduces participants' inertia.	It further increases the discrepancy between fees (prices) and marginal costs.
Repression of transfers	It discourages investment in marketing and cream skimming by incumbent firms.	It does not address the causes of participants' inertia. Additionally, it increases market power by decreasing demand elasticity. Finally, it increases barriers to entry by reducing the effectiveness of the marketing of new entrants.
Monopsony agreements	They discourage investment in marketing and cream skimming by incumbent firms, thus allegedly reducing barriers to entry.	Barriers to entry are artificially raised because new entrants cannot attract existing customers. Such agreements are politically unstable and facilitate the possibility of regulatory capture by the industry.
Caps on fees	They are effective in reducing administrative fees.	They do not address the causes of participants' inertia but only the consequences (high administrative fees). They are disconnected from the cost structure of pension services, and they may lead to redistribution in favor of pension firms' third parties. Their establishment generates lobbying and exposes the regulator to possible capture. Finally, they quickly become obsolete because of trends in the fee base.

Source: Authors' compilation.

Uniform Fee Rates

All jurisdictions prohibit price discrimination and favor the use of uniform fee rates. Such rules are intended to reduce inertia by increasing transparency. At the same time, they attempt to achieve equity across contributors. However, they sacrifice efficiency and encourage high marketing expenditures and price wars. In other words, they represent a less than fully satisfactory compromise between efficiency, equity, and transparency.

Uniform fee rates sacrifice efficiency in favor of transparency. Because different pension services have different production costs, uniform rates imply a divergence between prices and marginal costs across services. Efficiency in supply could be increased to promote lower administrative fees, but such an approach would require the use of different fees equal to the marginal cost of each pension service. Multiple fees would come at a possible high cost in terms of transparency, because participants would be less able to compare prices across pension firms charging a large menu of different prices.

Uniform fee rates also sacrifice efficiency in favor of equity, because they redistribute from high-income, high-asset participants in favor of low-income, low-asset participants. Although redistribution is per se a desirable policy objective, uniform rates applied to heterogeneous bases imply that different participants represent different rents for pension firms. This situation encourages excessive investment in marketing and cream skimming, and it compounds the negative impact of participants' inertia on price distortions by increasing barriers to entry.

Finally, price distortions are bound to increase over time. Fee rates are applied to trends in their bases, and pension services have a large fixed-cost component. Hence, individuals tend to pay more and more over time for the same quality of service while pension firms' operational profits increase.

In summary, uniform fee rates applied to heterogeneous bases may be more transparent and equitable, but in the end, they reinforce market power (and more so over time) and, therefore, price distortions.

Simplification of Fee Structures and Bundling of Pension Services

Simplifying fee structures and bundling pension services are commonly used ways to increase transparency, but they too sacrifice efficiency. Hence, the ultimate effect of these policies on price distortions depends on whether the alleged increased transparency really increases price elasticity sufficiently to offset the negative impact on prices caused by the decrease in efficiency.

For instance, many countries (most recently, Mexico in 2007) have required pension firms to charge participants on only one base. The tradition among regulators is that less complex fee structures simplify price information and facilitate comparison and learning by participants—that is, such structures contribute to increasing demand elasticity. However, the simplification of fee bases further increases the discrepancy between prices and marginal costs. In addition, changes in fee bases create intergenerational transfers in favor of younger cohorts when a shift occurs from an earnings- to an asset-related base. Conversely, the transfer is in favor of older cohorts when the shift is from an asset-related base to an earnings-related one.

A similar trade-off exists with bundling of pension services. The rationale supporting bundling of pension services is that it minimizes reliance on participants' choice; therefore, it limits the consequences of participants' inertia. However, when services with different cost structures are bundled, the highest price equilibrium that will arise with separate services will likely be extended to all other services in the bundle. Consequently, if policy makers fail to establish institutions for the centralized provision and procurement of services with high economies of scale, barriers to entry will be artificially extended. This situation, in turn, would increase market power and price distortions.

Repression of Transfers, Monopsony Agreements, and Caps on Fees

The ineffectiveness of the previous ad hoc regulations in increasing demand elasticity has prompted many jurisdictions to adopt even more draconian policies. These measures include (a) repression of transfers, (b) monopsony agreements between the regulator or supervisor and the pension firms, and (c) price controls in the form of price caps.

The main conclusion drawn from the discussion on repression of transfers and monopsony agreements is that they do not affect the fundamental incentive for firms to invest in marketing—namely, the presence of rent heterogeneity across consumers. They generally decrease the effective elasticity of demand and increase barriers to entry; that is, they increase the market power of incumbent pension firms. In particular, alternative policies based on monopsony agreements sponsored by regulators to repress transfers are politically unstable and facilitate the possibility of regulatory capture by the industry.

Finally, the main conclusion drawn from the discussion on the use of price controls is that they, too, do not directly address the causes of price distortions. Therefore, they suffer from a long list of drawbacks that, in great part, relate to the disconnection between price ceilings and cost structures. This disconnection could potentially discourage investment in asset management quality and result in the failure to redistribute in favor of participants; it also implies that caps could quickly become obsolete. Nevertheless, in the absence of more effective and market-based tools to increase demand elasticity and enable participants to recapture lost rents, price controls could be an effective (albeit undesirable) means by which providers' market power can be curbed.

Improving on Existing Administrative Fee Policies

The trade-offs embedded in the existing policies can be mitigated, as shown in table 5.2.

Flat Fees and Subsidies

A more aggressive use of flat fees would reduce price distortions because fixed costs are a large component of the cost structure of the majority of pension services. Furthermore, flat fees discourage marketing and cream skimming because all participants provide the same rent to pension firms. However, flat fees are not equitable per se if not accompanied by a flat subsidy, as done in Mexico or New Zealand (Mexico, however, does not allow flat fees to be charged). Within the fiscal space available to achieve a desired redistribution, a subsidy that redistributes across the whole population of contributors would represent a more efficient mechanism than uniform fee rates that redistribute simply across the clients of any given pension firm. Finally, flat fees do not reduce per se price distortions caused by low demand elasticity.

Pure Procurement

Alternative industrial organization models involving elements of procurement can be used to increase the elasticity of demand. For instance, some jurisdictions have been using procurement by a centralized public board. The merits of procurement arise directly from its primary objective, which is to deal in a radical manner with consumer inertia. When one demand block is granted to each firm that wins the contest, the incentive of providers to spend on marketing to attract clients is removed. In addition, by establishing competition for the market rather than in the market, barriers to entry and rent extraction activities are eliminated.

However, pure procurement may lead to underinvestment in financial technology for various reasons. For instance, a procurement board can exercise monopsony power and limit the compensation of financial innovators because providers do not have outside options for marketing their innovations. In addition, lack of competition in procurement may induce the board to reduce investment in innovation because it does not affect market share. In addition, public procurement boards are subject to strong transparency standards; therefore, eventual innovators are likely to suffer more imitation than in the case of a private pension firm. Finally, no valid benchmark exists for measuring the performance of a single public procurement board, and additionally, boards may be subject to undue political influence.

Table 5.2 How to Promote Lower Administrative Fees with Fewer Policy Trade-Offs

Policy	Pros	Cons
Interventions that minimize trade-offs (win-win policies)		
Flat fees	They are more efficient and reduce price distortions. They eliminate excessive marketing and cream skimming.	They do not allow redistribution and do not address the problem of participants' inertia.
Flat subsidies	They redistribute more efficiently than do uniform fee rates applied to heterogeneous bases.	They could be fiscally expensive if too generous.
Hybrid industrial organization models	They help address the problem of participants' inertia.	Flat fees and unbundling of pension services are needed to increase viability. Strong debate exists on the relative superiority of stock versus flow design.
Interventions that improve on caps on fees		
Pure procurement	It helps address the problem of participants' inertia.	It may lead to underinvestment in financial technology.
Cost-based tariffs	They are effective in reducing administrative fees.	Like caps on fees, they do not address the causes of demand inelasticity but only the consequences (high administrative fees). They are disconnected from the cost structure of pension services, and they may lead to redistribution in favor of pension firms' third parties. Their establishment generates lobbying and exposes the regulator to capture. Finally, they quickly become obsolete because of trends in the fee base. However, the connection with the cost structure of pension services reduces overall limitations. The cost structure needs to be estimated and audited accurately.

Source: Authors' compilation.

Hybrid Industrial Organization Models

Other jurisdictions have been using hybrid industrial organization models involving procurement and quasi-markets. These models share the merits of pure procurement, while the presence of a quasi-market mitigates the drawbacks.

In particular, the quasi-market component reduces the monopsony power of procurement boards. It represents a valid benchmark for measuring a board's performance and an outside option for the board's suppliers. Pension firms in the quasi-market segment are a well-tuned benchmark allowing the political authorities and public opinion to make a better assessment of the performance of the public procurement board. Finally, the existence of a pension quasi-market with multiple providers improves the outside options for suppliers to the public procurement board.

The main conclusion drawn from the discussion on hybrid industrial organization structures is that they represent a valid alternative to reduce pension firms' market power. However, the design of a well-functioning hybrid model needs to take into account several policy considerations discussed in detail in chapter 3. Here, it may be worth recalling that the winners of the auction for the procured segment are vulnerable to cream skimming during the period of service, and protection against cream skimming cannot be guaranteed as long as fee bases are heterogeneous. Hence, hybrid structures are likely to be more viable when flat fees are used.

Within hybrid models, a debate is ongoing regarding the relative superiority of two competing alternatives. These models differ in the way they allocate participants to the procured segment: either from the stock of participants or from the flow of new entrants. With the stock design, providers in the procured segment are allowed to serve the full set of participants (the whole set of inert customers) that would benefit from procurement. In addition, target participants can spend their whole working career in the procured segment because they will be served by a sequence of providers selected through periodic procurement auctions. With the flow design, providers in the procured segment are allowed to serve only a fraction of the set of participants (typically the inert customers who recently joined the system). In addition, no periodic auctions occur for the same target participants, so inert participants can spend their whole career served by the same provider.

The main conclusion that can be drawn from such debate is that the stock design presents attractive characteristics, such as targeting all inert participants and protecting them from dynamic predatory pricing schedules. However, it may induce bidders to raise their prices if they fear that their clientele will be lost in a future auction. This drawback could be mitigated by reducing barriers to entry through further unbundling of pension services.

Summary

In summary, the use of flat fees, separate subsidies, and hybrid industrial organization models appears to represent a superior package of policies to increase participants' welfare, especially if hybrid models are reinforced by the use of flat fees and unbundling of pension services. However, many jurisdictions have adopted price controls, and the political capital needed to implement alternative policies may be lacking. These jurisdictions could implement measures to increase the efficiency of price controls.

Most of the drawbacks of the design of current price caps could be mitigated if ceilings were linked to costs in the form of cost-based tariffs, as are commonly used in utilities industries. However, no country has yet tried to adapt tariff-setting techniques to mandatory DC pension quasi-markets. This book argues that the adoption of such techniques would greatly improve the transparency and due process with which caps are established.

The book also acknowledges the difficulties related to the adequate estimation of model firm costs and to the accurate audit of actual production costs. In addition, it stresses the need to revise tariffs periodically to reflect trends in the bases and the critical requirement of a regulatory authority with very strong technical capacity and the necessary independence to avoid capture.

Current Policies Focusing on Investment Performance

Chapter 4 discusses the second policy challenge of this book: how to improve fund managers' risk-adjusted investment performance when participants are inert. There is a clear trend toward providing more investment choice to cater for heterogeneity in risk aversion across individuals in many jurisdictions. The extent to which individuals are allowed to choose across pension firms and funds differs from country to country. Countries such as Australia and Sweden allow considerable choice, whereas countries in Eastern Europe and Latin America allow a more limited choice of funds.

Despite the increased investment choice, participants do not always profit from it. Participants in mandatory DC pension schemes exhibit a high level of inertia. Even when participants do make choices, empirical evidence suggests that individuals follow heuristic methods to solve investment problems and implement investment strategies, leading to systematic biases. In addition, the investment incentives of asset managers and the long-term retirement goals of participants might be unaligned because asset managers do not face a pension liability or an explicit long-term investment target. These concerns suggest that a rationale exists for designing policies that address problems emanating from the large number of inert participants, the systematic biases in investment behavior, and the misalignment of the incentives of asset managers with the long-term retirement targets of participants.

Default Investment Options in the Form of Multifunds

Several countries have introduced—or are in the process of introducing—limited default investment options for inert individuals that attempt to exploit the aforementioned systematic biases in portfolio selection. These schemes are commonly known as *multifunds* in Latin American countries. The idea behind the design of these default options is to expose younger individuals to equity risk and gradually move them into bond or money market funds toward retirement. The basic rationale supporting the design of multifunds is the generally accepted notion that equities exhibit a risk premium and their returns are mean reverting.

However, this book argues that, while representing a step in the right direction, the multifund design suffers from key weaknesses:

- *Inadequacy of supporting investment rules.* For instance, it is unclear whether investment rules in most jurisdictions are sufficiently flexible to (a) construct efficient portfolios, (b) allow a good match between the risk profile of admissible assets and the risk profile of individual liabilities, or (c) allow portfolios that adequately reflect the heterogeneity in risk aversion of the covered population.
- *Static and discrete glide paths.* The glide paths for rebalancing portfolios over time are not continuous but exhibit three to five steps (depending on the jurisdictions). The static nature of glide paths could imply a severe welfare loss for inert individuals who remain in a given default fund for a long time.
- *Inability to allocate cash balances to more than one fund.* Very few countries allow participants to hold account balances in more than one fund. Hence, in countries where options are more limited, the allowed investment universe may not adequately cater for risk-aversion heterogeneity.
- *Inadequate consideration of human capital and annuitization risks.* Important background risks, such as human capital and annuitization risks, are not explicitly taken into consideration in the regulation of investment choices and the design of associated default options. For instance, the explicit consideration of human capital risk suggests that the hedging demand for equities should be much higher than that suggested by simple mean reversion. Therefore, the default fund at young ages (when human capital is high) should be more aggressive than that currently provided for in most jurisdictions. Similarly, the explicit consideration of annuitization risk would justify the introduction of long-term bonds or deferred annuities in the default portfolios toward retirement to hedge the interest rate risk associated with the conversion of savings into an annuity.

In addition to the design weaknesses of multifunds, evidence shows (at least in Chile) that both strategic and tactical asset allocations of pension fund managers may not necessarily be compatible with the long-term objectives of participants. Hence, there is a need to tie the hands of fund managers.

Improving Default Investment Options

The rest of this chapter discusses simpler policies that would improve the current design of default investment options and can be safely implemented within the rule-based framework in which multifunds currently operate. It then discusses more complicated policies that require more sophisticated, deep, and liquid markets. These policies may present more serious trade-offs that require careful assessment.

Within a Rule-Based Framework

A first set of policies could be readily implemented in countries that have adopted a system of multifunds to improve the expected performance of default investment options (table 5.3). These policies would entail maintaining the current rule-based framework where products and investment rules are defined in regulations; therefore, such policies would present no implementation obstacles.

For instance, investment regulations could be reviewed in numerous countries to allow pension firms to construct portfolios that are more efficient and more adequately cater for local risk-aversion heterogeneity. In particular, annuitization risk could be effectively hedged in a rule-based framework by requiring default funds toward retirement to be invested in deferred annuities, long-term (inflation-indexed) bonds, or both.

At the same time, the review of investment rules should be aimed at reducing the macrofinancial stability effect of pension firms' trading activities. Pension firms have accumulated a large amount of assets in many countries, and their trading activities often exacerbate price pressures in the market for local securities and reduce liquidity artificially, to the detriment of local issuers and the capital market more generally.

Additionally, the number of default options currently offered in countries such as Hungary or Peru could be revised to reflect the larger heterogeneity of risk tolerance in the covered population. Along the same lines, two additional policies could be implemented by (a) allowing individuals to allocate their cash balances to more than one fund and (b) reducing the time during which individuals are allocated by default to any given fund. In practice, this change would entail maintaining the current deterministic glide paths for rebalancing portfolios over time, but making them more continuous by essentially increasing the number of default options along the life cycle of individual workers.

Table 5.3 Improving Default Investment Options within a
Rule-Based Framework

Policy	Criticism of current design
Gradually liberalize the investment rules.	Current investment rules are often too restrictive. They allow inadequate geographic risk diversification and likely limit the ability to construct efficient portfolios. The risk profile of admitted assets may not match the risk profile of participants' liabilities.
Require the use of deferred annuities and long-duration bonds toward retirement.	Current default option design exposes individuals to annuitization risk. This policy allows the accumulation phase to be partially reconnected with the decumulation phase by providing a (regulatory) hedge for annuitization risk.
Increase the number of default options.	Glide paths are static and force individuals into a default fund for long periods.
Allow individuals to allocate cash balances to more than one fund.	Current investment rules and the number of funds are often too restrictive. Current options may not adequately cater for heterogeneity in the risk appetite of participants.

Source: Authors' compilation.

Within a Risk-Based Framework

Although welfare gains could be achieved by improving the rules of multifunds and default investment options, major gains can be achieved only if pension firms are required to actively manage important risks. This second set of policies would entail progressively moving away from the current rule-based framework toward a risk-based framework. In such a framework, fund managers design investment products while the policy makers define their minimum standards and focus on monitoring their implementation.

Chapter 4 suggests that the weaknesses in the design of current investment choices and associated default options could be addressed largely by requiring providers to offer target annuitization funds (table 5.4). Target annuitization funds are essentially life-cycle funds that have a target retirement date and an investment portfolio whose construction is driven by a long-term financial target (that is, desired retirement

Table 5.4 Improving Default Investment Options within a
Risk-Based Framework

Policy	Pros	Cons
Require providers to offer target annuitization funds.	• Annuitization funds improve expected risk-adjusted long-term performance by diversifying risk intertemporally (that is, they reduce the investment risk borne by individuals). • They allow full consideration of important background risks such as human capital and annuitization risks. • They do not create liabilities for asset managers during the accumulation phase because the long-term target (liability) is defined only in probabilistic terms. • They are compatible with the physical separation of providers in the accumulation (asset managers) and decumulation phases (annuity providers). • They provide an adequate benchmark for monitoring long-term performance. • They minimize a key concern associated with DC arrangements (volatility of replacement rates) while maximizing a key benefit associated with defined benefit arrangements (stability of replacement rates), albeit only in probabilistic terms.	• Annuitization funds increase model risk borne by individuals. • The stochastic strategic asset allocation is complex and information intensive. • They require supporting investment rules, sophisticated capital markets, and general availability of risk management skills. • They require adequate estimation of liabilities, including good mortality tables. • Overall contribution levels need to be endogenous. • Supervisors need to evaluate and monitor model risk. • They are costly if not defined at the level of cohorts.

Source: Authors' compilation.

benefit). They are target-driven investment products that effectively reconnect the accumulation and retirement phases of the life cycle of individuals, but without creating liabilities to fund managers during the accumulation phase.

The proposal for target date annuitization funds does not drastically deviate from current institutional arrangements, which should ease concerns related to their eventual implementation, but it improves on the current design for three key issues.

First, target date annuitization funds are target-driven investment funds, and as such, their implementation requires the estimation of the consumption needs of individuals during retirement. The investment target could be expressed (a) as a consumption path or wealth level or (b) as a replacement rate at retirement compatible with the consumption path. The target would not represent a liability for the pension firm (in line with the DC nature of second pillars) but simply a probabilistic benchmark to guide tactical decisions and monitor long-term performance. Hence, the presence of a long-term investment target would provide a better means to align the incentives of asset managers with those of participants in mandatory DC pensions than would overly complicated investment rules.

Second, the strategic asset allocation during the accumulation phase would explicitly consider human capital and annuitization risks and be implemented with at least four basic asset classes: cash, equities, inflation-indexed long-term bonds, and deferred annuities. Each of these asset classes would serve a particular purpose:

- Cash could leverage the initial position in equities and hedge inflation risk in labor income.
- Equities could hedge human capital risk and benefit from the equity risk premium in particular.
- Long-term bonds could hedge interest rate risk in the initial stages of the accumulation phase and mitigate the annuitization risk toward retirement (if deferred annuities are not available).
- Deferred annuities could hedge the annuitization risk.

In addition, the solution for the strategic asset allocation for the target annuitization funds would imply continuous (rather than discrete) rebalancing strategies, thereby preventing individuals from remaining for too long in any given portfolio while the relative importance of the underlying background risks change.

Third, use of an asset management target, even if only probabilistic, implies increased volatility in contributions. For example, the current value of the pension fund may fall short of the level needed to reach the long-term investment target because of poor equity returns, and the only way to rectify the shortfall may be to increase contributions to the plan. This possibility raises a critical policy trade-off. Policy makers could make contributions endogenous to the mandatory DC plan, or they could expect participants to meet the financial gap by increasing contributions to their voluntary plans. The answer is likely to be country specific, balancing the individual appetite for volatile contributions and the willingness to minimize the potential fiscal costs of any implicit or explicit pension guarantee.

Target annuitization funds provide a framework for aligning the incentives of asset managers with those of participants in mandatory DC pensions. Their implementation, however, presents some challenges, and the model might not be suitable to all countries. Most important, the stochastic investment strategies implicit in target annuitization funds may be too complex and information intensive to be easily and safely put into operation in the context of many countries' mandatory DC pensions. In such circumstances, the stochastic solution to the optimal strategic allocation may need to be substituted with a simpler deterministic (ruled-based) solution with linear (or quasi-linear) glide paths to rebalance portfolios over time.

Index

Boxes, figures, notes, and tables are indicated by b, f, n, and t, respectively.

poor price performance, analysis
of, 33–35, 37
structure and governance of
pension firms in, 22
endogenous fixed costs, 53*n*4
entry
barriers to, 19, 20*b*, 26
new entries, 50–51, 59*n*75, 76,
159*f*, 164
switching costs and, 52,
59*n*73–74
equity funds, 127–28, 131, 145–47
equity risk premium in
U.S., 138–39*b*
Estonia
global financial crisis of 2008,
effects of, 115
mandatory second pillars in, 9*n*6
Europe, Eastern. *See* Eastern Europe
European Union (EU), structure
and governance of pension
firms in, 21–22
exogenous fixed costs, 53*n*4
extended CPPI strategies
(dynamic core-satellite
strategies), 149*b*

F

fee bases
defined, 57*n*48
in hybrid models, 85–86,
89, 95, 164
regulatory price controls,
76, 77–78, 81
simplification and bundling
requirements, 72–73,
159*t*, 161
uniform fee rates, 32, 69–71,
69*b*, 87, 158, 159*t*
fees and pricing, 6, 67–105, 157
alternative industrial
organization models,
82–86, 162–65
hybrids, 83–86, 88–89,
95–99, 163*t*, 164
pure procurement,

82–83, 88, 89–94,
93–94*b*
changes in prices, low
responsiveness to, 18–19
collusive agreements, 74
cost-based tariffs, 5, 80, 88,
102*n*27, 163*t*, 165
cream skimming, 5, 78, 81,
85–86, 94–95, 97, 158
endogenous and exogenous
fixed costs, 53*n*4
existing policy responses to, 4
flat fees and flat fee subsidies,
78–79, 79*t*, 85, 88,
158, 162, 163*t*
heterogeneous fee structures,
33–37, 33*t*, 34*f*, 35*t*,
36*g*, 37*t*, 38*f*, 40*f*, 40*t*
improving pricing schemes and
price regulation, 77–82,
79*t*, 162–65, 163*t*
justification for regulating, 68
new policy approaches to, 4–5
policy trade-offs, 67, 86–89,
158–61, 159*t*
poor price performance, analysis
of. *See under* markets for
mandatory DC pensions
problem of, xi, 2, 3
regulatory price controls and
caps, 75–77, 75*t*, 80–82,
88, 159*t*, 161
search costs, 52
simplification and bundling
requirements, 71–73, 87,
159*t*, 160–61
switching costs.
See switching costs
tradeoffs entailed, policy
interventions ordered
by, 86–89
uniform fee rates, 31–32, 32*t*,
68–71, 69–71*b*, 87,
159*t*, 160
financial crisis of 2008, xi, 107,
115–18, 116–19*t*,
122, 129, 157